Developing Health Promotion Programs

David J. Anspaugh, Ed.D., CHES, PED
The University of Memphis
Memphis, Tennessee

Mark B. Dignan, Ph.D., M.P.H.
University of Alabama at Birmingham
Birmingham, Alabama

Susan L. Anspaugh, Ph.D.
The University of Memphis
Memphis, Tennessee

Boston   Burr Ridge, IL   Dubuque, IA   Madison, WI   New York
San Francisco   St. Louis   Bangkok   Bogotá   Caracas   Lisbon
London   Madrid   Mexico City   Milan   New Delhi   Seoul
Singapore   Sydney   Taipei   Toronto

McGraw-Hill Higher Education

A Division of The **McGraw-Hill** *Companies*

DEVELOPING HEALTH PROMOTION PROGRAMS

This book is printed on acid-free paper.

1 2 3 4 5 6 7 8 9 0 DOC/DOC 0 9 8 7 6 5 4 3 2 1 0

ISBN 0–8151–4374–5

Vice president and editorial director: *Kevin T. Kane*
Publisher: *Edward E. Bartell*
Executive editor: *Vicki Malinee*
Senior developmental editor: *Michelle Turenne*
Senior marketing manager: *Pamela S. Cooper*
Project manager: *Mary Lee Harms*
Production supervisor: *Sandy Ludovissy*
Coordinator of freelance design: *Michelle D. Whitaker*
Senior photo research coordinator: *Lori Hancock*
Compositor: *Interactive Composition Corporation*
Typeface: *10/12 Times Roman*
Printer: *R. R. Donnelley & Sons Company/Crawfordsville, IN*

Freelance cover designer: *Z Graphics*
Cover images: © *PhotoDisc, Inc.*

Library of Congress Cataloging-in-Publication Data

Anspaugh, David J.
    Developing health promotion programs / David J. Anspaugh, Mark B.
Dignan, Susan L. Anspaugh. — 1st ed.
        p. cm.
    Includes index.
    ISBN 0–8151–4374–5
    1. Health promotion—Philosophy. 2. Health planning—Philosophy.
I. Dignan, Mark B.   II. Anspaugh, Susan L.   III. Title.
RA427.8.A57   2000
613—dc21
                                                    99–34740
                                                       CIP

www.mhhe.com

Brief Contents

Detailed Contents

Chapter 6 Management Issues in Health
Promotion Programs   123

Chapter 7 Marketing and Maintaining Involvement   150

Preface

Developing Health Promotion Programs is a comprehensive text that examines the philosophy, rationale, and guidelines for developing health promotion programs for the corporate and community sectors. The goal of the text is to help the health promotion student and specialist in planning, developing, implementing, and evaluating programs in a variety of settings, particularly at the worksite. Practical guidelines and an easy-to-read format familiarize the preprofessional and the professional health promotion specialist with the processes necessary for successful program development.

AUDIENCE

Anyone looking for a realistic, easily understood process for planning health promotion programs will find *Developing Health Promotion Programs* useful. The text will be valuable to preprofessionals seeking to enhance their perspective on health promotion programs, and to the professional seeking to utilize a workable format for planning, implementing, and evaluating health promotion programs. Individuals from the disciplines of health promotion, fitness, wellness, nursing, psychology, and nutrition will also find the text useful.

FEATURES

Previous texts in health promotion planning have tended to be lengthy or heavily theoretical, thus making applications of content difficult. Our goal is to provide insight into the theoretical basis for health promotion planning while providing a practical and straightforward approach. Every chapter has been written to provide information useful to the health promotion planner.

- Administrative issues such as staffing and budgeting are examined to help demonstrate how to interact with management and the "corporate culture."
- A variety of marketing concerns, including campaigns, promotions, incentives, and special events, are discussed to demonstrate how health education providers can best market themselves.
- How to successfully utilize available resources and programs such as health risk appraisals, weight management and diet analysis programs, stress reduction programs, smoking cessation programs, and the Internet are examined to assist the health promotion specialist in achieving the dual goals of cost effectiveness *and* behavior change.
- Theories of motivation and modification are covered separately in chapter 3 to enhance the coverage of behavior change.

- The framework for evaluating programs to demonstrate that the programs implemented are serving the client as well as contributing to the welfare and cost-effectiveness of the organization is examined.
- *Profiles in Health Promotion* are practical case studies that conclude with questions and/or suggestions to provide practical and realistic applications of content in every chapter.
- *The Check It Out* feature provides activities that address issues found in each chapter.
- Comprehensive appendixes of health promotion materials include Web sites, sample health histories, sample consent forms, physician release forms, fitness facilities development guidelines, and a directory of professional associations and publications that provides additional resources.

PEDAGOGICAL FEATURES

Numerous pedagogical tools are provided in each chapter to help reinforce learning. These include:

- chapter objectives
- *Profiles in Health Promotion* sections
- *Check It Out* sections
- bulleted summaries
- chapter bibliographies

ACKNOWLEDGMENTS

We would like to acknowledge and thank our reviewers whose comments, suggestions, support, and enthusiasm were valuable to us in developing and improving the manuscript:

Bradley O. Boekeloo, Ph.D. *The George Washington University*

René McEldowney, Ph.D. *Auburn University*

Patricia M. Legos, Ed.D. *Temple University*

Katherine J. Riggen-Santiago, Ph.D. *South Dakota State University*

Susan Cross Lipnickey, Ph.D. *Miami University (OH)*

Catherine A. Heaney, Ph.D. *Ohio State University*

A special word of thanks must be expressed to Vicki Malinee for helping to bring this project to fruition, and for her willingness to publish a text designed to be "user friendly" for both corporate and community settings. After several years of working with Michelle Turenne, we must once again thank her for her caring concern that we develop this text to be the ultimate product for our profession, and for refining it to help ensure the best quality possible. We also would like to thank Mary Lee Harms for her hard work and dedication to the project. As project manager, she was a joy to work with and indeed a driving force to see the project come to fruition.

David J. Anspaugh
Mark B. Dignan
Susan L. Anspaugh

The Need for Health Promotion

OBJECTIVES

CHAPTER OBJECTIVES

After reading this chapter, you should be able to

- define health and wellness.
- discuss the difference between health education and health promotion.
- discuss the scope of health promotion activities.
- identify why opportunities for health promotion activities exist in the business venue.
- describe the qualifications needed for a health promotion professional working in the business/corporate setting.
- identify potential settings for health promotion activities.
- discuss benefits of corporate/business health promotion programs.
- describe potential activities in health promotion that can specifically meet the needs of the business/corporate sector.
- discuss the cost savings of health promotion programs in the business/corporate sector.
- identify factors that positively influence health promotion programs.

Costs related to health care, such as delivery and insurance, have risen steadily at twice the general inflation rate since 1950. In 1996 these costs represented 13.6 percent of the gross national product (GNP). This trend is expected to continue— *unless steps are taken to restructure the present health care system.* Some estimates predict that, by the year 2000, more than 18 percent of the GNP will be spent on health care (Health Care Financing Administration, 1998).

Over the past twenty years, American businesses and corporations have become increasingly aware of the potential that health promotion activities have for improving the health of employees and reducing care costs. This awareness, in addition to the nation's current health objectives (*Healthy People 2000: National Health Promotion and Disease Prevention Objectives,* as well as the soon to be announced *Healthy People 2010: Healthy People in Healthy Communities*), emphasizes the merit of developing and implementing strong, results-oriented health promotion programs that address the greatest needs of these companies now. The time to exert leadership ensuring the development of appropriate, goal-oriented pro-graming is now.

This text approaches the development of health promotion programs for the business/corporate sector. Although most of the points discussed are applicable to a variety of settings, including the community, hospitals, and schools, it should be clearly understood that this text emphasizes concerns found in workplace environments.

WHAT IS HEALTH/WELLNESS?

In recent years, our society has been inundated by health-related messages conveyed by the media and many other sources about how to live longer, look better, and be more healthy. Unfortunately, the actual meaning of "health" has often been left open to interpretation. Most people consider themselves healthy if they are not feeling ill. Others think they are healthy if they are young or they perceive they look good or they are engaging in some practice that fulfills their interpretation of being healthy (such as they are not overweight or they walk two miles several days a week). To make the concept of health less abstract, the Joint Committee on Health Education Terminology (1991) defined **health** as ". . . an integrated method of functioning which is oriented toward maximizing the potential of which the individual is capable. It requires that the individual maintain a continuum of balance and purposeful direction with the environment where he (she) is functioning" (p. 102). Conceptually, this definition is synonymous with what many professionals refer to as **wellness,** which is a multidimensional approach to living with the goal of obtaining an optimal quality of life.

Thus, an absence of sickness is certainly part of being "healthy" or "well," but more importantly, the road to health requires active participation. In other words, one's journey toward health is a challenge that mandates a certain amount of personal responsibility in the pursuit of balance among several factors (see fig. 1.1) and

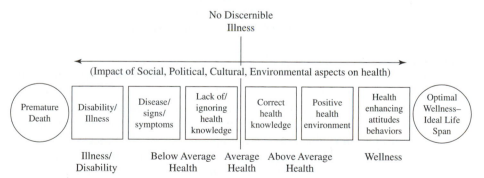

Although there is no guarantee of perfect health, one may be able to prevent, delay, or minimize the effects of environmental, social, political, or genetic predispositions through behavior change and through changes in environment.

FIGURE 1.1. The Health Continuum

FIGURE 1.2. The Components of Health/Wellness

To enhance quality of life and maximize personal potential, one must strive to maintain balance in the following areas:

1. *Spiritual*—the belief in a "higher level" force that unites human beings. This can include nature, science, religion, or a higher power. It includes morals, values, and ethics. Optimal spirituality is the ability to discover, articulate, and act on a (your) basic purpose and beliefs about/in life (Chapman, 1987).

2. *Social*—the ability to interact successfully with people and one's personal environment. The social component includes the capacity to develop and maintain intimacy and demonstrate respect and tolerance toward people with differing opinions and beliefs.

3. *Emotional*—the ability to manage stress in a positive manner and to express emotions appropriately. Emotional wellness includes the knowledge to recognize and accept human feelings and skills to not be defeated by setbacks and perceived "failures."

4. *Intellectual*—a striving for continued personal growth and willingness to learn and use new information effectively for personal, family, and career development.

5. *Physical*—includes the development of the health-related components of fitness (cardiorespiratory endurance, muscular strength and endurance, flexibility, and body composition), adequate nutrition, proper weight, avoiding abuse of drugs/alcohol, and non-use of tobacco products. Physical wellness also indicates appropriate sleep/rest for maximum physical care.

---

in the engagement of behaviors and adoption of attitudes that are conducive to an enhanced quality of life. Further, the definition of health/wellness is of a holistic nature and suggests that the spiritual, social, emotional, intellectual, and physical aspects of one's life should interact harmoniously if one seeks to maximize personal potential (see fig. 1.2).

WHAT IS HEALTH PROMOTION?

Two terms that frequently have been mistakenly used interchangeably are *health promotion* and *health education.* **Health promotion** is defined as "the aggregate of all purposeful activities designed to improve personal and public health through a combination of strategies, including the competent implementation of behavioral change strategies, health education, health protection measures, risk factor detection, health enhancement and health maintenance" (Joint Committee on Health Education Terminology, 1991, p. 102). Some health promotion professionals interpret this definition as somewhat narrow in focus, overly emphasizing individual change while overlooking broader, social perspectives. Another definition comes from the *Ottawa Charter,* which states health promotion is "the process of enabling people to increase control over, and to improve their own health" (First International Conference of Health Promotion, 1986, p. 102). This can be interpreted as the responsibility of the social/ecological environment to promote and enable individuals greater autonomy. By recognizing that people operate within their environments and that change can occur only as environments allow it, more responsibility is placed on the worksite to create an environment where employees can change. Appropriate health promotion activities do this.

Health education is one aspect of health promotion. Health education is the process of providing learning experiences for individuals to help them facilitate voluntary selection of behaviors conducive to positive health/wellness. The Joint Committee on Health Education Terminology (1991) has defined the health education process as the "continuum of learning which enables people, as individual members of social structures, to voluntarily make decisions, modify, and change social conditions in ways which are health enhancing" (p. 103). A very similar definition has been offered by Green and Kreuter (1991) who have defined health education as "any combination of learning experiences designed to facilitate voluntary actions conducive to health" (p. 2). Health education is learning specific and involves education, whereas the entire gamut of health promotion includes many other types of activities.

The definitions of health/wellness, health promotion, and health education are of special importance to health promotion practitioners. These definitions provide the basis for developing and implementing planned learning experiences for the purpose of supplying information, changing attitudes, and influencing behaviors. In other words, worksite health promotion is the process used to achieve understanding of the concepts of wellness, to implement activities that can initiate and execute the goals of wellness, and to promote individual responsibility/change environments for health enhancement or high-level wellness. Health education is a critical part of health promotion.

Health promotion tends to focus heavily on individual responsibility. Although individual responsibility is undoubtedly an integral part of behavior change, a social-ecological paradigm is also involved. Behavior change is complex and involves a cadre of sociocultural, political, and environmental conditions within and outside of organizations that influence behavior change (Stokals, Allen, and Bellingham, 1996). The issue of the complexity of behavior change will also be addressed in chapter 3.

Health promotion is not a panacea for every health care problem in our society. It is one piece of the puzzle for maximal quality of life for all individuals. To successfully implement a health promotion program certain assumptions must be made:

1. Health status can be changed.
2. Appropriate prevention strategies can be developed to deal with identified health problems.
3. An individual's health is affected by a variety of factors including, but not limited to, heredity, environment, and the health care system.
4. Changing behaviors and altering one's lifestyle can positively (or negatively) affect health status.
5. Individuals can be taught to assume more responsibility for their health.
6. For permanent change to occur, an individual must be motivated to change through personalizing of the information (McKenzie and Smeltzer, 1997) and achieving the appropriate stage of "readiness" (Prochaska, 1997).

PROGRAM OFFERINGS AT THE WORKSITE

In an ideal world, every worksite would offer a comprehensive health promotion program that included a variety of activities and health assessments and addressed many physical, emotional, psychological, and spiritual needs. Unfortunately, few companies are able to offer such comprehensive programs. In a study by O'Donnell (1988), the three types of interventions most frequently observed in the worksite were programs focusing on awareness, lifestyle change, and environmental support. **Awareness activities** increase the knowledge base and broaden perception of specific health problems or issues. **Lifestyle change programs** include various behavior change strategies designed to positively modify current lifestyle activities. **Supportive environments programs** provide encouragement, assistance, and reinforcement for positive health behaviors (O'Donnell, 1988). Based on web site information provided by the Association for Worksite Health Promotion (AWHP) in 1997, the majority of worksite programs tend to fall into either awareness or lifestyle change categories. Unfortunately, for long-lasting changes to occur, programs that seek to change culture and provide employee support are needed. When investigating some of the current offerings, it is sometimes difficult to determine what types of interventions are occurring. A selected list of the more frequently offered programs are identified in figure 1.3. A list of web sites related to health promotion is in appendix A.

FIGURE 1.3. 1997 Worksite Health Promotion Activities and Percentage of U.S. Worksites Offering

Activity	Percentage of Worksites Offering (%)
Job hazard/injury prevention	66
Exercise/physical fitness	43
Smoking control	42
Stress management	39
Alcohol/other drugs	38
Back care	34
Nutrition	32
High blood pressure	31
AIDS education	30
Cholesterol screenings	29
Mental health	27
Weight control	26
Cancer (screenings and education—authors' interpretation)	25
Off-the-job accidents	20
Medical self-care	19
STDs	12
Prenatal education	11

Source: Taken from the AWHP web site, September 1997, http://www.awhp.com/whatis.html.

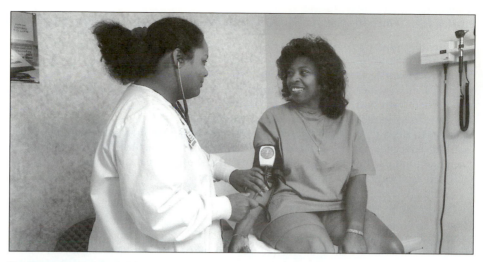

Health promotion activities can occur in a variety of settings.

A WINDOW OF OPPORTUNITY

Driven by both the desire to improve employee health and to lower health care costs, worksite health promotion programs have shown significant growth over the last two decades. *Business Week* reported that medical costs in the very near future will exceed $900 billion with 51.7 percent paid by employers, 33.7 percent by the federal government, and 14.4 percent by the states in Medicare and Medicaid (Pelletier, 1993). In addition, the Health Care Financing Administration (HFCA) projects that by the year 2000, Americans will spend more than $1.6 trillion, or 16.4 percent, of that year's GNP on health care. A report in the *Harvard Business Review* projected that by the year 2000, if health costs continue to escalate, the medical costs of all the Fortune 500 companies will equal their after-tax profits. At the economic conference held in Little Rock during President Clinton's first administration, the chairperson of Ford Motor Company stated that health care costs accounted for almost 20 percent of their total budget, which was close to rivaling their budget for steel (Polling, 1992).

As we move into the next century, the greatest challenge in health care will be to deliver quality, affordable care for all people. It is estimated that by the year 2000, the median age in the United States will have risen from 29 years in 1975 to 36 years of age. By the year 2000 the number of individuals over the age of 65 will increase to more than 35 million plus, representing about 13 percent of the population. Many problems related to rising health care costs are and will continue to be related to lifestyle and, thus, can be influenced through positive lifestyle change. This idea was highlighted at the 1990 conference that reviewed the document *Healthy People 2000: National Health Promotion and Disease Prevention Objectives.* At that time the Public Health Service stated that mobilizing ". . . the nation in the interest of disease prevention and health promotion is an economic imperative" (*Healthy People 2000,* 1990). With a current workforce of more than 110 million

TABLE 1.1. Worksite-Related Goals in Healthy People 2000 Objectives

*Increase the proportion of worksites offering employer-sponsored physical activity and fitness programs as follows:

> 20% of worksites with 50–99 employees
> 35% of worksites with 100–249 employees
> 50% of worksites with 250–749 employees
> 80% of worksites with greater than 750 employees

*Increase to at least 50% the proportion of worksites with 50 or more employees that offer nutrition education and/or weight management programs for employees.

*Increase to at least 75% the proportion of worksites with a formal smoking policy that prohibits or severely restricts smoking at the worksite.

*Extend the adoption of alcohol and drug policies for the work environment to at least 60% of the worksites with 50 or more employees.

*Increase to at least 40% the proportion of worksites employing 50 or more people that provide programs to reduce employee stress.

*Increase to at least 85% the proportion of the worksites with 50 or more employees that offer health promotion activities to their employees, preferably as part of a comprehensive employee health promotion program.

*Increase to at least 20% the proportion of hourly workers who participate regularly in employer-sponsored health promotion activities.

*Increase to at least 70% the proportion of worksites with 50 or more employees that have implemented programs on worker health and safety.

*Increase to at least 50% the proportion of worksites with 50 or more employees that offer back injury prevention and rehabilitation programs.

*Increase to at least 50% the proportion of worksites with 50 or more employees that offer high blood pressure and/or cholesterol education and control activities to their employees.

Source: Healthy People 2000, 1990.

men and women who spend a majority of their time at the worksite, a built-in opportunity is provided for promoting health and for providing the support neces-sary to adopt and maintain positive lifestyle patterns. From the hundreds of objec-tives set forth in *Healthy People 2000,* many are directly related to the worksite (see table 1.1).

Along with the direct impact health promotion programs can have on employ-ees' health, considerable opportunity also exists for reinforcing a myriad of business incentives, such as improving productivity and effectiveness while decreasing the costs associated with illness and injury. Health promotion activities at the worksite are an investment in human capital. The AWHP recognized that businesses and cor-porations cannot ignore the importance of initiating positive health activities when it stated that worksite initiatives can

- reduce risks for targeted diseases and health conditions.
- improve health, productivity, and employee morale.
- offer tailored programs/assessments to meet business needs.
- link employees with community and medical resources.
- evaluate outcomes and identify new opportunities.
- serve as recruiting and retention tools, protecting the investment in employee training and development (AWHP web site, April 1997, http://www.awhp.com).

SKILLED PROFESSIONALS NEEDED IN WORKSITE HEALTH PROMOTION

As the field of health promotion continues to expand, many professional groups envision more opportunities for developing, implementing, and evaluating programs. Included in the list are exercise physiologists, health educators, nurses, nutritionists, sociologists, and health psychologists. The variety of professional groups interested in these opportunities increases the competition for positions in health promotion. For this reason, anyone interested in the area of corporate wellness needs to be adequately prepared to meet the demands of the job.

Appropriate preparation for a health promotion practitioner in the business/corporate sector requires the student or preprofessional to accumulate skills and expertise from the traditional health promotion curriculum (which typically includes coursework such as stress management, smoking cessation, nutrition, back care, and exercise), but also from studies/experience in business and marketing and adult education. For instance, to conduct a successful health intervention program, it is beneficial to understand personnel management, budget development, marketing strategies, evaluation strategies, adult learning theories, counseling theories, and behavioral change techniques. In other words, today's health promotion specialist must have the facility to be as comfortable in the boardroom as in an exercise or classroom setting.

Thus, a comprehensive health promotion curriculum embodying a broad range of disciplines (such as business, marketing, management, health, exercise physiology, nutrition, psychology, counseling, and sociology) will better prepare the preprofessional. If this type of preparation is not included during the baccalaureate years, then seminars, professional conferences, and additional preparation at the university level can help provide the broad, comprehensive background necessary to successfully expand and advance health promotion into the next century. Schools with graduate-level degrees in public health have formal competencies that are part of program accreditation that should ensure adequate skills for professionals. Table 1.2 provides a partial list of the skills essential for successful health promotion professionals.

In addition to the skills mentioned previously, there are other abilities that cannot be obtained solely in a formal learning environment. It is paramount that the health promotion professional possess the following attributes:

1. *People skills.* Anyone entering health promotion needs to enjoy interacting and working with diverse people both individually and in group situations. Knowing how to interact successfully, remaining sensitive to others' needs, demonstrating appropriate care and concern about individual needs, and treating clients fairly and equally are skills and attitudes that must be developed.
2. *Leadership skills.* Successful programs must have exceptional leadership. A good leader leads by setting a good example and displaying energy and enthusiasm for the program. If leaders do not believe in what they are doing, the health promotion program will not achieve the efficacy desired. Only the leader can create an environment where staff and clients perceive themselves as integral to the program and where their ideas and input are valuable and taken seriously.

TABLE 1.2. Skills Advocated for Successful Health Promotion

Business/Manager Skills	Marketing/Promotional Skills
Develop needs assessments	Develop marketing strategies
Develop mission statement, goals, objectives	Develop marketing programs
Develop and administer budget	Develop sales strategies
Hire and train staff	Select promotional materials
Supervise staff	**Educator/Motivator**
Evaluate staff	
Communicate with staff	Develop educational programs
Motivate staff	Develop assessment programs
Purchase equipment	Hire/train staff
Develop schedules	Develop evaluations
Understand company culture	Teach educational programs
Analyze facilities needs	Motivate clients
Maintain facilities	Provide support to clients
Understand legal regulations for	Support behavioral change
fitness/wellness	Consult with clients
Communicate with upper management	Understand the adult learner
Evaluator	**Counselor**
Design program evaluation tools	Advise clients
Design staff evaluation	Consult with clients
Analyze data	Interpret assessment results to clients
Interpret results to management,	Persuade clients to change
wellness committee	Serve as role model for staff/clients

3. *Communication skills* (written and verbal). A knowledgeable and respected leader always communicates professionally, both verbally and in written documents. Learning how, what, and when to say something can provide motivation, win friends, and influence behaviors. Practicing good communication skills can help prevent misunderstandings among clients, management, and staff, and will facilitate "yes" when negotiating with upper management for new programs, staff, equipment, or facilities.

4. *Creative skills.* One of the pitfalls of health promotion is becoming "stuck" in doing/thinking only one way. Creative individuals leave their options open for new ways of approaching the same old problem. For instance, a concept or suggestion that may seem initially silly may not be. Unique or unusual approaches to a problem or issue should always be considered. The question remains, "How can we do this better?," and the answer may be surprising.

As stated in the introduction, the focus in this text is the business/corporate sector. However, because health promotion activities occur in numerous places other than the worksite, it is wise to acquaint the reader with these possible sites. It is not the intent to provide a comprehensive presentation of all these settings, but hospitals; clinical facilities; the community, elementary, and secondary schools; and colleges are just some of the venues for health promotion. Many health promotion activities take only a few minutes, such as a quick health screening or a visit to an educational booth in a shopping mall, whereas other programs are more longitudinal (occurring over time) in nature and may occur over several months or years. Sometimes participants volunteer eagerly and thus represent a "captive audience." Other times, participants must be persuaded to become involved in health promotion activities. Because the field of health promotion is so diverse and occurs in many different settings, each with its own set of challenges and populations, there is tremendous opportunity and challenge for finding an occupational fit between health promotion practitioners and their interests/talents.

HEALTH PROMOTION IN OTHER SETTINGS— AN OVERVIEW

Although health promotion in other settings is not the focus of this text, worksite health promotion sometimes goes beyond just the worksite and into the community, medical environments, and schools. Often these organizations incorporate worksite activities, but they are not limited to them. For instance, hospitals frequently have activity areas on-site that are usable for employees, their families, and the community at large. In cases such as this, worksite health promotion activities may also involve areas for patient education as well as more "traditional" worksite activities. In any case, it would be difficult to completely isolate worksite activities from all other kinds. Often a worksite specialist will be involved in activities that extend beyond the worksite environment. At the same time, strategies used in more diverse settings can be beneficial when incorporated into the worksite. Although we are not attempting to provide a comprehensive look at other types of activities, it is important for worksite specialists to be aware of other kinds of settings in which they may have some interaction.

Community Settings

Green and Kreuter describe two types of interventions at the community level. **Community interventions** seek small but important changes that relate to the *majority* of the population within an identified community. **Interventions in a community** focus on producing change in a subpopulation in the community (Green and Kreuter, 1991). The latter approach targets a specific site and an identified subgroup within the community. In both types of interventions, the objective is to reduce, correct, or eliminate health problems and improve health.

Most community programs involve forming coalitions and focus on creating ownership of the program by the people in the community. A variety of strategies are then designed to impact on an identified situation or problem. Understanding the concepts of social marketing (see chapter 7) and knowing how to effectively utilize the mass media are important considerations, especially when planning and implementing health on a large scale. Just a few of the more frequently adopted community health education projects are screenings for diabetes and hypertension, HIV and AIDS education, smoking and alcohol education, and immunization awareness.

Hospital/Clinical/Agency Settings

For the past ten to fifteen years, there has been a growing movement for health education and health promotion activities to occur in hospitals, physicians' offices, and pharmacies. Health promotion activities in these settings commonly include activities for employees, their families, and even the community at large. Therefore, they are applicable to the traditional worksite.

In the medical area, efforts have been made to increase patients' knowledge and compliance with treatment and enhance their sense of self-responsibility for personal care. Patient education programs can be accomplished via personal and group counseling and by dissemination of health literature. For instance, many pharmaceutical companies have developed pamphlets and data printouts to help consumers understand drug interactions, side effects, and proper procedures when using a prescription. Similarly, hospitals and physicians are now more willing to help patients understand their illnesses or conditions and more likely to advise patients of their rights when under treatment. Hospitals and many other clinics now have patient advocates who represent patients and their concerns and serve as liaisons between the patient, family, and hospital staff.

For many years agencies such as the American Heart Association, the American Cancer Society, and others have had health education and health promotion programs that employed educators to inform the general public regarding particular conditions. These agencies have provided information, education, and services for individuals and families and the communities in which they serve.

Colleges and Universities

Colleges and universities across the country are increasingly offering opportunities outside normal classroom instruction for students, faculty (worksite), and, in some cases, the general public to enhance the quality of their lives through educational and exercise programs. Designated wellness facilities, either on or off campus, often house exercise equipment and provide classrooms for educational seminars and training and are sometimes operated and managed by fitness and wellness specialists other than regular faculty. Examples of topics addressed in wellness programs at the university level include HIV and AIDS, stress reduction, smoking cessation, nutrition, diet and weight loss, alcohol and drugs, safe living, contraception and safer sex, relationships, and parenting skills. Much of what is done at this level is a result of the attempts to meet the needs of today's college student with an emphasis on personal responsibility through greater knowledge, attitude assessment, and behavioral change.

School Health Education

Perhaps there is no place more appropriate for health promotion activities than in our public and private elementary and secondary schools. Although many approaches to health education have been taken in the school systems over the last few decades, the current philosophy regarding "what works best" is a well-planned curriculum consisting of a comprehensive program that begins as early as possible and continues through the high school years. The present comprehensive program was formulated by Allensworth and Kolbe and consists of eight different components. The different components consist of School Health Instruction; School Health Services; School Physical Education; School Nutrition and Food Services; School-Based Counseling; Schoolsite Health Promotion; and School, Family, and Community Health Promotion Partnerships. Within each school setting there should be opportunities for the children, staff, and administrators to become more healthy as a result of the personal and cultural changes that a comprehensive program has to offer.

Content curriculum should include, but not necessarily be limited to, the following areas: community health, consumer health, environmental health, family life, mental and emotional health, injury prevention and safety, nutrition, personal health, prevention and control of disease, and substance use and abuse (Joint Committee on Health Education Terminology, 1991). These major topics provide an umbrella under which a plethora of potential subtopics can be addressed.

The potential for positively affecting young people's lives with a sound health education curriculum is significant. This is particularly true if the curriculum is based on enhancing cognitive skills and providing opportunities for attitude and value assessment to positively impact behavior. To accomplish this, a variety of appropriate learning experiences and strategies that are grade-level specific must be utilized. Effective health education must be based on a realistic assessment of pupil needs, interests, and capabilities. Community and parental values and support must also be considered when determining curriculum content. Several states are moving from the traditional health education model to the wellness model. The topics addressed using the wellness model are those the students can control directly through positive health behavior and effective management of their environment.

When beginning a school-based health education program, initial efforts usually involve a team approach involving fitness specialists, health educators, nutritionists, nurses, faculty, administration, and maintenance personnel. Program content can run the gamut from behavioral change workshops to activities that develop parenting skills, strengthen the family, develop personal empowerment, and enhance self-esteem and self-efficacy (Butler, 1994).

WHY HEALTH PROMOTION PROGRAMS AT THE WORKSITE?

Health promotion efforts at the worksite have demonstrated success at reducing health care costs and, as such, hold considerable potential for future endeavors (Fries et al., 1994; Golaszewski et al., 1992; Harvey et al., 1993; Pelletier, 1993). The basic goal of health promotion is to provide opportunities for participants to engage in screenings/assessments, self-help activities, and educational programs with the goal of improving their quality of life as well as their life span. This remains the goal for all efforts, regardless of the venue in which they occur.

The American lifestyle has become more sedentary as products and services have been developed that make life "easier." Unfortunately, achievement of an easier life is not without costs. Sedentary lifestyle is a significant risk factor associated with the leading killers in modern history, including coronary artery disease, cancer, and work-related injuries. When the habits associated with an inactive lifestyle, such as a high-fat diet, high alcohol intake, and smoking, are factored into the equation, the major contributors to the leading causes of death and disability are identified (Anspaugh, Hunter, and Mosley, 1995).

The underlying intent of health promotion is to motivate individuals, provide incentive and support, and promote the opportunity for people to personalize information in such a fashion that they will make positive health decisions for themselves, their family, and their community. Research has repeatedly indicated that health promotion programs are associated with positive lifestyle changes that can reduce risk factors associated with disease, improve productivity, and morale at the worksite. In the business/corporate sector, companies are increasingly adopting health promotion strategies for the purpose of reducing health care costs, improving employee morale, decreasing absenteeism, and developing behaviors associated with enhanced productivity.

Results of Selected Health Promotion Programs

Medical care costs may well be the financial termites for any size company in the United States. Uncontrolled, these financial termites will weaken, and ultimately destroy, the structure of a company. Many companies already recognize the need for successful methods of empowering employees to accept responsibility for their own health and providing opportunities for better health management. Many employee illnesses can be prevented, diminished in severity, or delayed in onset if detected early through some intervention. Further, health promotion programs can serve to improve morale and lower absenteeism. Table 1.3 presents profiles of several companies and agencies that have implemented health promotion programs that have achieved positive results.

SOCIAL AND CULTURAL CONSIDERATIONS

Before health promotion programs can be implemented, the specific needs of the target population must be assessed. Groups will invariably differ, depending on the nature of the organization and the type of work individuals within the organization do. For instance, blue-collar workers may have health risks related to safety, whereas white-collar workers may have a greater need for time management programs or ergonomics, such as for prevention of carpal tunnel syndrome. Further, since most health care plans also cover the employee's family, health promotion efforts should extend beyond just the employee and the worksite.

Social and cultural differences will also play a role in the types of programs implemented. For example, smoking rates among Asian immigrants are very high. Seventy-two percent of Cambodian males smoke. Lung cancer rates are currently 18 percent higher for Asian males than for white males (Chen and Hawks, 1995).

TABLE 1.3. Results of Selected Health Promotions Programs

Company	Activity	Results
Adolph Coors	The wellness program offers complete health appraisal services. Programs include smoking cessation, nutrition, exercise, diet, stress management, senior aerobics, pre/postnatal exercise, lifetime parenting, and divorce. Many discussion groups.	In one year the cardiac rehabilitation program saved more than 2.3 million in wages ordinarily lost due to missed work and placement hiring salaries and $1.9 million in rehabilitation costs. It estimated a return per year of $5.50 for each $1.00 invested.
AT&T Communication	Employees were offered a health promotion program that included a health risk appraisal (HRA) and various intervention modules.	Program participants increased their level of exercise and reduced risk factors from smoking, coronary artery disease, and physical inactivity. Improved perceptions of their energy, productivity, and quality of life. Estimated a potential savings of $312.2 million over ten years if all AT&T employees had participated.
Duke University	Employees who were employed for four years voluntarily participated in some component of the "The Live For Life" program. Only hourly employees were eligible.	Hourly employees who participated in the HP program experienced 3.3 fewer absences during the first year.
The City of Birmingham	A five-year grant by the National Institutes of Health allowed the city to assess the effectiveness of a comprehensive health program. Part of this assessment was a comprehensive worksite health promotion program.	Over the five-year program there was a 1.4% increase in health care costs for employees in the health promotion program compared with an increase of 11–14% for nonparticipants.
General Electric Aircraft Engines	Utilized an employee fitness center to promote health and wellness.	Members of the fitness center reduced their medical costs to approximately $787 while nonmembers medical costs were around $941.
General Mills	Of sales employees who were employed for three years, 64% volunteered to participate in the HP program. Participants were required to complete one of three optional lifestyle activities every three months. Each client received a quarterly newsletter and incentives based upon accomplishments.	Participants were absent 2.0 days less than nonparticipants during the first year. During the second year the participants were absent 1.7 days less than the nonparticipants. It is estimated that General Mills return of the HP investment was $3.10 & $3.90 returned for every $1 invested for the two-year program.

(continued)

TABLE 1.3. (continued)

Company	Activity	Results
General Motors	A three-year program in which worksite screening was conducted at four manufacturing sites. The three experimental plants received different levels of health promotion activities. 75–80% of employees participated.	Employees at the two most comprehensive sites experienced a greater number of health-risk reductions or relapse prevention compared with the less comprehensive site and control site. To achieve a 1% reduction in risks the more comprehensive sites spent $.65.
J.P. Morgan Company	The HP program conducted different theme programs each year. During the *Year of the Body* different screenings were conducted, including breast cancer screening and mammography.	552 women participated with six early cancers identified among the women. Two received mastectomies and four received lumpectomies. As a result of this early detection and immediate treatment, medical costs were much less, there was a reduction in morbidity, missed days of work, less lost productivity, and insurance costs were reduced.
Martin Marietta Energy Systems, Inc.	Developed a program to help impact on the $1 million a year in low-back injuries. Began a back program that included back classes, instruction regarding fitness, stretching, flexibility, sports injuries, posture, ergonomics, and lifting.	Due to the program the company reported a net savings of approximately $830,000 a year, or a 9:1 benefit to cost ratio.
Orgill Brothers	Initiated an HP program that included an on-site physical examination coupled with an HRA. Orgill Brothers offered all participants a "wellness voucher" equal to 75% of the annual deductible on their health insurance as an incentive to participate in health promotion activities.	Participation rates were in excess of 95%. As a result, a reported reduction of health care costs of 35% below their projections for the time period under consideration.
Steelcase, Inc.	Conducted a three-year study utilizing HRAs in which measures were taken regarding employee levels of alcohol consumption, smoking, activity, stress, and the amount of absenteeism.	Determined that medical costs for inactive employees was $869.98 in comparison to $478.61 for active employees, a difference of 46%.

Depression, stress, and posttraumatic stress syndrome are major problems, with depression rates as high as 90 percent for some groups within the Asian-American population (Frye, 1995). Another example of cultural differences is found in African-Americans. Currently African-Americans experience higher death rates due to cancer, cardiovascular disease, and cirrhosis; are more likely to smoke; and have greater risks of obesity, diabetes, and hypertension than their white counterparts (Neighbors, Braithwaite, and Thompson, 1995; Pugh, 1992). Minority women employed in the workplace report factors of "caregiver stress" compounded by racism and sexism. They report frequently being called on to serve as translators for clients, patients, and customers in addition to the normal pressures and requirements of their work (Walcott-McGuigg, 1994).

It is imperative that people in the work environment be understood from a social and cultural perspective. The needs of employees are paramount to the types of programs and activities undertaken. In instances where the perceived needs of the health promotion staff are drastically different from those of the employees, resulting programs will not succeed. Recognizing the social/cultural pressures of smoking for an Asian male population requires the development of antismoking programs that address, not just how to quit smoking, but how to overcome the social pressures associated with that situation.

NONPARTICIPATION AND ATTRITION IN HEALTH PROMOTION PROGRAMS

A survey of worksite health promotion programs in Fortune 500 companies revealed that of the 61 percent of companies who responded ($N = 247$), less than half of all eligible employees participated (Hollander and Lengermann, 1988). Estimates of on-site participation rates ranged from 20 to 40 percent, whereas off-site program participation rates were 10 to 20 percent (Conrad, 1988).

In addition to low participation, adherence can be a problem. For example, completion of smoking cessation courses resulted in only a 17 to 20 percent abstinence rate after one year. A study of workers who began a coronary heart disease prevention program revealed that only 25 percent continued to participate after one year (Kotarba and Bently, 1988). Since adherence and participation are essential elements in the cost-benefit equation, the ultimate challenge in health promotion programs is not just to motivate employees in the use of services and activities, but to find ways to attract and maintain participation among individuals who will benefit most (Anspaugh, Hunter, and Savage, 1996).

Individuals who initially volunteer to join health promotion programs may be healthier from the onset (Conrad, 1988). Thus, it has been argued by critics that health promotion programs are merely "preaching to the choir." Research indicates that those who join a health promotion program tend to be more physically active, are less of a health risk, have lower medical costs, and demonstrate less absenteeism than individuals who choose to not participate (Glasgow and Terborg, 1991). Consequently, to maximally achieve the goals of health promotion, it is imperative to include and motivate the segment of the workforce that does not already participate in health-promoting activities.

The worksite provides a unique setting in which high-risk and underserved individuals can be reached. To help ensure that long-term health promotion efforts are successful, the health promotion practitioner must recognize, actively recruit, and include nonparticipants; identify their perceived and real barriers to participation; and promote adherence.

ACHIEVING EMPLOYEE PARTICIPATION

Getting employees to participate in activities and programs requires a variety of interesting strategies as well as awareness of the practical and psychosocial concerns of potential participants. The following section discusses introductory concepts and activities often used to spark interest in programs, types of programs that can be implemented, and a brief introduction to motivational components involved in health promotion (see chapter 7).

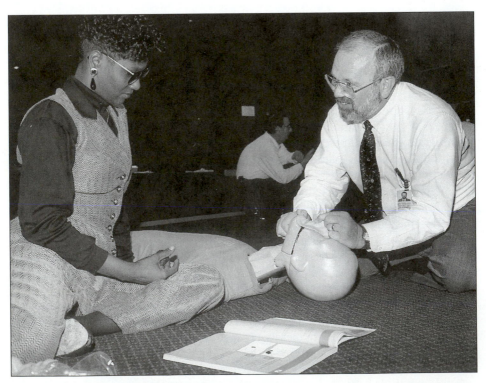

Business and corporations utilize a variety of health promotion activities to reduce health care costs.

Reaching a variety of diverse target groups requires multiple strategies. Current methods such as health risk appraisals (HRAs) and various screening examinations, such as blood pressure, are valuable preventive health measures as well as tools to "hook" potential participants into health promotion activities. However, nonparticipants often need encouragement to initially utilize screenings before they become involved in any subsequent wellness initiatives.

Programs with a fitness orientation are very popular and may attract participants for a variety of reasons. As Conrad notes, "'Fitness' drives the health promotion program; it is likely without exercise and fitness activities the program would attract fewer participants" (Conrad, 1988, p. 548). Johnson & Johnson's "Live for Life Program" and AT&T's "Total Life Concept Program" have shown exercise to be a popular intervention (Conrad, 1988; Gebhardt and Crump, 1990). However, while fitness programs may attract participants, fitness itself does not guarantee commitment to other lifestyle changes. For instance, many employees for whom the fitness aspect of the program is ostensibly appealing may actually view it as a social outlet or an extension of our culture's obsession toward losing weight and staying attractive.

Although a variety of motives may serve as viable selling points to encourage program participation, Kotarba and Bently (1988) suggest that nonmedical reasons for participation may ultimately result in a trivial, short-lived commitment to exercise. Even when participants are aware of the association between exercise and reduced risk for disease, participation tends to gradually decline. For instance, a heart disease prevention program for public employees had a 61 percent participation rate at the end of one year, a 42 percent rate at the end of three years, and a 25 percent rate at the end of five years (Conrad, 1988). Further, in a study of 1,172 males and females at two worksites, only 20 percent of the sample exercised regularly, and approximately 25 percent did not intend to start in the next six months (Marcus et al., 1992).

Perceived major barriers to exercise must be considered when motivating employees to participate and when marketing the program. The desire to exercise may be short-lived when the reason to begin is to "stay in shape" or "look good." Hopefully, employees will remain in an exercise program because of the intrinsic motivation developed due to feeling better and other observable health improvements. People do change negative lifestyle habits once they learn to enjoy a program because of how good it makes them feel.

Pugh (1992) addressed other practical concerns that may affect the motivational component of health promotion programs. Program literature or educational material must be adapted to the demographic characteristics of the audience, especially the educational level on which the group is functioning. Class times should be convenient to all employees so all workers have equal program accessibility options. More employees will participate in a health-promoting activity or program if it is accessible, affordable, and convenient. For instance, when one company adapted its on-site fitness center to meet the needs of its blue-collar workers, participation increased from 3 to 15 percent (Gebhardt and Crump, 1990).

Ultimately, the driving force of the health promotion program may depend on the psychosocial aspects of the individual. Self-efficacy, locus of control, and self-worth contribute to personal feelings and resulting decisions (Walsh, 1988). Researchers have concluded that prior to a decision to join a particular program, participants must develop a sense of security or competence about the activity in which they are involved. Competence can be influenced by interpretation of prior experiences, anxiety of the unknown, and family structure and dynamics (Kotarba and Bently, 1988).

Since competency involves members believing they will fit in and do well, encouraging employees to join health promotion programs may entail marketing and educating strategies that focus on alleviating fears and enhancing competence. Prior negative experiences or perceptions such as feeling awkward, incurring an injury, or not being able to perform a task or achieve designated goals would require addressing self-efficacy issues. It is important for marketing efforts to convey messages that encourage everyone to join activities, regardless of their experience or abilities. Similarly, it is important to alleviate fears by projecting positive, nonintimidating messages toward potential participants. For instance, the typical media image of a young, well-conditioned exerciser in color-coordinated tights might intimidate the overweight or out-of-shape employee from joining a fitness program. These issues certainly need to be considered when planning marketing efforts.

POTENTIAL PROBLEM AREAS FOR HEALTH PROMOTION PROGRAMS

If health promotion programs are to remain viable over a long period, professionals must be aware of potential problems that can impede or even halt the program. Larry Chapman (1991) identified eight different areas where the potential exists for problems to arise that would hinder successful programs. We prefer to emphasize that if strength is demonstrated in each of the areas listed, a high probability exists for success. The following list includes the strengths needed if programs are to be successful:

1. Strong management support for the program
2. Sufficient funding for the program(s)
3. High levels of employee participation
4. Creation of long term behavior change
5. Exciting, motivating, creative programming, taught/led by enthusiastic, competent educators
6. Sense of employee ownership in the program
7. Documentation of program impact on employees
8. Demonstration of the program's strengthening of economic and social impact on the organization (adapted from a list by Chapman, preface).

The remaining chapters will present the skills and tools necessary for you to deal with each of the preceding areas, which will facilitate the success of health promotion activities.

TABLE 1.4. Return on Investment by Selected Companies

Company	Dollars Saved per One Dollar Invested
Coors	$6.15
Bank of America	$6.00
Kennecott Copper	$5.78
Equitable Life Insurance	$5.52
Travelers Insurance	$3.40
Blue Cross/Blue Shield of Indiana	$2.50
DuPont	$2.05

Source: "Economic Impact of Worksite Health Promotion," April 1, 1998, http://www.fitwellinc.com/noframe/hlthpro.htm.

THE FUTURE OF WORKSITE HEALTH PROMOTION

Health promotion programs can be a significant part of future cost containment options. In addition, these programs can serve as tools for attracting exceptional individuals to the workplace and developing a cooperative environment where production can flourish. Through the evolution of comprehensive programs and utilization of a wide range of creative intervention strategies, positive results can be achieved while providing a custom-made experience for employees. As the previously mentioned studies have indicated, health promotion programs do work. Recently, additions to the AWHP Web page indicate savings reported by several other companies. Table 1.4 contains some of the information on the return on investment by seven large companies due to their health promotion activities. These companies indicate that savings range from $6.15 to $2.05 for each dollar they invested in health promotion activities.

In the future, lifetime health care may be provided for all U.S. citizens through national health care reform. This does not mean health care costs will be reduced for corporate America specifically. Indeed, as the demand for more health care rises, the need to cover costs will also increase. If worksite health promotion programs are going to achieve their potential, a long-term, comprehensive approach is necessary. This requires time and commitment on the part of the company. Trained personnel who are knowledgeable concerning data and strategies to achieve specific results are mandatory. The ability to recognize the value of the total person is critical to achieving long-term goals. The rise in health care costs can be slowed and possibly reduced. Employee morale can be improved. Providing the type of cohesive environment where healthy change occurs is vital to the total success of a health promotion program. Worksite health promotion is a link in the chain that can benefit all who participate.

If a business/corporation is paying for health care costs for the family, these costs can be most readily impacted when the whole family becomes a part of the health promotion program. Program involvement should emphasize self-responsibility and allow for multiple types of interventions. The company should have the option of choosing those interventions that work best for its employees. By recognizing and fulfilling the localized needs of an organization, health promotion efforts will benefit the company and the profession of health promotion.

Profiles in Health Promotion

Avery Distribution Company employs seventy-five individuals. Two-thirds of the employees are female ranging in age from 25 to 60. The males range in age from 23 to 64 years of age. The average age for female employees is 39, and the average age of male employees is 45. Over the previous five years there has been more than a 40 percent increase in health care costs. The company has become alarmed at the potential impact on the company's ability to maintain a profitable operation. The personnel manager has suggested that perhaps a consultant be contacted to suggest possible cost-saving measures. Imagine that you are the consultant contacted by Avery Distribution. They are interested in how other companies are handling the increasing health care costs, and what steps should be taken to help impact on their own costs. What types of information would you provide and what initial steps would you suggest the Avery company take? Provide examples of the types of data you would supply.

Check It Out

Listed below are a variety of terms. How would you define each of the terms, and why are they important for health promotion?

Term	Your Definition	Implication for Health Promotion
A. Wellness	_____	_____
B. Health Education	_____	_____
C. Health Promotion	_____	_____
D. Awareness Activities	_____	_____
E. Lifestyle Change Programs	_____	_____
F. Supportive Environment Programs	_____	_____
G. Healthy People 2000	_____	_____
H. Professional Skills	_____	_____
I. Ethics and Health Promotion	_____	_____

Summary

- Health/wellness can be defined as "an integrated method of functioning which is oriented toward maximizing the potential of which the individual is capable."

- Health promotion is the aggregate of all purposeful activities designed to improve personal and public health through a combinations of strategies.
- Health education is one aspect of health promotion and is the process of providing learning experiences to facilitate the voluntary selections of behaviors conducive to positive health/wellness.
- Program offerings at the worksite fall into three categories: awareness activities, lifestyle change programs, and supportive environment programs.
- A plethora of program offerings are available at worksites ranging from injury prevention to prenatal education.
- Because of increasing health care costs and the national goals established in *Healthy People 2000,* opportunities in the business sector for health promotion activities have never been better.
- Working in health promotion today requires skills in business, management, marketing, counseling, health, and education.
- Ethical issues such as how to conduct business practices, marketing techniques, the right to privacy, and professional behavior are important considerations for health promotion specialists.
- Health education and health promotion activities can take place in a variety of settings including hospitals/clinical facilities, colleges, communities, and the elementary/secondary schools.
- Regardless of the setting, health promotion programs can provide a better quality of life, reduce health care costs, and help each individual develop a sense of personal empowerment.
- Medical care costs are the financial termites for any size company. Unless checked and reduced these costs can destroy a company's ability to remain financially solvent.
- Numerous companies have been able to demonstrate savings by offering various types of health promotion programs. These companies include J.P. Morgan, AT&T, Quaker Oats, Adolph Coors, Steelcase, Inc., and the City of Birmingham, Alabama.
- For health promotion programs to be successful, special attention must be given to the social and cultural differences of employees.
- It is also imperative to attempt to develop high participation rates and prevent attrition.
- Successful programs must have comprehensive marketing strategies.
- Every health promotion program needs to have employee involvement through participation of an employee advisory committee. Employee ownership for the various health promotion programs is vital to a successful effort.
- A strong employee advisory committee can help develop goals, objectives, plan, evaluate, and market health promotion programs.
- Potential problem areas for health promotion programs are (1) lack of strong management, (2) insufficient funding, (3) low levels of participation, (4) insufficient long-term behavioral change, (5) poor programs, (6) lack of employee ownership, (7) poor evaluation of programs, and (8) economic impact.
- Through the development of comprehensive and innovative programs and effective evaluation, the future of health promotion is exceptional in the business/corporate sector.

Bibliography

ALLENSWORTH, D. D., and KOLBE, L. J. 1987. The comprehensive school health program: Explore an expanded concept. *Journal of School Health* 57(10): 409–412.

Access- U-M. A Worksite Health Promotion Abstracting Service. 1994. U-M study confirms hunch; employees who improve their health habits can cut medical costs significantly for their employers. In *Worksite Wellness: Costs Benefits 1993 Analysis and Report* (Vol. 5). Ann Arbor, MI: The University of Michigan Fitness Research Center.

ANSPAUGH, D. J., HUNTER, S., and MOSLEY, J. 1995. The economic impact of corporate wellness programs—past and future. *American Association of Occupational Health Nurses* 43(4): 203–210.

ANSPAUGH, D. J., HUNTER, S., and SAVAGE, P. 1996. Enhancing employee participation in corporate health promotion programs. *American Journal of Health Behavior* 20(3): 112–120.

Association for Worksite Health Promotion. 1997. http://www.awhp.com/whatis.html.

BUTLER, J. T. 1994. *Principles of health education and health promotion*. Englewood, CO: Morton.

CHAPMAN, L. S. 1991. *Tough problems: Wellness solutions that work*. Seattle: Corporate Health Designs.

CHEN, M. S., and HAWKS, B. L. 1995. A debunking of the myth of healthy Asian Americans and Pacific Islanders. *American Journal of Health Promotion* 9(40): 261–268.

CONRAD, P. 1988. Worksite health promotion: The social context. *Social Science and Medicine* 26: 465–489.

Economic impact of worksite health promotion. World Wide Web, http://www.fitwellinc.com/noframe/hlthpro.htm.

First International Conference on Health Promotion. 1986. *Ottawa Charter for Health Promotion* 1(4): 3–4.

FRIES, J. F., HARRINGTON, H., EDWARDS, R., KENT, L. A., and RICHARDSON, N. 1994. Randomized controlled trial of cost reductions from a health education program: The California Public Employees' Retirement System (PERS) study. *American Journal of Health Promotion* 8: 216–223.

FRYE, B. A. 1995. Use of cultural themes in promoting health among southeast Asian refugees. *American Journal of Health Promotion* 9:40, 269–280.

GEBHARDT, D. L., and CRUMP, D. E. 1990. Employee fitness and wellness programs in the workplace. *American Psychology* 45: 262–272.

GLASGOW, R. E., and TERBORG, J. R. 1991. Occupational health promotion to reduce cardiovascular risk. *Journal of Consulting and Clinical Psychology* 56: 363–373.

GOLASZEWSKI, T., SNOW, D., LYNCH, L. Y., and SOLOMITA, D. 1992. A benefit-to-cost analysis of a work-site health promotion program. *Journal of Occupational Medicine* 34: 1164–1172.

GREEN, L. W., and KREUTER, M. W. 1991. *Health promotion planning—an educational and environmental approach* (2nd ed.). Mountain View, CA: Mayfield.

HARVEY, M. R., WHITMER, R. W., HILYER, J. C., and BROWN, K. C. 1993. The impact of comprehensive medical benefit cost management program for the city of Birmingham: Results at five years. *American Journal of Health Promotion* 7: 296–305.

Health Care Financing Administration. 1998. Office of the Actuary: Data from the Division of National Health Statistics. http://www.hcfa.gov/news/nhetbl1.htm.

Healthy people 2000—National health promotion and disease prevention objectives (Conference ed.) 1990. Washington, D.C.: U.S. Department of Health & Human Services.

HOLLANDER, R. B., LENGERMANN, J. J. 1988. Corporate characteristics and worksite health promotion programs: Survey findings from 500 companies. *Social Science and Medicine* 26: 551–558.

Joint Committee on Health Education Terminology. 1991. Report of the 1990 joint committee on health education terminology. *Journal of Health Education* 22: 97–108.

KAOTARBA, J. S., and BENTLY, P. 1988. Workplace wellness participation and becoming self. *Social Science and Medicine* 26: 551–558.

MARCUS, B. H., ROSSI, J. S., SHELBY, V. C., NIAURA, R. S., and ABRAMS, D. B. 1992. The stages and process of exercise adoption and maintenance in a worksite sample. *Health Psychology* 11: 136–395.

MCELROY, K., BIBEAU, D., STECKLER, A., and GLANZ, K. 1988. An ecological approach to health promotion programs. *Health Education Quarterly* 15(4): 351–377.

MCKENZIE, J. F., and SMELTZER, J. L. 1997. *Planning, implementing, and evaluating health promotion programs* (2nd ed.). Boston: Allyn & Bacon.

NEIGHBORS, H. W., BRAITHWAITE, R. L., and THOMPSON, E. 1992. Health promotion and African-Americans: From personal empowerment to community action. *American Journal of Health Promotion* 9(40): 281–287.

O'DONNELL, M. P. 1988. *Design of worksite health promotion programs* (2nd ed.). Birmingham, MI: American Journal of Health Promotion.

PELLETIER, K. R. 1993. A review and analysis of health and cost-effective outcome studies of comprehensive health promotion and disease prevention programs at the worksite: 1991–1993. *Update* 8(1): 50–62.

POLLING, H. A. 1992. (Comments). Clinton Economic Conference, Little Rock, AR.

PROCHASKA, J. O., D. CLEMENTE, C. C., and NORCROSS, J. C. 1997. In search of how people change: Application to addictive behaviors, *American Psychologist* 47(9): 1104–1114.

WALCOTT-MCGUIGG, J. 1994. Gender and cultural diversity issues. *American Association of Occupational Health Nurses* 42(11): 528–533.

WALSH, D. C. 1988. Toward a sociology of worksite health promotion: A few reactions and reflections. *Social Science and Medicine* 26: 569–575.

CHAPTER 2

Planning Health Promotion Programs

OBJECTIVES

CHAPTER OBJECTIVES

After reading this chapter, you should be able to

- define the process of planning health promotion programs.
- identify the procedures for securing management support for the health promotion program.
- discuss the importances of understanding corporate culture.
- describe the procedures for developing and implementing needs assessments.
- identify the tasks necessary to successfully establish a health promotion program.
- develop a mission statement, goals, priorities, and objectives for a health promotion program.

Planning, implementing, and evaluating a health promotion program is a complex task. Unfortunately, what works at one worksite will not necessarily work at another. Program planning should be predicated upon the needs of a particular organization, not what worked at another worksite. Although it is not always necessary to "reinvent the wheel," it is necessary to examine, through a planned process, the administrative support, logistical needs, company culture, budgetary requirements, and perceived needs of the clients to be served.

To **plan** means to "engage in a process or a procedure to develop a method for achieving an end" (Breckon, Harvey, and Kancaster, 1994, p. 11). In the corporate/business sector, planning a health promotion program is a multiphase process requiring time, commitment, and insight into the social culture of that company. Every program should be tailored to the corporate philosophy, the company's desires for the health promotion program, and the employees' needs and desires. In this chapter, the process, tools, and insights necessary for successfully bringing a health promotion program to fruition will be discussed.

DETERMINING MANAGEMENT SUPPORT

The beginning point for any health promotion program at the business/corporate level is determining the level of support and commitment of senior management. To be successful, a program must have strong corporate backing from a philosophical, moral, and financial perspective. The desire for a health promotion program may be initiated from an employee, employee committee, a company executive, or even a federal/state mandate. Ideally, the stimulus for health promotion will come from upper-level management. In this case, the concept of the program will not have to be "sold" to decision makers in order to obtain their support. Unfortunately, this is not the case in every business/corporate setting. Upper management must then be shown the potential that health promotion holds for enhancing employees' lifestyles. A variety of strategies can be used to substantiate the value of health promotion programs, such as providing research demonstrating health cost savings, supplying examples of model programs at other worksites, and furnishing results of employee surveys conducted concerning employee needs/interests.

The best way to secure top management support is a face-to-face interview with the chief executive officer (CEO) of the company. Through such a meeting, the lines of communication can be established, insight into the company culture determined, and, hopefully, a financial commitment for beginning the health promotion program can be determined. In addition to the CEO, it is essential to conduct individual interviews with all managers, since these individuals are in charge of allocating financial resources, and provide logistical support. A well conducted interview with a manager can be the opportunity to assess his/her personal perceptions & expectations for a health promotion program and ascertain the amount of company support and personal involvement she/he will be willing to supply. Further, by first talking to and securing the CEO's blessing, other top managers are usually more willing to provide their commitment and endorsement for the program. The process of securing top management support is not necessarily a simple or an easy task. Sometimes it may take months of efforts to bring to fruition the endorsements and cooperation of top management. However, without such commitment for the long haul, programs can be doomed to failure at the first indication of economic downturn within a company or if success is not immediate.

During the initial meeting with the CEO every effort should be made not only to discover the level of commitment and involvement, but also to educate and

Support from management is critical to success for health promotion programs.

broaden the CEO's vision of the possibilities a health promotion program offers to the company. This time allows opportunity to share the successes other corporate/business programs have experienced and to identify a vision for the program under consideration. Finally, this interview time can be used to determine the standard of performance the CEO feels would best reflect a successful program (Bellingham and Tager, 1986). One word of caution for this interview time with top and middle management: It is important to not make promises that cannot be fulfilled. For example, extravagant claims of health cost reductions probably cannot be achieved during the first few years of a new program. Such claims will only result in loss of support of mid and upper management, reduced enthusiasm, and lessening of resources; lowering of financial commitments are also possible. Figure 2.1 contains potential questions that can be asked during interviews with the CEO and other management personnel.

UNDERSTANDING CULTURAL NORMS

Webster's New Collegiate Dictionary defines **culture** as "the integrated pattern of human behavior that includes thought, speech, action, and artifacts and depends on man's capacity for learning and transmitting knowledge to succeeding generations." Corporate culture, as defined by Mainiero and Tromley (1989, p. 31), views worksite culture as the "shared values, beliefs, norms, and assumptions that guide (often unconsciously) the behavior of the members of an organization." For health promotion specialists working in the business/corporate sector, it is imperative to know and understand their corporate cultural environment. Company culture describes the informal cultural elements of a particular business or "the way things get done" within an organization.

Every organization has a culture. Sometimes it is fragmented and difficult to identify, and at other times it is fairly apparent. Whether the cultural aspects of a business/corporation are readily identified or less obvious, they can have a powerful influence throughout the organization. Cultural climate affects who gets promoted, what decisions are made, how employees dress, in what activities employees engage, the informal channels of communication, office protocol, break times, and, perhaps most important, whether employees choose to participate in health promotion activities.

To use the company culture to advantage in health promotion, it is necessary to define what that culture is within any given environment. It is vital to comprehend that while all companies have a culture and many companies share cultural values, each corporation and each worksite situation is unique in their professional and personal values and priorities. In any organization, the details and specifics of that culture need to be assessed and properly defined before situation-specific programming can occur. Very few health promotion programs really fit all circumstances. Therefore, the more health promotion specialists develop sensitivity toward their particular situation and environment, the better prepared they are to design, adapt, incorporate, and include programs, events, and activities that will truly meet the needs and find the support of the employees at their worksite. Inability to understand the culture of the environment within which health promotion functions will

FIGURE 2.1. Potential Interview Questions for Management Support of Health Promotion Programs

---

1. Perceptions of Program Content

    A. What is your perception of what should be included in a health promotion program?
    B. What type of program(s) should be offered by this company?
    C. What type of participation rates would you envision as critical for success?
    D. What type of timeline do you see for the development of a comprehensive program?
    E. What type of programs should receive the highest priority?
    F. Are there other health promotion programs of which you are aware?

2. Management Support

    A. Would you participate in the health promotion program offerings?
    B. In which programs would you participate? How often?
    C. What would motivate you to participate?
    D. What would keep you from participating in the health promotion program?
    E. Would you encourage other managers and employees to participate in the program?
    F. How strong do you view the support of other managers for health promotion programs?

3. Financial Support

    A. What do you view as realistic start-up costs for a health promotion program?
    B. What type of financial commitment are you willing to make at this time?
    C. Do you have any projections on cost per employee for health promotion programs?
    D. In your opinion, should employees help underwrite the cost of the health promotion programs?
    E. Do you have any suggestions for additional revenue for the health promotion program?

4. Potential Benefits

    A. From a management perspective, what type of benefits are you expecting from the health promotion program?
    B. What short-term results does management expect from a health promotion program?
    C. What type of company benefits do you expect to occur over the long term?
    D. What do view as the most important benefits for the employees for the short term? Long term?
    E. What is a realistic timetable for the program to demonstrate long-term benefits for the company?

5. Strategies for Implementation

    A. What do you feel are the keys to a successful health promotion program?
    B. What needs to be done to ensure midmanagement support for the program?
    C. What corporate culture values should be considered when planning a health promotion program?
    D. What are the positive cultural norms of the company? Negative norms?

---

result in decreased results. In other words, lack of cultural perceptiveness can result in programs that are poorly attended, possibly resented by employees, have high levels of attrition, and poor prognosis for long-term success. Without the support of the employees, there is no program.

    Understanding of company culture is achieved by developing insight into what employers and employees value. By being able to define and list the key cultural concerns expressed by a company, the health promotion team will be able to determine: (1) the norms of the work environment: what standards are important—the behavior, dress, and interactions considered acceptable, desirable, and unacceptable; (2) the peer support for health promotion programs: which groups advocate which programs and who they will positively influence; (3) the organizational support for health promotion: the individuals within management who will sustain the program and how strongly they encourage such concepts; and (4) the organizational climate for health promotion: where and how health promotion fits into corporate goals and standards; the conceptual goal of what health promotion should achieve for the company; what risks the company will take to support programs, how long it will wait before requiring evidence of positive impact and what kinds of changes it expects to see.

A goal of health promotion specialists within an organization is to understand the culture of their organization. A variety of methodologies should be utilized to achieve this goal. Cultural norms and values can be assessed through observation, company interviews, surveys, questionnaires, suggestion boxes, requests or expressions of interest by personnel, and interpersonal interactions with management and employees.

Each company has its own social systems for defining and perpetuating its culture. The company's culture is developed and maintained via modeling, training, rewards, recognition, and communications within the company. Factors such as resource allocation; management and employee commitment to the company and its programs; and rituals, myths, and symbols that have developed within the company over the history of the organization (Allen, 1995) all provide insight into culture.

An important aspect of company culture is the informal communications facilitated by "storytellers," "spies," and "whisperers" within a company. This unofficial network serves to form a hidden, interconnected system of power within an organization. Recognizing who operates and manages this system and how this informal structure functions can be a key to securing support for programs, participation, and long-term corporate change. Having an inside track with the people who "spread the word" about events and happenings, both good and bad, can facilitate transmittal of information about events and activities as well as providing insight into the culturally perceived value of these events.

Companies tend to have their own "heroes." Heroes are individuals who others respect and look to as role models. These individuals may or may not hold official titles but are viewed as people who know how to get things done and who represent behavior(s) others admire. Heroes can be leaders and trendsetters. Identifying and soliciting the assistance of these people in developing health promotion programs can go a long way toward gathering initial employee support for health promotion efforts. People with power, who are supporters of health promotion, whether officially recognized by the company or not, can largely influence the success or failure of programming. It is imperative to involve these people and to find ways to incorporate them into activities that require the support of employees. Solidarity among workers can enhance participation, even if people attend simply to "be there" for the people they respect.

Incorporating company culture into health promotion can provide a powerful lever for change. Choosing to focus on events and activities aimed at or dovetailing off of culturally determined priority values will enhance participation and success. For instance, if the culture within the organization places high priority on taking care of children, then planned events need to include families where children can participate and perhaps play a key part in the event. A health fair with a parent-child baseball game might increase attendance. Activities or programs that are aimed at improving childhood health or can assist parents in developing parent-child relationships or even programs that emphasize the importance of taking care of one's health to ensure that they will be around for their children for a long time are all ways to "use" cultural values to achieve a result of improved health for employees. Gaining the support of the company culture can enhance health promotion programs, make them viable, and contribute to program longevity.

When a worksite culture is basically toxic, that is, the emphasis is on working double shifts, ignoring one's health, or drinking a couple of six packs of beer every night when work is completed, it becomes important to find ways to positively alter the environment and the norms. *Changing* a worksite culture seems to depend on a variety of factors. Allen (1993) has identified several factors that need to be included when planning programs to alter existing worksite culture(s). They include the following: (1) engage in a systematic change process—have a plan that will guide the effort from initiation through implementation and to evaluation; (2) develop multilevel programming—strategies for individuals as well as for groups within the worksite; (3) work from a sound information base—know/understand the worksite culture and use that information to the advantage of the program; (4) incorporate results-oriented activities into the program—use proven strategies and activities to achieve measurable results in relatively brief periods of time; (5) use win-win approaches—strategies and activities that do not "victim blame" groups or individuals (i.e., avoid programs that would indicate smokers are the cause of high insurance rates; rather, adopt programs that emphasize benefits of quitting smoking from a personal perspective and make people believe they can succeed); (6) show concern and empathy for both the individual and the

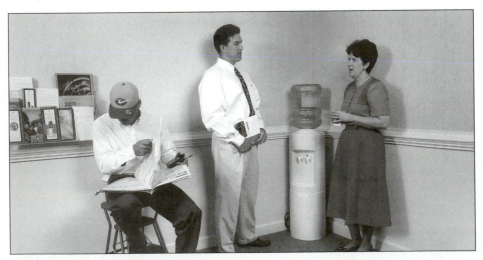

Understanding corporate culture is necessary when developing health promotion programs.

organization—both groups have needs and long-term goals that should be recognized and addressed; demonstrate how involvement in activities will facilitate these goals; (7) involve and empower people—individuals should be represented from all facets of the worksite so that personal values drive the agenda for cultural change and all groups are represented and recognized as having merit; and (8) articulate a clear vision of program themes and principles—develop a clear, shared vision for all workers and list the steps to be taken to integrate these goals into existing worksite culture.

NEEDS ASSESSMENTS

In any setting, it is necessary to determine the health needs of the group under consideration. Various terms have been used to define this process, including Dignan and Carr's *community analysis/community diagnosis* (Dignan and Carr, 1992). This term describes the process of determining what health problems exist in any given group of people within a particular setting. The term used most often in the planning of health promotion programs in the business/corporate sector is needs assessment. A **needs assessment** is defined similarly to the community analysis in that "needs assessment is a planned process that identifies the reported needs of an individual or a group" (Gilmore and Campbell, 1996, p. 5). Regardless of what term is used, carrying out a survey of the health needs of the group(s) for whom the health promotion programs are intended is an integral part of the planning process. In fact, the first step after interviewing the CEO and management personnel is to assess the needs of the intended clients. Three vital questions should be answered during the needs assessment: (1) What are the perceived health practices and needs of the client population?; (2) In what wellness topics and activities are the clients interested?; and (3) What level of readiness (interest) do potential clients demonstrate/vocalize (readiness is discussed in chapter 3)?

To assess the health practices and habits of clients, the utilization of health risk appraisals (HRAs) is recommended. The costs of an HRA may range from moderate to expensive; however, the information obtained can provide a comprehensive picture of the health status of the client population (HRAs are discussed in detail later in the text). To assess the topics and activities of interest to clients, questionnaires and surveys can also be developed. This same questionnaire/survey can be used to address the level of readiness of clients for various health promotion activities. Determining the level of readiness for action can reduce time spent in activities that will yield little or no results while providing data for the types of interventions that will be most positively received. An example of an interest/readiness survey is found in figure 2.2.

PREPARING SUMMARY REPORT

After interviewing management and employees, conducting a needs assessment, and determining current client health status, a summary report that establishes a strong position for an effective health promotion program should be written. This report provides the rationale for the program itself and for the goals of the program.

FIGURE 2.2. Sample Survey Instruments for Assessing Interests and Readiness for Health Promotion

Please take a few minutes to fill out the following survey. Individual information will not be disclosed; only summary results will be tabulated and reported. At no time will individual responses be reported.

1. Listed are various health promotion programs that might be offered by the Company X's Fitness and Wellness program. Please indicate your interest in each of the programs.

Program	Low interest				High interest
Nutrition	1	2	3	4	5
Weight loss	1	2	3	4	5
Cancer screening	1	2	3	4	5
Cardiovascular risk reduction	1	2	3	4	5
Hypertension control	1	2	3	4	5
Men's health issues	1	2	3	4	5
Women's health issues	1	2	3	4	5
Parenting skill	1	2	3	4	5
Developing communication skills	1	2	3	4	5
Assertiveness training	1	2	3	4	5
Healthy back	1	2	3	4	5
Stress management skills	1	2	3	4	5
Time management	1	2	3	4	5
HIV and AIDS education	1	2	3	4	5
Alcohol education	1	2	3	4	5
Drug education	1	2	3	4	5
Home and personal safety	1	2	3	4	5
Exercise and fitness programs	1	2	3	4	5
Smoking cessation	1	2	3	4	5

Other suggestions_____

2. What classes/programs would you attend if the time of the program was convenient to you?

	Would Definitely Attend	Would Probably Attend	Would Not Attend
Nutrition	_____	_____	_____
Weight loss	_____	_____	_____
Cancer screening	_____	_____	_____
Cardiovascular risk reduction	_____	_____	_____
Hypertension control	_____	_____	_____
Men's health issues	_____	_____	_____
Women's health issues	_____	_____	_____
Parenting skill	_____	_____	_____
Developing communication skills	_____	_____	_____
Assertiveness training	_____	_____	_____
Healthy back	_____	_____	_____
Stress management skills	_____	_____	_____

(continued)

FIGURE 2.2. (*continued*)

Time management	_____	_____	_____
HIV and AIDS education	_____	_____	_____
Alcohol education	_____	_____	_____
Drug education	_____	_____	_____
Home and personal safety	_____	_____	_____
Exercise and fitness programs	_____	_____	_____
Smoking cessation	_____	_____	_____

3. What would be the best time to attend these programs?
   ___A. Prior to work   ___B. Lunch time   ___C. After work   ___D. Weekends

4. Would your spouse or significant other take part in the health promotion program?
   ___Yes   ___No   ___Maybe

5. Would you participate in an exercise program with males and females (coed)?
   ___Yes   ___No

6. In what type of exercise programs would you participate?
   ___Aerobics   ___Swimming   ___Walking   ___Jogging
   ___Weight Lifting   ___Tennis   ___Racquetball   ___Other (please list)

7. Are you a ___Female ___Male?

8. What is your age range?
   ___20–30   ___31–40   ___42–50   ___51–60   ___Over 60

9. Are you   ___Upper Management   ___Middle Management
   ___Staff   ___Production?

A well-documented and well-written report can be a persuasive tool as well as a guideline for health promotion/disease prevention development. A comprehensive report should contain at least four sections to best provide an integrative perspective. These main four sections are (1) representation of the needs, interest, and support for health promotion within the organization; (2) demographic data; (3) the current health status of employees; and (4) recommendations for an effective health promotion program at this organization.

In the first section of the report, a precise summary of the CEO's vision and support, management's vision and support, and employee vision/needs/interest should be included. The second section should deal with the company demographics. This section would indicate the number of employees who participated in the surveys, the average age(s) of these employees, percentage of males and females, racial and ethnic composition, proportion of management/staff, employee family size, on-site versus off-site employees, and any other data that could be useful in program development. The third section should present a breakdown of the current health status of the employees, as gathered by an instrument such as an HRA. It is imperative that client confidentiality be maintained throughout the report and that no individuals are mentioned in the course of developing the summary health status report. Confidentiality increases client accuracy in reporting personal information, reduces fear of reprisal, and protects clients' right to privacy. The health status summary will define the most prevalent problems found in the workforce. An accurate health status report will determine the number of employees who are hypertensive, diabetic, have high cholesterol, suffer from low-back problems, smoke, or experience high stress levels. Any problems indicated in the employee population should be discussed in this section of the report.

The fourth section of the summary report consists of the recommendations for the health promotion program for the company. Justification for these recommendations should be based on the data gathered in the survey(s) (Wellness Councils of America [WELCOA], 1995). Recommendations must reflect the interests and needs of the employees and management, as well as the current health status/problems within the company. For a program to succeed, a strong sense of ownership within the employee community must exist. The starting point for that sense of ownership is an honest, true reflection of employee desires, needs, and interests embodied in the initial report. *Above all,* the recommendations should *not* be the desires of health promotion specialists who believe they know what is best for an organization. Although health promotion specialists may realize a need not recognized by the employees, initial efforts should be focused on the stated desires of the employees. Other programs can be added as health promotion efforts mature.

THE EMPLOYEE HEALTH PROMOTION COMMITTEE

The support of top management is a key ingredient to the success of any health promotion program. However, the ultimate success or failure of a program will depend on acceptance by employees at all levels of the organization. A highly effective method of developing such support is to form an employee health promotion committee. This committee should have representation from all levels of management and from all departments within the organization. It should be composed of not only those who are very prohealth promotion but also people who are nonhealth promotion clients or reluctant participants. By creating a committee of this type, a diversity of opinions and viewpoints can be gathered regarding important issues for promoting successful health programs. Unfortunately, governance by committee is slow, highly political, and most members of an employee committee are not health promotion professionals (Frank, 1989); therefore, it is imperative that the committee not be the decision-making authority for the health promotion program. However, the committee serves an appropriate role as an advisory group, helping with program design, providing invaluable marketing suggestions, and selling the various components of the program to their respective groups. An effective committee contributes to a sense of ownership by employees and delivers health promotion personnel access to channels of communication needed for policy review, program planning, implementation, and evaluation. This group can be particularly effective in interpreting policy to the various subgroups or union representatives.

The employee committee should be selected carefully and be in philosophical agreement with the mission of the health promotion program, goals, and objectives

FIGURE 2.3. Schematic of the Process of Developing a Health Promotion Program

1. Determine Management Support

A. Top Management
B. Middle Management
C. Financial Commitment

2. Needs Assessment Survey

A. Management
B. Employees (all levels)
   –needs, interest surveys
   –health status—HRAs

3. Summary Report

A. Health Status of Employees
B. Needs and Interest
C. Recommendations for Program(s)

4. Form Employee Committee

A. Representative of All Employees
B. Advise, Promote, Develop Programs
C. Represent All Employee Groups, Not
   Just Those Who Are Pro Health
   Promotion

5. Mission Statement/Goals/Objectives

A. Philosophy and Scope
B. Approved by Management/Employees
C. Long-Term and Short-Term Goals
D. Long-Term and Short-Term Objectives
E. Staff Hiring and Training
F. Equipment Purchases

6. Programs

A. Program Selection
B. Program Marketing Plan
C. Program Development
D. Program Implementation
E. Program Evaluation

(fig. 2.3). Members can either be appointed or volunteer for the committee. Whatever the selection process, members should represent all segments of the company, have an outgoing personality, be enthusiastic, be accepted among their peers, and be creative. Not all members need to be role models for fitness and wellness, since viewpoints of the fit, as well as the unfit, are important for success. Committee members must understand their roles and be willing to meet and participate on a regular basis. If the members are to be selected, these concepts should be clearly communicated to those making the selection (Association for Fitness in Business, 1992). Usually membership is for a year so others will have an opportunity to participate and burnout can be avoided (Bellingham and Tager, 1986).

TIMETABLE FOR DEVELOPMENT

The process of developing a comprehensive health promotion program or even a single component takes a much longer time than is generally expected. In the case of a comprehensive health program, the time framework necessary for development may be a year or more. For new individual programs, it may require up to six months of planning to implement a health promotion effort. Adequate time for all facets of planning is essential. Not only is appropriate administrative support needed, but proper staff selection and training is required, adequate equipment and materials need to be obtained, an effective marketing campaign must be planned, and evaluation procedures must be established, if a program is to experience both short- and long-term success.

FIGURE 2.4. A Task Development Time Line for a Comprehensive Health Promotion Program

Task	Monthly Time Line for Accomplishment											
	J	**F**	**M**	**A**	**M**	**J**	**J**	**A**	**S**	**O**	**N**	**D**
Interview CEO	X											
Determine Financial Commitment	X											
Interview Upper/Middle Management	X											
Interview/Survey Client Groups		X										
Administer HRA		X										
Write Summary Report		X										
Form Employee Committee			X									
Development Mission Statement			X									
Develop Goals and Objectives			X									
Determine Programs			X									
Determine Staff Needs			X									
Determine Equipment Needs			X									
Train Staff			X									
Program Planning				X	X	X	X					
Program I				X	X	X	X					
Program II				X	X	X	X					
Program III				X	X	X	X					
Program Marketing Developed								X	X			
Comprehensive program								X				
Individual Components								X	X	X	X	X
Program Evaluation Planned				X								X
Program Implementation										X		
Program I										X		
Program II										X		
Program III										X		
Evaluation of Program												X
Program I										X		
Program II												X
Program III												X

To promote success in planning a project, some type of time framework must be established. Figure 2.4 illustrates a **Task Development Time Line.** This type of conceptualization identifies the tasks needed to complete the project and the month or time period in which those tasks will be accomplished. Figure 2.5 is an example of a Gantt chart, which provides a slightly different presentation of a project outline. A **Gantt chart** is defined as a visual portrayal of tasks that includes the projected starting and completion dates for various activities. The task development time line illustrates the planning of a comprehensive, long-term health promotion program, whereas the Gantt chart illustrates a shorter education program for the worksite.

FIGURE 2.5. Gantt Chart for Developing a Stress Management Class

Task	June			July				August	
	1	14	28	1	8	15	30	1	5
Plan Class	+++++++++								
Order Materials		+++++++++							
Plan Marketing Strategies		++++++++++++++++++							
Begin Marketing Campaign				++++++++++++++					
Registration for Class						++++++++++			
Teach Class								+++++++++	
Evaluate Class									+

PROGRAM PHILOSOPHY

During the health promotion assessment process, there should be an emerging framework of basic program beliefs and of the types/nature of programs to be offered. This framework of program reference is the **philosophy** of the program. The philosophy should mirror what management and employees envision concerning the commitment and expectations for the health promotion program. The statement of philosophy need not be lengthy, but it should reflect a clear vision for the emerging program. This philosophy represents the guiding principles upon which the entire health promotion program will be built. The philosophy is unique to each particular organization. Program philosophy cannot be taken from another organization and transplanted because these beliefs are the road map for developing the mission statement (see next section), establishing short- and long-term goals and objectives, selecting program priorities, and planning the evaluation component(s) of the program.

The actual formulating of the philosophy can best be accomplished by a small group of two to three people. These individuals should be able to analyze and communicate in written form the feelings of management and the desires of the employees as determined by the needs assessment phase. The philosophical statement should then be reviewed by the employee advisory committee and approved by upper-level management before moving forward with the creation of the mission statement. The following considerations are important when defining program philosophy:

1. Purpose of the program (public relations, morale, cost containment)
2. Goals (what type of impact is expected)
3. Wellness model to be used/created
4. Depth and scope of the program
5. Image of the program and the company
6. Internal versus external development/operation of the program (Association for Fitness in Business, 1992).

FIGURE 2.6. Example of a Statement of Philosophy

Avery Architectural Consulting & Planning, Inc., firmly believes that all employees and their families are valuable members of the company family. Based upon this belief, it is the desire of Avery Architectural Consulting & Planning, Inc. to provide a workplace environment enabling opportunity for optimal personal and professional growth for every employee. The opportunities provided are designed to promote and enhance quality of employees' personal and corporate life. Participation in these activities and events will be voluntary in nature and open to all adult family members. To help facilitate greater personal and company well-being, the Avery Corporation is committed to creating a comprehensive health promotion program designed to fulfill individual and groups needs and aspirations. The health promotion program seeks to be proactive in meeting the identified goals of the individual as well as those of the organization. Some programs will be specifically designed for individuals via counseling, personal tailoring to individual needs, follow-up consulting, and cultural support to sustain positive health actions. Group programs will be developed which provide a broader perspective and will aid in group changes, company cultural changes, and a supportive environment enhancing health-related actions and behaviors.

Figure 2.6 illustrates one example of what a company might institute as a guide to the development of a mission statement, goals, and objectives.

DEVELOPING THE MISSION STATEMENT

After completing the assessment phase, establishing the need for a health promotion program, writing the summary report, organizing the employee committee, and developing and approving the statement of philosophy, the process of organizing the actual health promotion program(s) begins. The **mission statement** is a statement of what the expectations of the program are, who is eligible for the program (groups within the company, spouses, family members, retirees, etc.), the scope for the program (what types, depth), and the evaluation criteria (indicators of success). The mission statement should reflect management philosophy, management and employee goals, employee interest, and company culture. All this should be stated in a fairly short, precise statement. The mission statement is what the company embraces as the guideline for directing the development of the health promotion effort. Like the philosophical statement, it is the company "mind-set" for the actual program.

The mission statement can be developed one of two ways. The health promotion director can write an initial draft and then have it approved by the CEO of the company, or the health promotion committee can formulate the mission statement. Either way, the final mission statement must be approved by management as the representative reason for the development and existence of the health promotion program. Examples of two mission statements are provided in figure 2.7.

FIGURE 2.7. Examples of Mission Statements

Example 1

It is the mission of the ABC Company to provide a work environment conducive to facilitating a healthier lifestyle both at the worksite and in the employees' personal functioning. The programs will focus on enhancing activity levels, following proper nutritional guidelines, reducing stress, and promoting a nonsmoking environment.

Example 2

The mission of the Healthy Employee Wellness Program of the XYZ Company is to promote and support health-enhancing lifestyles of its employees and their spouses by providing opportunities to enhance health-related awareness, increase personal knowledge, influence attitudes, and change behavior, leading to a higher level of personal wellness. The secondary mission is to have at least 85% of the employee population and 50% of spouses engaged in the Healthy Employee Wellness programs.

GOALS AND OBJECTIVES

As an outgrowth of the mission statement, goals and objectives for the health promotion program can be developed. Both goals and the objectives should reflect and further identify the organization of the health promotion program. A **goal** is defined as a general statement(s) concerning a desired outcome. Goals should be developed for both the short term and long term and be subject to periodic review. Each goal should have related objectives. **Objectives** are precise statements of outcome defining criteria necessary for successful outcomes. To develop effective objectives, the following four elements should be included:

1. *Doer of Action:* The client(s) or person(s) who will perform the desired activity (employees with diabetes; all managers; on-site staff, etc.)
2. *Outcome or What Will Change:* What will change as a result of the health promotion program (knowledge, attitudes, action, or behavior due to the program)
3. *Conditions:* Conditions under which the outcome will be observed or when the change will occur (at lunch; during break time; at home)
4. *Criteria:* What standard will be utilized to indicate success has been achieved (three times a week; daily; 90% of the time)

Knowing how to construct objectives is an important skill for health promotion specialists. Constructing well-written, measurable objectives requires time and practice, with the process usually requiring several rewrites to convey the intent. This process is important because objectives provide the link between needs assessment, the mission statement, goals, and the planned actions of the health promotion program. The following are some considerations when developing objectives:

1. Can the objectives be realistically achieved?
2. Can they be realized during the life of the program?

3. Does the program have enough resources (personnel, budget, space) to meet the requirements of the objective?
4. Are the objectives consistent with the mission, policies, and procedures of the company?
5. Do the objectives violate any of the rights of clients?

In addition, health promotion planners must deal with several types of objectives. Deeds (1992) identified these objectives on several levels and placed them in a hierarchy that covers several areas of concern for health promotion professionals. The types of objectives formulated by Deeds (1992) include:

1. *Administrative objectives.* Administrative objectives focus on evaluating intervention strategies, targeting population attendance and participation, procuring materials utilized, and finding appropriate space/environment for programs.
2. *Learning objectives.* There are four types of learning objectives: awareness, knowledge, attitude, and skill development. The objectives progress from least complex (awareness) to most complex (skill development). Complexity depends on the time, effort, and resources required to meet the objective (Parkinson & Associates, 1982). These objectives are developed to measure increased awareness, expansion, deeper understanding of knowledge, development of attitude(s) that enable clients to deal with specific concerns, and the acquisition of skills to engage in more positive health behavior.
3. *Behavioral and environmental objectives.* These are behaviors in which clients will engage to help solve their problems. These objectives commonly deal with adherence, compliance, prevention, self-care, access, or the psychological/emotional climate of the environment.
4. *Program objectives.* Program objectives are described by Deeds as the ultimate objectives because they are designed to provide changes in health status, social benefits, or quality of life. These objectives are written in terms of morbidity, mortality, disability, or quality of life.

Every program must determine objectives in the preceding areas. Obviously, it requires some time and insight to formulate all the objectives utilized in developing all facets of a health promotion program. One or two objectives will not meet the needs of a comprehensive program. In fact, a variety of objectives that cover all levels will better enable an extensive review and evaluation of all components of a program. Figure 2.8 illustrates a program goal with the accompanying program objectives. Figure 2.9 illustrates the relationship of the mission statement to goals and objectives.

ESTABLISHING PRIORITIES

As a result of the needs assessment and other information gathered during the process, it should become evident that certain programs are needed more than others. Occasionally, several identified needs will appear to be of equal importance. Unfortunately, decisions may have to be made that delay or even eliminate certain types of programs. These decisions may be based on budget requirements, company

FIGURE 2.8. An Example of a Program Goal and Accompanying Objectives

Program Goal I

Reduce the incidence of job-related low-back injuries.

Short-Term Objectives

(1) All employees will attend the "Operation Safe Back" program on correct lifting and strengthening of low-back and abdominal muscles.
(2) All employees will receive the brochure "Healthy Back" demonstrating correct lifting technique and information on exercises for maintaining a healthy back.

Long-Term Objectives

(1) Within a four-month period of time the incidence of back injury insurance claims will be reduced by 75% as a result of employees participating in "Operation Safe Back" exercise program.
(2) Days lost from work as a result of low-back injury will be reduced by 75% due to 90% employee participation in the "Operation Safe Back Program."

Program Goal II

Reduce the job-related stress of all employees.

Short-Term Objectives—One Year or Less

(1) Relaxation classes for reducing stress will be provided with 65% participation rates of 75% of the employee population.
(2) All employees will receive the brochure "Effective Time Management."

Long-Term Objectives—More than One Year

(1) Fifty percent of the workforce will participate in some form of exercise program.
(2) Reported stress will be reduced by 50% over a three-year period.

FIGURE 2.9. Relationship of the Mission Statement to Goals and Objectives

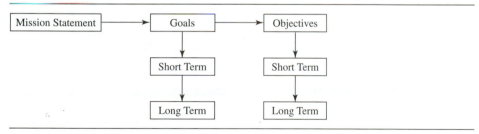

philosophy, or the most pressing needs and desires of the employees. Priorities for programs help make the planning process manageable and allow for creative, exciting programs. Establishing priorities will help in training and hiring professionals who can facilitate excellent programs that address the requirements of the company. This is especially important since one poorly done program can create a negative image among the employees that will be difficult to overcome in further health promotion efforts. Overall priorities should reflect the philosophy as well as the needs

Profiles in Health Promotion

Suppose you are the health promotion manager charged with gathering information for a needs assessment for the Gnome Manufacturing Company. It has been decided that, during the needs assessment phase, information will be gathered from the CEO, middle managers, and potential clients of the health promotion program. Your task is to decide what type of information is needed and how it should be gathered. The needs assessment is to begin within the next few weeks. The CEO has agreed to be interviewed and has requested that a plan for gathering data for the needs assessment be shared at that time.

1. What types of information would it be important to determine when interviewing the CEO?
2. What questions would you ask the CEO?
3. What would be your plan for gathering information from middle management? potential clients?
4. What types of information would you gather concerning the company culture?

Check It Out

Listed below are several activities necessary for initiating an employee health promotion program. In the first column indicate the order that each step should occur beginning with number one. In the second blank indicate the rationale for doing that particular step.

Step	Order Done	Rationale for Doing
Develop interest survey(s)	_____	_____
Arrange for health status assessment	_____	_____
Survey employees	_____	_____
Interview the CEO	_____	_____
Determine priorities	_____	_____
Survey middle management	_____	_____
Write the mission statement	_____	_____
Development a summary report	_____	_____
Develop goals and objectives	_____	_____
Determine financial commitment	_____	_____
Develop program proposals	_____	_____

---

of potential clients. The employee committee can provide direction in establishing priorities. This also will encourage participation in potential programs by giving the employees a sense of ownership in the health promotion program.

Questions that might be asked in determining program priorities are:

1. What programs offer the most services to the greatest number of employees?
2. Will the employees participate readily in the program?

3. What programs are most congruent with the mission of the health promotion program?
4. Will the program(s) contribute to the short-term goals?
5. Will the program(s) contribute to the long-term goals?
6. Will the program(s) create visibility within the company for the health promotion?
7. Does the staff have the expertise to adequately develop and implement the program(s)?
8. Are there adequate facilities, equipment, and supplies to support the program(s)?
9. What are the problems associated with implementing the program(s) into the company culture?
10. Can the program(s) fit within the health promotion budget at the present time?

Summary

- Every worksite must be examined to determine the individual needs of that group; what works at one setting may not apply to another.
- The beginning point in the process of program planning is determining the senior management's level of support of and commitment to health promotion programs.
- A face-to-face interview with the CEO is the best way to determine top management support.
- The interview of the CEO is an excellent time not only to determine the commitment and involvement of the CEO but also to educate and broaden that person's vision of the possibilities of the health promotion program.
- Company culture is how things get done within an organization. Understanding a company's culture is important in developing support and in planning health promotion programs. Key to understanding company culture is what employees value, the peer support system, the informal lines of communication, and the norms of the work environment.
- A needs assessment is a planned process that identifies the reported needs of an individual or group.
- Needs assessments can be done through interviews, written surveys, and HRAs.
- Three important questions that can be answered through needs assessments are what are the perceived health practices; what wellness topics/activities are of interest to employees and their families; and what is the readiness of the employees to participate.
- To present the needed evidence for a health promotion program, a summary report should be prepared.
- The summary report should contain information about support for the program, demographic data of the employee population, the needs/interest of the employees, the health status of the employees, and recommendations for the health promotion program.
- A health promotion committee should be formed that represents all facets of the workforce.

- The employee committee serves as an advisory committee and can assist with program design, marketing, and selling of the program to fellow employees.
- A timetable for development of the health promotion program should be formulated. This should be for both the total program as well as the various components. Two types of time lines can be developed: a task development time line, and a Gantt chart.
- The philosophy and scope should reflect what management and employees envision for the various health promotion programs. Contained in the statement are the goals, level of program impact, and the expectations for the program.
- The mission statement consists of the program expectations, who is eligible for the program, program offerings, and what will be the indicators for the success.
- A goal is defined as a general statement concerning a desired outcome of a program. Goals can be both short term and long term.
- Objectives are precise statements of outcomes that are based on the various goals of the program. Objectives can be both short term and long term.
- Priorities need to be established for when programs will be offered. Program priorities should reflect the philosophy, need, interest, mission, goals, and objectives.

Bibliography

ALLEN, J. R. 1993. Practitioners' forum. *American Journal of Health Promotion* 7: 323–324.

ALLEN, J. R. 1995. Building a supportive workplace. In *Healthy, wealthy, and wise— fundamentals of workplace health promotion.* Omaha: Wellness Councils of America (WELCOA).

Association for Fitness in Business. 1992. *Guidelines for employee health promotion programs.* Champaign, IL: Human Kinetics.

BELLINGHAM, R., and TAGER, M. J. 1986. *Designing effective health promotion programs— the 20 skills for success.* Chicago: Great Performance.

BRECKON, D. J., HARVEY, J. R., and LANCASTER, R. B. 1994. *Community health education: Setting, roles, and skills for the 21st century* (3rd ed.). Rockville, MD: Aspen.

DEEDS, S. G. 1992. *The health education specialist: Self-study for professional competence.* Los Alamitos, CA: Loose Canon.

DIGNAN, M. B., and CARR, P. A. 1992. *Program planning for health education and health promotion.* Philadelphia: Lea and Febiger.

FRANK, A. 1989. Wellness committee management a flop. *Optimal Health* 4(1): 38.

GILMORE, G. D., and CAMPBELL, M. D. 1996. Needs assessment strategies for health education and health promotion (2nd ed.). Madison, WI: WCB Brown & Benchmark.

MAINIERO, L. A., TROMLEX, C. L. 1989. Developing managerial skills in organizational behavior. Englewood Cliffs. NJ: Prentice-Hall.

Parkinson and Associates. 1982. *Managing health promotion in the workplace: Guidelines for implementation and evaluation.* Palo Alto, CA: Mayfield.

Wellness Councils of America. 1995. *Health wealthy and wise—fundamentals of workplace health promotion,* edited by Sandra Wendel. Omaha: Wellness Councils of America (WELCOA).

CHAPTER 3

Models for Health Promotion Interventions

OBJECTIVES

The Social Ecological Approach to Health Promotion

Principles and Concepts of Adult Motivation

Change Theories

The Health Belief Model

The Transtheoretical Model

Learning Styles

Adult Learners

Profiles in Health Promotion

Check It Out

Summary

CHAPTER OBJECTIVES

After reading this chapter, you should be able to

- define five major concepts of adult learning theory.
- understand that how people change behavior is not clearly understood.
- explain several prevalent theories as to how people change their behavior.
- develop specific interventions based on specific behavior change theories.
- select behavior change activities based on a specific population and how it functions.

The goal of health promotion programs is to initiate and maintain change in behavior. However, behavior change is complex, at best, and results are frequently less than desired. One solution to improving the results from health promotion programs has been stated as the need for "stronger theoretical underpinnings" to improve program effectiveness (Chapman, 1997). We need to use what is known about behavior change to provide the basis for future success. Health promotion programs need to be designed according to solid research on behavior change. Professionals need to understand how and why people behave the way they do and what "things" can be done to impact on that behavior to change it for the better.

At its most basic, a theory is an explanation of factors or principles that are the underlying tenants of life happenings, such as behavior. Theory is the "how." Behavior change theories provide direction and justification for health promotion program activities and the basis for successful change processes that can be incorporated into the programing (Cowdery et al., 1995). Understanding the tenets of *how people change* their behavior and recognizing that change involves complex factors, both overtly discernible and indiscernible, helps when dealing with the frustrations that inevitably arise because people do not respond "the way they should." An understanding of the complexities of behavior change also allows for the development of multiple interventions that can address *all* the components of change, increasing the likelihood of success.

This chapter introduces explanations (theories) for how people make behavior changes. Historically, health promotion interventions that have demonstrated success have incorporated more than one theory of change (Shea and Basch, 1990). Using accepted behavior change theories in health promotion efforts provides a research base as a guide for selecting specific programs. Correctly understanding the application of theory should result in improved compliance and more discernible results.

THE SOCIAL ECOLOGICAL APPROACH TO HEALTH PROMOTION

Many health promotion strategies seem to focus primarily on individual behavior, although not always by design. The Ottawa Charter definition of health promotion (chapter 1) speaks of "the process of enabling people to increase control over, and to improve, their own health" (First International Conference on Health Promotion, 1986). The *social ecological* approach to health promotion emphasizes the need for comprehending the complex interaction between the environment and the individual (as suggested by the Ottawa Charter) because patterns of health and illness are closely linked to numerous sociocultural, political, and physical-environmental conditions (Stokols, Allen, and Bellingham, 1996).

The social ecological model of health promotion views health as a product of the interdependent relationship between individuals and their ecosystems. Behavior can only be understood in the context in which people live. According to this view, health can only be promoted via an ecosystem that cultivates health and healthful lifestyles (Green, Richard, and Potvin, 1996). By definition, the social ecological approach states that the environment establishes the limits of the behavior that can occur within it and that by altering the environment, behavior will automatically be modified. It also means that environment influences how the individual acts; that is, the same person will act differently in different environments (Green et al., 1996).

Given this, by structuring the environment in the healthiest manner possible, people will automatically alter their behavior to some extent. Switching a working environment from one where smoking is allowed to a no-smoking one significantly alters behavior at the worksite. Increasing healthy food choices in the cafeteria or removing vending machines that supply less healthy foods are other ways of modifying the environment that increases opportunities and probabilities for positive health behavior at least at the worksite. The more a health promotion program integrates both environmental and individual targets, the more it is ecological (Richard et al., 1996).

Undoubtedly, people are influenced by their environments. It is extremely difficult to quit drinking alcohol if all of one's friends drink regularly and their main form of recreation is going to a bar. Change is more likely to happen when a person wishing to abstain from alcohol finds new friends with new hobbies. From a health promotion perspective, providing an environment where people have other options for recreational activities and forging new relationships would meet the criteria for a social ecological approach.

PRINCIPLES AND CONCEPTS OF ADULT MOTIVATION

Maslow's Theory of Human Motivation

Although commonly referred to as "Maslow's Theory of Human Needs," Maslow's hierarchy (figure 3.1) is really a humanistic concept of *motivation* (Maslow, 1943).

FIGURE 3.1. Maslow's Hierarchy of Needs

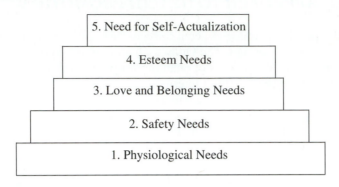

According to Maslow's theory, people generally experience five levels of "need" and their "needs" motivate them to act. For instance, an individual who lacks the first level, physiological needs, will spend his or her energy trying to achieve a level of comfort in this area. Someone who is hungry will seek food, especially if there is a continual lack of food and fear of starvation is real. Once basic food needs are met and there is some level of comfort with the continued ability to satisfy them, an individual will look at other needs and attempt to satisfy them. According to Maslow, this occurs in a particular order. As other physiological needs are met (adequate sleep, water, oxygen, sex, etc.), people will seek to fulfill the needs at the next level—safety. A brief description of the levels of need follows:

- *Physiological needs.* The most basic and influential needs related to survival, Maslow considered physiological needs *deficiency needs*—ones that result from a lack and must be met by external, environmental sources. For instance, a person cannot manufacture air or food without external assistance.
- *Safety needs.* Generally, a safe environment involves a certain amount of structure where "what will happen next" is pretty well known; for instance, one's house will be there upon arriving home or having a secure job. Safety needs are also considered deficiency needs.
- *Love and belongingness needs.* Next, people desire to feel love, affection, and a sense of belonging. Love and belongingness needs are also deficiency needs in that external sources (others) are required.
- *Esteem needs.* People have a need to feel good about themselves and to believe others think well of them. Actual achievements, such as successfully quitting smoking, must occur to develop self-worth and increase self-confidence. Success in achieving health goals can significantly contribute to esteem needs.
- *Self-actualization needs.* Maslow considered self-actualization needs to be *growth needs.* Self-actualization involves the personal desire to become all one can. People at the level of self-actualization are seeking ways to expand their horizons. Trying new things and finding new ways to be challenged are cornerstones of meeting self-actualized needs.

Lewin's Field Theory

Kurt Lewin's work has provided the basis for several theories, including the health belief model (later in this chapter). He also developed a tool that can be used to explain the multiple forces that interact in people to directly affect their behavior (Lewin, 1935, 1961). His theory, called the *force field concept,* states that behavior is the result of two sets of forces. The first set of forces is composed of the *change or driving forces.* These are all the variables that pressure groups and/or individuals to change how they behave. Change variables can be the desire to "be healthier," look "better," or obtain certain rewards, such as health cost incentives or even a T-shirt. The second set of forces includes the *resisting or restraining forces.* Resisting or restraining forces are all the pressures individuals feel that cause them to resist change. Lack of energy, lack of time, or negative feedback from family or friends can all be forces that contribute to a lack of change, even for an improved quality of life.

According to Lewin, these two sets of forces are constantly working against each other (figure 3.2). When resisting forces are matched in power with change forces, nothing happens. Essentially the individual is frozen, moving in no direction. When resisting forces outweigh change forces, individuals may not only *not* engage in new behaviors, they may actually regress to a previous behavior. For instance, a person who has quit smoking cigarettes may actually resume the habit, even though he has ceased for a number of years, if a highly stressful event occurs and he has previously used smoking as a stress management tool.

It is only when change forces are strong and the resisting forces are weakened that change actually occurs. When motivation is high and resistance is reduced, people are more likely to participate in health promotion programs, especially if they have not been previously involved. This theory of behavior change emphasizes the need to plan strategies that motivate while simultaneously finding ways to reduce resistance to participation.

FIGURE 3.2. Lewin's Force Field Concept

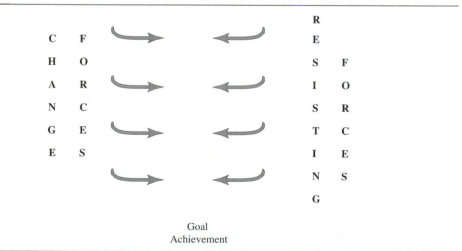

Goal
Achievement

In real life the relative influence of change and resisting factors is constantly fluctuating. A person's change desire to regularly engage in an exercise program after work may be resisted by family problems, work demands, energy level, or other commitments. For this reason, it is important for health promotion specialists to clearly delineate the factors that contribute to resistance and to change and then find ways to increase change forces while minimizing resistance forces. The more individualized a program is, the more these issues are specifically addressed. An example of a strategy for this program is talking to potential participants about their resisting forces; for example, asking "What keeps you from becoming involved in . . .?" while also asking about the kinds of things that will motivate them. According to this theory, strategies designed to change human behavior must (a) increase the strength of change forces (find out what the population considers to be motivating factors), (b) reduce the influence of restraining forces (work with the target population on types of programs or best times to offer them), or (c) simultaneously reduce restraining forces and increase change forces. Strategies that emphasize decreasing restraining forces tend to be the most successful.

Lewin's theory includes a five-step process of learning and change. These steps are *unfreezing, problem diagnosis, goal setting, the new behavior,* and *refreezing. Unfreezing* is the point where an individual becomes ready to consider change. Until someone perceives a need for change, change will not be a consideration. When a different behavior is viewed as desirable, unfreezing occurs. *Problem diagnosis* is the point where the client seriously considers the ramifications of an unhealthy behavior. Health professionals can assist clients in recognizing the problems associated with an undesirable behavior and in understanding why they currently engage in that behavior. This is when a client must also consider the difficulties associated with change.

Goal setting implies a commitment toward a new, more healthy behavior. At this point, a new behavior is defined and ways to achieve that goal are defined. Realistic expectations of behavior change can determine success or failure. Many people simply set highly unrealistic goals, setting themselves up for failure. A carefully planned goal-setting session that provides contingency options is crucial and is the strategy most beneficial at this stage.

Next the client engages in the *new behavior.* This is another challenging step, since people may become too easily discouraged, especially if they have unrealistic goals. Over time, with consistent participation in the new behavior, *refreezing* occurs. This is the point where the new behavior becomes an integral part of the person's life.

Skinner's Operant Conditioning

B. F. Skinner has long been recognized as a primary figure in the behaviorist tradition. Behaviorists traditionally define behavior in terms of observed action. While ignoring, or at least minimizing, the role of the intellect in behavior, Skinner's theory of *operant conditioning* states that human behavior can be changed by manipulating reinforcers (an *operant* is a behavior that operates on the environment causing either a positive or negative response; a *reinforcer* is something added to the environment that increases response). At its most basic, Skinner's "law of conditioning" states that a response (behavior) followed by a reinforcing stimulus (reinforcer, sometimes called a "reward") or a negative reinforcement (where an aversive consequence is removed) is strengthened, making it more likely to reoccur (Catania and Harnard, 1988).

Skinner did not like the use of the term "reward," but as an application in health promotion the term is useful. When people engage in behaviors that result in immediate positive feedback or results, they tend to continue to do that behavior. One reason people continue to eat certain, less-healthy foods, such as chocolate or a high-fat cut of steak, is the immediate sense of sensory pleasure they experience. At the same time, they may consider the immediate physiological response to exercise (sweating, heavy breathing, fatigue, pain) unpleasant and thereby something to be avoided. The behaviorist would then need to find some way to change that perception either with a positive reinforcement (a reward, such as encouragement for the healther behavior) or a negative one (a decrease in sensations of pain or sweating) at least part of the time. Better yet, find a way to get chocolate to taste "bad" and exercise to feel "good"!

How a person perceives a reward or reinforcer is individual and can vary greatly. Factors such as culture, background, personal values and goals, age, and other characteristics all influence what is perceived as a reward. When establishing reinforcers for behavior or activities, it is important to understand what will serve as positive and negative reinforcers for the targeted audience. If a large portion of the target population consists of mature males at elevated risk for a heart attack, they may be interested in the health benefits of exercise and unconcerned with developing a buffed body. In this case, improving fitness levels (positive reinforcer) or lowering cholesterol levels (negative reinforcer) may be more important than measurable weight loss using a scale.

CHANGE THEORIES

Social Cognitive Theory

Social cognitive theory was formerly referred to as social learning theory. Social learning theory has its roots in behaviorism but has evolved to include many cognitive aspects; hence, the change in names. Social cognitive theory concerns the learning that occurs within a social context (Ormand, 1995) among humans. Basic conceptualizations in social cognitive learning include the importance of reinforcement for behavior, but they emphasize the role of personal expectations. This means that what an individual learns is a result of three things: the environment, the person's cognitive process (what he or she expects to occur), and the actual behavior of the person. Learning is therefore a dynamic, interrelated process where a change in one component may well initiate a change in another.

Social cognitive theory has some general principles that separate it from behaviorism, where only observable actions are the basis for change. Social cognitive theorists believe that, first, *people can learn merely by observing the behavior and the outcomes of that behavior in others* rather than needing to experience behaviors directly. In other words, according to this theory, *modeling* behavior can have a powerful influence on others. As role models for health behavior, health professionals can positively impact those around them without directly interacting with them. Individuals never know who is watching or what effect they are having on the people who observe them every day. Rest assured, it can be a powerful influence.

Second, *an observable change in behavior is not necessary for learning to occur.* Behaviorists base everything on observable behavior, but social cognitive theory states that, because people can learn through observation, their learning will not necessarily be reflected in their behavior. For instance, it is possible for a person to make a decision at an early age to never smoke after observing a family member die of emphysema resulting from a lifetime habit of smoking. This is a learning situation where no change in behavior was observed, but a definite decision was made to not smoke.

Third, *reinforcement is valuable but may act less directly on the actual learning process.* Reinforcement may be *direct* (i.e., immediately telling someone what a good job they have done or how hard they have worked), *vicarious* (i.e., seeing a friend lose 20 lb. after taking up walking for a year and observing how much better she looks and feels); or *self-managed* (i.e., a person rewards himself with a trip to Ireland after he lowers his blood pressure through exercise and proper diet).

Fourth, *cognitive processes are necessary for learning to occur.* While behaviorists consider cognitive processes irrelevant, social cognitive theorists have been placing increasing importance on the role of thinking in the learning process. Constructs directly applicable to health promotion state: If people are to engage in a specific behavior they must know (1) what that behavior is and (2) how to do it. This sounds simple enough, but, in fact, many people decide to engage in what they perceive as healthy behaviors without really understanding what they are or knowing the appropriate way to do them. For example, everyone knows they should "eat right." However many people think this means simply choosing one of the new, highly processed, zero-fat/low-fat products available, may then overeat such products and believe they are eating healthy.

For people to be healthy, they need to know what "healthy" means. They need classes at the worksite on topics such as "What is healthy eating?" People also need to know how to eat in a healthy manner, not by buying a dozen boxes of low-fat cookies and eating them for dinner but by understanding what healthy food is. They need to know how to shop for healthy foods and how to prepare them so they are palatable. Likewise, they need to know how to make healthier selections from a menu when they eat out, whether at a fast-food establishment or a more expensive restaurant. Proper weight training is another area where people may recognize the need to participate, but they may not be sure why or what the outcomes should be. Chances are they don't know how to engage in resistance exercises correctly. Walk into any weight room at any time and at least 30 percent of the participants will be lifting incorrectly. They then run the risk of injury or results that are less than satisfying, and they provide poor modeling for others who don't know the mechanics but are watching them and imitating their behavior. Any worksite offering fitness classes and equipment for use needs to provide proper instruction, as well as the reasons why activities are performed using specific techniques.

The other construct related to the cognitive component of this theory that has been widely received in health promotion is "self-efficacy" (Bandura, 1977; Bandura and Adams, 1977; Bandura and Schunk, 1981). Self-efficacy is one's situational perception of his or her ability to succeed or fail at a particular task. For instance, an individual may be convinced he cannot adhere to a regular exercise regimen because he has been unsuccessful in the past. That same person may feel perfectly confident in his ability to rebuild a car or do his job effectively (things he may have successfully achieved previously), but, in the area of exercise, he lacks self-efficacy, that is, the belief that he can succeed. People who "expect" to fail are more likely to fail, whereas people whose expectations are that they can accomplish a particular task (e.g., run a mile in eight minutes) are more likely to initiate the attempt and achieve their goal, even working at achieving it longer and trying harder than people who expect to fail.

Self-efficacy is usually related to prior experience, but may not be. An individual may have done really well at a task, but because her perception is that she did poorly on it, her sense of self-efficacy about it is that she can't do it. At the same time, another person may not have done very well, but because he believes he did do well, he is more likely to attempt the same or a similar task again and to be more confident about succeeding. According to the theory of self-efficacy, it is one's perceptions that have the most profound effect on future behavior—more than what actually happens.

Using self-efficacy as a theory of behavior change requires understanding people's perceptions about their ability to succeed. Building self-efficacy is done by setting very short-term goals that people can accomplish quickly to achieve feelings of success. As clients begin to reach goals successfully, they develop not only improved self-efficacy about their future ability to succeed at more difficult tasks but also increased interest in the topic (Bandura and Schunk, 1981). Success breeds success. However, it is extremely important that set goals are short term and can be achieved successfully in a brief time. A goal to run a marathon would not be viable for people who have never exercised or trained before, even if they considered it the greatest accomplishment in the world. A goal of walking twenty minutes at lunch a couple of times a week with friends may be better. At the end of the week, see how it went (What problems were encountered? Was lunch a good time for this activity? Would another time be better?). Small moves consistently made over time help build self-efficacy.

Theory of Reasoned Action and Theory of Planned Behavior

The theory of reasoned action and theory of planned behavior both present frameworks to study attitudes toward behaviors rather than behaviors themselves. According to the theory of reasoned action model (figure 3.3), a person's attitude toward a behavior (positive or negative) along with his or her beliefs about what significant others (spouse, parents, boss, friends) think the person should do and how important their opinions are to him or her (the subjective norm) form the individual's *intention* to engage in a certain behavior. The intention is the person's statement of intent along with the probability he or she will perform the behavior.

FIGURE 3.3. Theory of Reasoned Action

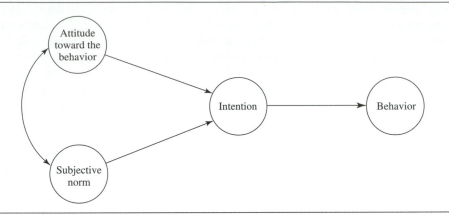

The *strength* of the intention determines if the person will actually perform the behavior. The merit of this theory is that it takes into account the influence other people have over someone's behavior. For example, it is difficult to stay after work and exercise if one's family complains about the person getting home late. The perception is that the family does not value the attempts to exercise (which may or may not be true). If the person views the family's complaints as a lack of support, however, the *intention* to exercise can be weakened. If, however, the family verbally states how wonderful it is the individual is exercising after work, the intention to exercise will probably be strengthened.

The theory of reasoned action states that ultimately behavior change is the result of changes in what people believe (Ajzen, 1988). If they believe that being twenty-five pounds overweight is normal for their age group ("I'm 50 and I just don't care about how I look"), then they may see no need to exercise and eat better. If their belief system about appropriate weight ("Weight is important because it impacts my health no matter how old I am") becomes altered, then behavior change is more likely. The implication for health promotion is that, to be successful, programs need to work on changing what people perceive to be true (their subjective norm). If the target population believes that developing elevated blood pressure is an inevitable part of aging, they are not going to do things that might lower it. If their doctor implies that 140/85 is "OK" for a 65-year-old person and transmits this belief to them, they are going to believe they are "OK." Since increasing blood pressure is more a product of culture than of age and 140/85 is not desirable at any age, the job of the health promotion professional is to get that message across—along with data about the deleterious effects of elevated blood pressure—in a way that can be integrated into individuals' belief systems.

The theory of planned behavior takes the preceding model one step further (figure 3.4). This theory acknowledges there are situations that may include a component not under voluntary control—such as an addiction. In this instance, an addiction to tobacco or lack of resources to help quit may overrule or dilute the

FIGURE 3.4. Theory of Planned Behavior

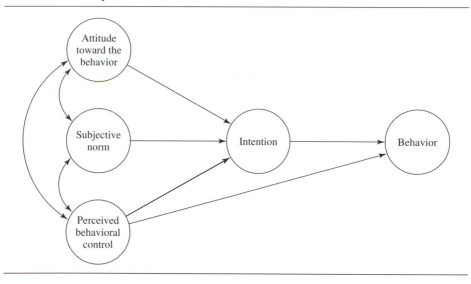

other factors influencing behavior. Of course, due to varying reasons, people quit smoking all the time in spite of their addiction. The theory of planned behavior includes the four elements in the theory of reasoned action but adds the construct of "perceived behavioral control." This element is considered to be the result of past experience and anticipated problems that determine the person's *perceived* ease or difficulty of performing the behavior. People who view quitting smoking as "no big deal" may find it easier to quit than others who believe they simply cannot survive without their cigarettes.

Perceived behavioral control can be affected through appropriate health promotion techniques. This can be done by programming that allows for cognitive and behavioral changes to occur in small steps so that confidence about success is developed. If the targeted population is at high risk for heart disease and views the possibility of reducing that risk as beyond their reach, they are hardly going to be motivated to engage in activities that might help them. If, however, the health promotion department can change people's perceptions so that the population (a) has a positive attitude about changing behavior (just because something is difficult does not mean it cannot be accomplished), (b) thinks important others (bosses, friends, family) believe it would be good for them to adapt heart healthy behaviors, and (c) feels like they have some control over making changes (selecting from a variety of stop smoking aids), individuals are more likely to change. The role of health promotion, then, would be to get people to that point by convincing them that quitting is possible (motivating), providing opportunities for them to succeed at making life changes (encouraging), explaining about multiple types of interventions that can be used (educating), and offering different stop-smoking aids and having day long "smoke-outs" (providing opportunities for those changes to occur).

THE HEALTH BELIEF MODEL

The *health belief model* (figure 3.5) has been widely used both in medical compliance and disease prevention and in health education as an explanation for why people do the things they do (Becker, Drachman, and Kirscht, 1974; Janz and Becker, 1984; Lewin, 1935; Rosenstock, 1988). The health belief model is very comprehensive, looking at components of behavior not examined in any other model of behavior change. The health belief model provides a unique perspective on the complexity of understanding behavior and considers multiple social, ecological, and environmental factors that can influence behavior. Basic precepts of the model are that people, even healthy ones, must believe they are susceptible to health problems and that those health problems have undesirable consequences before they will make the effort to change current behavior. People must also believe that those health problems can be prevented, delayed, or minimized. Consider an organization where several of the women employed are of Ashkenazi Jewish origin and have family histories of breast cancer. If these women believe they are destined to develop breast cancer and probably die from it, like many female members in their families, they are more unlikely to attempt to engage in behaviors that might result in early detection and treatment because the women believe these behaviors will do no good. They may be so frightened by the prospect, they prefer to avoid the topic altogether. If, on the other hand, the women's perception is that, if they get regular checkups, perform monthly self-exams, have regular mammograms, exercise regu-

FIGURE 3.5. The Health Belief Model

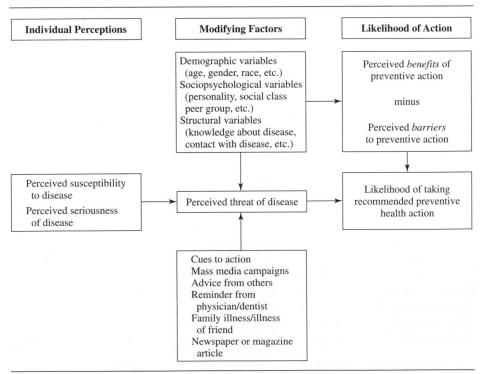

larly, keep alcohol intake at low levels, maintain healthy body weight, and keep up with the latest information about breast cancer and breast cancer treatment, they can reduce their chances of developing it, or, if they do develop it, can find it early enough to prevent metastasis and early death, they are more likely to engage in these behaviors (*USA Today,* 1998).

In the health belief model, perception is the basis of all behavior; that is, people must believe they are *susceptible* to a condition or they will not act. Many deceased cigarette smokers failed to really believe they would develop lung cancer. In addition, people must consider that the condition to which they are susceptible is *serious* enough to do something about. The drug of choice among many people is caffeine. Caffeine can have fairly serious side effects, including elevated blood pressure and tachycardia (irregular heartbeats) in some people. For most people, however, the fear of side effects or the potential negative side effects (sleeplessness, agitation, anxiety, rebound fatigue) are not serious enough to completely give up caffeine, even though any regular user has experienced these side effects at some time. The seriousness of the problem is insufficient to motivate change in most people.

Even if a person considers a condition a serious problem and realizes that he or she has a significant chance of developing it, other factors can intervene to negatively (or positively) influence what eventually occurs. While the role of health promotion is to encourage change via information, motivational activities, encouragement, and consultation, people are also exposed to negatively modifying influences. Perhaps individuals consider themselves too old to make a change or so

Self-efficacy is an important component of successful behavioral change.

young that they can worry about it later. Perhaps they lack self-efficacy. Maybe they think they lack sufficient funds or time or simply do not know *how* to make the necessary change. As mentioned, people know they should "eat right," but they may not know what that means. Only a few years ago, a "good" breakfast would include bacon and eggs, whole milk, and toast with butter on it. Now that breakfast is considered an invitation to a heart attack by many. A good breakfast now would be one that includes fruit, carbohydrates, some protein, and, especially if a female, a low-fat dairy product, such as a high fiber bowl of cereal with skim milk and a banana or cut-up cantaloupe and a piece of toast with cheese toasted on it. Many people think eating low-fat or fat-free cookies or eating chicken twice a day is a healthy diet. Inadequate information can be the most detrimental factor of all, especially if people think they are doing what they should.

Unfortunately, even people who have suffered a heart attack or undergone open heart surgery tend to be noncompliant, with drop-out rates of 30 to 70 percent within six months (Nieman, 1995) of initiating an exercise program, even with all the evidence stating that exercise can help prevent a second attack or future surgery. Why? Maybe the barriers of time or cost or transportation or lack of family support or personal lack of discipline altered individuals' original perceptions of susceptibility. Maybe they think the surgery fixed the problem and they don't have to worry any more. In any case, it is the interactions of multiple factors that lead to the ultimate result of behavior change or not, and the health belief model allows for interventions to be developed addressing many of the issues being considered.

THE TRANSTHEORETICAL MODEL

The transtheoretical model (Prochaska and DiClemente, 1983; Prochaska, Diclemente, and Norcross, 1992; Prochaska and Velicer, 1997; Velicer and Prochaska, 1997) provides a different perspective on health behavior change. Drawing on diverse theories of behavior change, this model is considered a systematic integration of the heterogenous field of psychotherapy. Using studies of people with addictive behaviors, researchers noted that people change, with and without assistance, but that, in all cases, people who change tend to move through a series of stages *toward* change before they actually *do* change. Prochaska's version of the stages of change (see Lewin's field theory for another stages-of-change process) is as follows:

1. *Precontemplation.* At this stage, people, even ones with high-risk behaviors, have no intention of taking any kind of action concerning their behaviors in the foreseeable future (usually defined as six months). People in this stage may "undersee" the problem or fail to recognize it at all. Or they may recognize a need to change but are not interested in doing anything about it at this time. Precontemplators need information about their problem behavior via educational programs, bibliotherapy, media campaigns, and feedback from others. Hearing testimonials from others may influence the emotions of people at this stage and cause them to think more about their behaviors. The tragic consequences of someone else suffering from the same behavior may affect them also.

2. *Contemplation.* Contemplators are thinking about changing sometime in the foreseeable future, but not today. Typically, contemplators struggle with the positive effects they see as the result of a behavior change and the amount of effort, energy, and sense of loss required to overcome the problem. It is possible to remain stuck in this phase for indefinite periods of time, including years. The kinds of strategies used with precontemplators also prove effective for contemplators. Family interventions may augment awakening emotions about need for change. Recognizing that they serve as role models can be useful.

3. *Preparation.* During this stage, people are preparing to take action during the next month. Frequently, they have unsuccessfully taken action during the past year, but failed to move into maintenance. Instead, they "fell back and regrouped" and are now ready to try again. Often, preparers will begin to make small behavioral changes, such as reducing smoking, or will prepare to become involved in exercise classes or weight loss clinics. People in this stage are greatly concerned they will fail when they do take action. As people move from being contemplators to preparing to change, they tend to reevaluate their self-image and clarify their values about who they are and what they want to represent. Strategies of benefit in the preparation stage are ones that enhance commitment, such as giving individuals options (up to three) about how to change. This is a time to solidify commitment to change.

4. *Action.* In the action stage, people actually begin to modify their behavior or environment to overcome their problem (change their behavior). This is the stage where people generally let others know what they are doing, even though they may have been preparing to do something for a long time. Successful action requires complete alteration of the behavior to the required goal for at least six months. Most of the time people will relapse rather than succeed for this very reason—they do not realize they will encounter difficulty and will need to maintain action for an extended period of time. Very few people are prepared to work really hard for six months or longer. They expect the change to occur much more quickly. Relapse occurs most frequently during times of emotional distress.

Action and maintenance use many of the same strategies. These include building a helping relationship with important others who can provide encouragement and support. This is the time for promotion personnel to call personally and encourage individuals. During this time, people in transition need to find ways to reward themselves. This can include group recognition of gains. Healthy alternatives for times of difficulty need to be substituted for previously unhealthy ones. For instance, a person trying to lose weight needs to learn the cues that set off binge eating episodes and find substitutes for those situations. Behavior modification techniques may be beneficial.

5. *Maintenance.* During maintenance, people have managed change for at least six months and now must work to prevent relapse. Prochaska considers maintenance a continuation of the action stage where more work must be done to ensure new behaviors are totally integrated into a person's life. Maintenance may be a temporary stage, lasting six months or longer, or it may continue

throughout the rest of one's life. The behavior largely determines if the person making the change can move beyond maintenance to the last stage.

6. *Termination.* Termination implies *total confidence* that relapse will not occur in any high-risk situation and there is no temptation to return to unhealthy behaviors.

According to Prochaska, traditional health promotion programs fail because they all focus on the *action* portion of change, the point in time when someone is actually willing to do something to bring change. Unfortunately, at any given time about 40 percent of people are in the precontemplation stage, 40 percent are contemplators, and 20 percent are preparers. Since about 80 percent of all people are *not* in the action stage but are in some other stage of change, efforts that focus on getting them to do something will not succeed.

If successful behavior change programs involve doing the right things (using the correct techniques) at the right time (i.e., when the technique will be most effective in supporting behavior change), then it becomes necessary to identify the stages of change the target audience is experiencing and then match programs/promotions to those stages (figure 3.6 and table 3.1). If only 20 percent of the population is in the action stage at any given time and if, as statistics indicate, they are unlikely to achieve behavior change with a single attempt, it becomes vitally important to develop programs and interventions that match *all* the stages of change. Nonaction stage people will become overly discouraged if they are unsuccessful, or they will not attempt change at all, when they really are just unprepared to change at this time.

It must also be noted that people rarely move linearly through the stages. Patterns of change may be (a) *stable,* where people remain "stuck" in one of the stages and move neither forward nor backward (e.g., someone may be constantly planning on starting an exercise program in the next few weeks [contemplator], but never quite get there), (b) *progressive,* where changers tend to move linearly from one stage to the next without relapse or regression, (c) *regressive,* where people tend to move back to an earlier stage of change and stay there, and (d) *recycling,* where there is a pattern of movement up and down the stages of change, never terminating but never quite giving up.

FIGURE 3.6. Stages of Change in Which Particular Processes of Change Are Emphasized

Precontemplation	Contemplation	Preparation	Action	Maintenance
Consciousness raising				
Dramatic relief				
Environmental reevaluation				
Self-reevaluation				
		Self-liberation		
			Reinforcement management	
			Helping relationships	
			Counterconditioning	
			Stimulus control	

TABLE 3.1. Definitions of Ten Change Processes

Consciousness raising	Increases information about self/problem/increased awareness about causes, consequences, and cures; i.e., "I read articles about quitting smoking": bibliotherapy, media, confrontation, education, feedback
Self-reevaluation	Values clarification/healthy role modes/assessments of one's self image; i.e., "I get upset when I think about my smoking"
Self-liberation	Choosing to act/self-efficacy/belief one can change; i.e., "I tell myself I can choose to smoke or not": two or three choices used to make change
Social liberation	Increased social opportunities/alternatives, especially for deprived/oppressed: advocacy, empowerment, smoke-free zones, better options (e.g., salads for lunch)
Counterconditioning	Substituting alternatives for problem behaviors; i.e., "I do something else when I want to relax": relaxation techniques to manage stress, low-fat foods for high-fat foods
Stimulus control	Avoiding stimuli that elicit problem behaviors/adding prompts for healthier behavior: parking farther away so must walk farther to office.
Contingency management	Rewarding self/being rewarded by others/consequences for behaviors: contingency contracts, positive self-statements, group recognition
Helping relationships	Social support; being open and trusting with other(s): rapport building, therapeutic alliances, counselor calls, buddy system
Dramatic relief	Expressing feelings about problems and solutions/increased emotional experiences: psychodrama, role playing, personal testimonies, grieving
Environmental reevaluation	Assessing how one's problem affects the environment/serving as role model for others; i.e., "Smoking may be harmful to the environment": empathy training, documentaries, family intervention

Since most behavior change programs are action oriented, the majority of people are overlooked. And since the majority of people simply are not in the action stage, the ability of health promotion programs to affect behavior is seriously impaired. Efficient self-change depends on doing the right things (processes/techniques) at the right time (stages) (Prochaska, DiClemente, and Norcross, 1992). In fact, the National Institutes of Health has noted worksite-based interventions that are the most successful at reducing cardiovascular risk are those that use intense counseling as their technique (National Heart Memo, 1997). Steven Blair, senior scientific editor for the Surgeon General's Report on Physical Activity and Health recently stated that the "greatest void in health promotion programs is the lack of behavioral intervention" (Blair and Pfeiffer, 1997). The transtheoretical model purports that to make change effective it is necessary to meet individuals where they are and work with them as they move individually through the stages of change. The stages of change paradigm requires identifying the stage of change, developing programs specific for each stage, and then proactively reaching out to the target population and compelling them to become involved. Figure 3.7 summarizes several different intervention models.

FIGURE 3.7. Application of Selected Theories to Health Promotion Interventions

Maslow's Hierarchy of Needs: Understanding the level of client needs should influence the types of programs being offered. If the target audience is overwhelmed with physiological or safety needs, activities that can assist in these areas would be most beneficial and can develop "trust" between potential participants and health promotion professionals. A safety level program might be about financial management skills or how to increase home security or how to parent. Once people feel they have a grasp on these needs, they can move to "higher" ones, such as feeling better about yourself.

Skinner's Operant Conditioning: Positive and negative feedback can influence behavior. Health promotion professionals need to incorporate frequent, immediate feedback with participants, especially for those who are new to behavior change objectives.

Social Learning Theory: Since people learn in part by observing others, health promotion professionals should model appropriate behavior at every opportunity (without appearing self-righteous). Providing an environment where healthy behavior is accessible and social support from other employees is an integral part of activities can significantly encourage behavior change.

Self-efficacy: Because change is frequently so difficult and people often lack belief in their ability to achieve certain health goals, they need the opportunity to develop confidence in themselves and their ability to engage in new and different behaviors. Often, their perceived failures are erroneous, based on unrealistic standards, and/or compounded by other problems. In health promotion, this indicates the need to assist employees in developing plans that are reasonable and divided into more easily achievable steps (changes). Also, success needs to be experienced before proceeding on to more complicated changes.

Health Belief Model: Using a more ecological approach, understanding family, cultural, environmental, educational, and social background and conceptualizations can contribute to developing programs specific to group needs. Success begins with meeting people "where they are" by understanding the diverse influences that affect their perceptions of the world. The culture of the people must be addressed and programs designed that can interface with that culture as well as seek ways to influence negative behaviors in a way that is culturally appropriate. Recognizing the complexity of change demands multifacted approaches to programming.

Stages of Change: Frequently, the target population is simply not "ready" to change. Since, at any given time, most people are actually moving somewhere along a continuum toward change or away from it, programs need to be developed that can provide the education necessary to realize the need for change and to assist individuals on an individual level with preparedness as well as preventing relapse after change has occurred. Learning how to manage stress to prevent relapse is vital. Stages of change emphasizes the need for "one-on-one" interaction.

LEARNING STYLES

Understanding theories of behavior and behavior change is vital to success in the area of health promotion. The more professionals in health promotion comprehend about people, their motivation, their point of view, their needs, their frame of reference, their desires, how they think, and how they learn, the better prepared professionals are to address all health promotion issues from as many angles as possible. Multiple interventions and approaches increase probabilities of achieving desired goals. Understanding how people learn new information can further contribute to appropriate interventions that help people initiate new behaviors and attain healthful behavior goals.

People learn or intake new information in different ways. Using a learning methodology that is not "comfortable" to people (i.e., one that does not "fit" with their learning style) will result in an inability to process information so it can be used successfully. Having a basic understanding of differences in learning styles and planning programs that address the differences can contribute to successful outcomes (behavior change).

There are different theories of learning styles and it is not within the scope of this book to address all of them. However, most theories of learning styles are similar in conceptualization, even if the labeling/wording of the components are different. Following is a synthesized conceptualization of how people learn.

First, people tend to learn using different *modalities.* A *modality* is the sensory component used to receive information (seeing, hearing, doing/touching). When analyzed, most people demonstrate a preference for a *kinesthetic* modality; that is, they understand information best when they are involved in touching and feeling it. Other people learn best by viewing pictures: they use a *visual* modality as their primary means of acquiring new information. In their case, a picture truly is worth a thousand words, because seeing it is the format that has the most meaning. Fewer people yet seem to process new information best when they assimilate it *auditorily,* or they hear it. The difference in the different modalities is that a visual learner can read about something and process the information satisfactorily by seeing it. An auditory learner (such as this author) needs to hear information to fully understand and assimilate it. For an auditory learner following written directions can become a real problem. Auditory learners do well with lecture formats. A kinesthetic learner would tend to be bored at a lecture. Since very few people use only one modality to learn and most persons are, in fact, multimodal, the more modalities used, the better people can comprehend and assimilate and the wider the audience that can be reached. Therefore, it is never sufficient to simply send a memo about something. The information must be talked about (for the auditory learner) and events must transpire that include participation (for the kinesthetic learner).

People *perceive* and *process* information differently. Perception has to do with how we conceptualize reality. Some people *experience* reality; that is, they determine what is real and what is not based on sensation. They absorb life experiences through their senses; learning is a form of intuition. Experiential learners are sometimes called "feelers," and they will learn best in situations where their emotions are used or where they can interact with someone who "has been there and done that."

"Feelers" can literally *feel* what a person is saying and absorb the information. A feeler will be more likely to be affected by hearing someone talk about how exercise positively affected his or her life from a personal perspective. Other people perceive reality by thinking about it. Often called "thinkers," they are analytical by nature and they approach new information logically. Rather than attempting or caring about feeling, they will look at data objectively and attempt to distance individuals from information in order to be free of bias. A thinker will respond more favorably to data that can be analyzed and a conclusion drawn. Lists of statistics and facts would be a more effective presentation for a group composed only of thinkers.

Information *processing* is how people take information or data and integrate it into their lives. Some people are "doers." They take the action oriented trail and "jump right in." Doers are often leaders when it comes to new things because that is how they make new information real. Other people are "watchers"; that is, they reflect on new things, think about them for a while, and consider what is the meaning of what they see (McCarthy, 1987).

Combinations of how people perceive (whether predominantly feelers or thinkers) and how they process (by doing or by watching) can reflect, therefore, four different styles of learning (figure 3.8). People who take in information by feeling and process it by watching are said to learn by "reflective observation" (aka "watchers"). People who perceive by thinking rationally and process by watching are designated as "abstract conceptualization" learners (aka "thinkers"). People who take in information by analysis and then process it through action are said to use "active experimentation" (aka "doers"), and those who perceive through their feelings and act according to what they feel are designated "concrete experience" learners (aka "feelers"). Figure 3.9 provides a description of these four psychological "types" (Jung, 1976).

FIGURE 3.8. Learning Styles

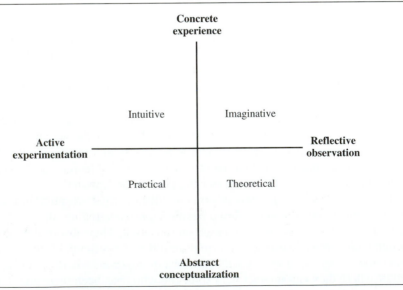

FIGURE 3.9. Psychological Types

Feelers:	Validate events and perceptions based on emotions; tend to be very aware of other people and their feelings; people oriented and sympathetic; need love and harmony.
Thinkers:	Arrange life events into rational categories; do not readily show emotion; judgment monitors categories and their content; make decisions impersonally.
Sensors:	Consciously perceive events but do not categorize them; do things in established ways; good at precise work; work steadily; patient with details.
Intuitors:	Apprehend instinctively; like solving problems; reach conclusions quickly; works in bursts of energy with slack time in between; patient in complicated situations.

Using the four types as models, learners "learn" best when issues are addressed using the basic concepts to which they respond best. For instance, concrete experiencers (feelers) are interested in personal meaning. They want to have a reason to learn new information or adapt new behaviors. They like to discuss. They need to know "why." Reflective observers (sensors) are most interested in data. They want to use facts to provide them with a deeper understanding of what needs to be done and how to do it. Abstract conceptualizers (thinkers) will want to try new things. They want to think about what needs to be done and then have the opportunity to do it. The role of the health promotion specialist is to facilitate opportunities for them to "do." Active experimenters (intuitives) want the opportunity for self-discovery. They want to "feel" the experience by interacting with others.

Very few people will be purely one type but will have some characteristics of even opposing types of learning styles from time to time. How people learn can be affected by vocation and environment and can change over time. However, one type of learning will tend to be more comfortable and the way in which a person accommodates new information best. Using approaches to health promotion that allow for individual learning differences will facilitate knowledge assimilation, and knowledge that is assimilated and accepted can influence behavior change.

Understanding learning styles helps in the development of programs that will influence the most people who attend. Although a health specialist may love information and feel that anyone who is exposed to the facts should "have enough sense to make a change," this approach will *not* succeed with someone who is more interested in "understanding" what change is like. A rational approach will have no effect on a person who approaches information from a sensing perspective. Therefore, programs that include components and opportunity to both supply data and to interact with others become imperative.

One technique will not work. Perhaps the reason why specialists are leaning more toward the intensive, counseling model and why it has proven so successful is that it addresses so many issues—from reinforcement to modeling to working through barriers to change to information dissemination to understanding why change needs to be made.

ADULT LEARNERS

The majority of the population in the workplace are adult learners, so it is important to understand how adult learning differs from that of "traditional" (younger) students. Figure 3.10 describes the characteristics of adult learners. For instance, knowing that adult learners express interest in the applicability of what they learn means they will want programs consisting of information pertinent to improving their lives. Adult learners tend to be more discriminating about information they are willing to spend time accumulating, since time is at a premium. Impressing upon adults the value of a program in their personal lives can influence the learning situation.

FIGURE 3.10. Characteristics of Adult Learners: How Adults Learn

---

* Depend on themselves for support/life management; self-directed
* View selves as doers, building on previous learning to achieve success
* Learn best what contributes to their own development/success
* Have differing views on what is important to learn
* Learning groups tend to be diverse
* Want to use time more effectively
* Have a broad, rich experience base to relate to new learning
* Learn more slowly, but just as well
* Tend to reject/explain away new information contradictory to personal beliefs
* Readiness to learn related to personal and professional "needs"
* Learn because of immediate applicability
* Tend to be internally motivated
* Have higher level expectations, sometimes negative ones

Adapted from The National Center for Research in Vocational Education.

 Profiles in Health Promotion

Joan has been working at the Gordon Manufacturing Company for the past ten years. She is now a midlevel manager who enjoys her job and the relationship with the company. Joan has been a smoker for the past fifteen years and has never really considered giving up cigarettes until recently when the company announced that it would become smoke free within the next six months. For the past five years the company has had a designated smoking area, but now plans to eliminate smoking from all company property. As a result of the new smoking policy the company has decided to offer smoking cessation classes to all employees who desire to take them. Joan has registered for one of the classes, but she really enjoys smoking and is unsure she wants to quit or if she will be able to quit after fifteen years of smoking. As a health professional, you have been asked to design a program that would help employees such as Joan quit smoking. Utilizing the concepts of adult motivation, select a theory of behavioral change model and describe the steps necessary for the program to be successful.

Check It Out

One theory that many health promotion professionals prescribe to for facilitating behavioral change is the transtheoretical model. Listed below are the six stages of that theory. For each stage, describe the type of strategy that might be used to keep clients either compliant or moving toward behavioral change.

Stage of Change	Strategy/Technique
Precontemplation	
Contemplation	
Preparation	
Action	
Maintenance	

Summary

- Behavior change theories provide direction and justification for health promotion activities.
- Maslow developed a theory of human motivation that views motivation as a drive to get certain "needs" met.
- Maslow's list of human needs includes physiological needs, safety needs, love and belongingness needs, esteem needs, and self-actualization needs.
- Very few people reach the level of self-actualization, which is an intrinsically driven desire to become all one can.
- Lewin's field theory views behavior change as the result of conflicting forces (called driving forces and resisting forces). Change can only occur when driving forces are strengthened and resisting forces are weakened.
- Lewin conceived of change as a five-step process that includes unfreezing, problem diagnosis, goal setting, the new behavior, and refreezing.
- B. F. Skinner's theory of operant conditioning emphasizes that when a behavior is immediately followed by a reinforcing stimulant, it is strengthened. Behaviors not followed by reinforcing stimuli tend to be weakened.
- Social cognitive theory, aka social learning theory, views learning as taking place in a social context.
- Social cognitive theory states that people can learn by observing others, that learning can occur without an observable change in behavior, that reinforcement may be indirect, and that learning can only occur when cognitive processes take place.
- Social cognitive theory requires people to know what a new behavior is and how to do it.

- Self-efficacy is one's situational perception of one's ability to succeed or fail at a particular task/behavior.
- Self-efficacy may or may not be related to an actual experience; self-efficacy has to do with perception about events.
- The theory of reasoned action views behavior change as a result of individuals' attitudes toward the behavior and their belief about what others think that forms their intention to change.
- The theory of planned behavior includes the preceding concepts and adds the component of "perceived behavioral control," which is how easy or difficult the change is perceived to be.
- The health belief model provides a comprehensive framework for why people do the things they do.
- Certain factors must occur if behavior change is to occur. These factors include feelings of susceptibility to disease/problems and perceived seriousness of potential health problems.
- The transtheoretical model provides a systematic integration of several theories of behavior change.
- The transtheoretical model views change as movement through a series of stages that include precontemplation, contemplation, preparation, action, maintenance, and termination.
- Movement through these stages is not always linear and frequently involves relapse to previous behaviors.
- Successful health promotion programs need to provide activities aimed at all the stages of change, rather than just the action stage.
- People learn in different ways. They learn using different modalities (seeing, hearing, touching/doing), perceive information differently (feeling vs. thinking), and process information differently (doers vs. watchers).
- Varying combinations of how people perceive and process information results in four primary learning styles/psychological types (feelers, thinkers, sensors, intuitors).

Bibliography

AJZEN, I. 1988. Attitudes, personality, and behavior. Chicago: Dorsey Press 3–16.

BANDURA, A. 1977. Self-efficacy: Toward a unifying theory of behavioral change. *Psychological Review* 84(2): 191–215.

BANDURA, A., and ADAMS, N. E. 1977. Analysis of self-efficacy theory of behavioral change. *Cognitive Therapy and Research* 1: 287–305.

BANDURA, A., and SCHUNK, D. H. 1981. Cultivating competence, self-efficacy, and intrinsic interest through proximal self-motivation. *Journal of Personality and Social Psychology* 41(3): 586–598.

BECKER, M. H., DRACHMAN, R. S., and KIRSCHT, J. P. 1974. A new approach to explaining-sick-role behavior in low income populations. *American Journal of Public Health* 64: 205–216.

BECKER, M. H., and GREEN, L. W. 1975. A family approach to compliance with medical treatment, a selective review of the literature. *International Journal of Health Education* 18(3): 2–11.

BLAIR, S., and PFEIFFER, G. 1997. What the surgeon general's report means for you. AWHP's Worksite Health, Winter 4(1): 9–11.

BUTLER, J. T. 1994. *Principles of health education and health promotion.* Englewood, CO: Morton.

CATANIA, A. C., and HARNARD, S. 1988. *The selection of behavior: The operant behaviorism of B. F. Skinner: Comments and consequences.* Cambridge: Cambridge University Press.

CHAPMAN, L. S. 1997. Reactions to the article. *The Art of Health Promotion* 1(1): 7–8.

COWDERY, J. E., WANG, M. Q., EDDY, J. M., and TRUCKS, J. K. 1995. A theory driven health promotion program in a university setting. *Journal of Health Education* 26(4): 248–250.

DiCLEMENTE, C. C., PROCHASKA, J. O., and GIBERTINI, M. 1985. Self-efficacy and the stages of self-change of smoking. *Cognitive Therapy and Research* 9(2): 181–200.

DiCLEMENTE, C. C., PROCHASKA, J. O., FAIRHURST, S. K., VELICER, W. F., VELASQUEZ, M. M., and ROSSI, J. S. 1991. The process of smoking cessation: an analysis of precontemplation, contemplation, and preparation stages of change. *Journal of Consulting and Clinical Psychology* 59(2): 295–304.

First International Conference on Health Promotion. 1986. Ottawa Charter for Health Promotion. *Health Promotion* 1(4): 3–4.

http://archon.educ.kent.edu/~nebraska/curric/ttim1/aaal.html. 1995. Assumptions about the adult learner. The Nebraska Institute for the Study of Adult Literacy.

JANZ, N. K., and BECKER, M. H. 1984. The health belief model: A decade later. *Health Education Quarterly* 11(1): 1–47.

JUNG, CARL G. 1976. *Psychological Types.* New Jersey: Princeton University Press, p. 160.

KOLB, D. A., RUBIN, I. M., and McINTYRE, M. 1974. *Organizational Psychology: A Book of Readings* (2nd. ed.). New Jersey: Prentice-Hall.

KOLB, D. A. 1983. *Experiential learning: Experience as the source of learning and development.* New Jersey: Prentice-Hall.

KNOWLES, M. S. 1970. *The modern practice of adult education.* New York: Association Press.

LEWIN, K. 1935. *A Dynamic Theory of Personality.* New York: McGraw-Hill.

LEWIN, K. 1961. "Quasi-stationary social equilibria and the problem of permanent change." In W. G. Gennis, K. D. Benne, and R. Chin, editors, *The planning of change.* New York: Holt, Rinehart & Winston.

MASLOW, A. H. 1943. A theory of human motivation. *Psychological Review* 50: 370–396.

McCARTHY, B. M. 1987. *The 4-mat system.* Barrington, IL: Excel.

McKENZIE, J. F., and Smeltzer, J. L. 1997. *Planning, Implementing, and Evaluating Health Promotion Programs—A Primer.* Boston: Allyn & Bacon.

National Institutes of Health, National Heart, Lung, and Blood Institute. Summer, 1997. Taking it to the streets: community based interventions. *Heart Memo,* p. 16.

ORMAND, J. E. 1995. *Human Learning.* New Jersey: Merrill.

PROCHASKA, J. O. 1979. *Systems of Psychotherapy: a transtheoretical analysis.* Homewood, IL: The Dorsey Press.

PROCHASKA, J. O., and DiCLEMENTE, C. C. 1983. Stages and processes of self-change of smoking: Toward an integrative model of change. *Journal of Consulting and Clinical Psychology* 51(3): 390–395.

PROCHASKA, J. O. 1991. Prescribing to the stage and level of phobic patients. *Psychotherapy* 28(3): 463–468.

PROCHASKA, J. O., DiCLEMENTE, C. C., and NORCROSS, J. C. 1992. In search of how people change: Applications to addictive behaviors. *American Psychologist* 47(9): 1102–1114.

PROCHASKA, J. O., and VELICER, W. F. 1997. Introduction: The transtheoretical model. *American Journal of Health Promotion* (12)1: 6–7.

RICHARD, L., POTVIN, L., KISHCHUK, N., PRLIC, H., and GREEN, L. W. 1996. Assessment of the integration of the ecological approach in health promotion programs. *American Journal of Health Promotion* 10(4): 318–327.

ROSENSTOCK, I. M., STRECHER, V. J., and BECKER, M. H. 1988. Social learning theory and the health belief model. *Health Education Quarterly* 15(2): 175–183.

SHEA, S., and BASCH, C. E. 1990. A review of five major community-based cardiovascular disease prevention programs: Part I, rationale, design, and theoretical framework. *American Journal of Health Promotion* 4(3): 203–213.

SKINNER, B. F. 1953. *The Behavior of Organisms.* East Norwalk, CT: Appleton Lange.

STOKOLS, D., ALLEN, J., and BELLINGHAM, R. L. 1996. The social ecology of health promotion: Implications for research and practice. *American Journal of Health Promotion* 10(4): 247–251.

USA Today 1998. Cathy Hainer's personal journey D(4): 3–20.

VELICER, W. F. and PROCHASKA, J. O. 1997. The transtheoretical model of health behavior change. *American Journal of Health Promotion* 12(1): 38–48.

Conducting Needs Assessments

OBJECTIVES

CHAPTER OBJECTIVES

After reading this chapter, you should be able to

- define and discuss needs assessment and its role and function in the development of health promotion programs.
- distinguish between populations and program participants.
- describe and discuss the types of information collected for needs assessment.
- identify at least three different approaches to data collection for needs assessment.
- describe how needs assessment information is used in program development.
- demonstrate the process of goal and objective development.

In this chapter we turn to the task of collecting information about worksite environments for the purpose of developing health promotion programs. The process of collecting such information is called *needs assessment.*

AN INTRODUCTION TO NEEDS ASSESSMENT

Needs assessment is a phrase that describes a process that is perhaps the most critical part of program planning. We can define needs assessment as the process of collecting and analyzing information, to develop an understanding of the issues, resources, and constraints of worksite populations, as related to development of health promotion programs (McKenzie and Smeltzer, 1997; Windsor et al., 1994). In carrying out needs assessment, program planners collect information that reflects the desires (needs) of several different constituencies, including those who asked for the program to be developed (known as the "sponsors"), those who are the intended audience of the program, those who will deliver the program, and those who will deal with the aftermath of the program. As an illustration, a needs assessment for developing a worksite fitness program would include the management (sponsors) and employees at the worksite, and health promotion personnel who would provide the program. The needs assessment would also include medical professionals who would provide consultation for the program, and who might be called on to treat employees who develop program-related medical complaints.

It is important to realize that needs assessment is not a **product,** but a **process,** and that perceptions about the role and function of the program usually change as new information becomes available. Although it is necessary to draw conclusions from needs assessment for planning purposes, it is important to recognize that the process of collecting information should never really end, and that new information should be integrated into programs whenever possible.

The primary objective of needs assessment is to develop a level of awareness such that program planners will be able to accurately anticipate how program activities will be received by the intended audience. Achieving this objective requires developing a clear understanding of the context for the program and of the roles of the program sponsors and the intended audience. In addition, achieving the primary objective requires knowledge of the resources that are needed to implement the program.

The issue of resource availability is an important part of needs assessment. It is important to use needs assessment to develop estimates of the resources that will be needed to plan, implement, and evaluate the program. It is also critical to learn about processes for obtaining additional resources for the program.

Finally, needs assessment provides an opportunity to learn about any hidden agendas that may be operating. Hidden agendas are unspoken goals of management, employees, health promotion personnel, insurers, or others who may serve many different purposes. For example, an unspoken goal of sponsors of a worksite heart disease program may be to identify personnel who are most likely to develop heart diseases. This information would not be for health promotion purposes, but to identify personnel who may develop conditions that could cause insurance rates to increase.

In sum, program planning is doomed without a thorough needs assessment. Without understanding of those who have asked for the program (the sponsors) and what is expected, and the needs, interest, values, and past experiences of those who will receive the program (recipients) and who may be affected by the program, planning is likely to be misdirected.

POPULATIONS AND PROGRAM RECIPIENTS

Before delving into a discussion of the steps in needs assessment, we need to address the fundamental question of who might a health promotion program be designed to reach. The answer to this question provides the first step in focusing needs assessment. Program recipients (also known as the "intended audience," or "target population") are those for whom a health promotion program is designed. For a worksite, the intended audience may be all or a part or parts of a population that includes all of the employees and service providers outside the organization (company) that may have influence on the recipients, in the context of the health promotion program. For example, the intended audience for a worksite health promotion program focusing on reducing back injuries might include those at risk of back injury and their supervisors as the primary program recipients. The population would include the recipients and others who may become involved with issues related to back injuries such as management, health services provided at the worksite, physicians and others who provide health care for back injuries for employees, and perhaps insurance companies and other who may influence costs of care and certification for disability. From this example, it is clear that identification of the population and the program recipients can be quite complex. A useful way to simplify the process of defining the population, and to identify the intended audience, is to consider the concept of population from two points of view: *structural* and *functional* populations.

A **structural population** is defined in terms of the organization in which the program will be implemented. In other words, the structural population is the "company," and by definition includes all individuals who are employed. Although a structurally defined population may be convenient for descriptive purposes, the definition may be too limiting for planning. As the back injury program example provided earlier pointed out, the recipients of worksite health promotion programs often have important interactions and relationships that extend beyond the boundaries of the worksite or exist within subunits of a structural population. To capture these complex relationships that extend beyond the structural population, we can consider the population in functional terms. A **functional population** is one that can be defined in terms of the interactions of people at work and in other parts of their lives. In this case, a functional population would be one that includes employees and their daily interactions as related to a specific health issue. Such interactions may take place within and outside the structural population, so the structural population may be of relatively little importance. For example, employees may obtain health-related information, advice, and health care from sources in the community. The influence of these sources should be carefully considered in planning a worksite health promotion program. Employees may take information from the worksite program and apply it to their interactions at home and with community health care providers. If the information received from the program agrees with the opinions of health providers, then reinforcement occurs. If the sources disagree, however, then confusion will be the likely result. In practice, it is a very good idea to include both

Needs assessment should include information from individuals whenever possible.

structural and functional components in defining the population and recipients for worksite health promotion programs.

In some cases, the distinction between structural and functional communities is faint, while in others the differences are clear and important. Regardless, it is critical that needs assessment consider these two points of view and strike an appropriate balance that includes elements of both.

Now that we have an introduction to needs assessment and the concept of population, it is time to focus on the information that is to be collected.

INFORMATION FOR NEEDS ASSESSMENT

Table 4.1 presents a summary of the information that is required to carry out a needs assessment for planning a worksite health promotion program. The information collected for the categories in table 4.1 is adapted from a general format for conducting community analysis and represents consideration of the structural and functional populations and has the effect of transforming data into programming (Dignan and Carr, 1992). As table 4.1 shows, the information required is divided into six main categories: structural and functional population characteristics, health status indicators, health care delivery system, current and past health promotion programs, and, a very broad category, the community environment. It is important to note that all of the information shown in table 4.1 may not be relevant for every worksite, and it is important to sort through the categories and focus attention on those elements that relate to the specific worksite under scrutiny, the population, and the health promotion issues that the program will address. Deciding on the

TABLE 4.1. Types of Needs Assessment Information to Be Collected for Planning Worksite Health Promotion Programs

Information Type	Information Source(s)	Information to be Collected
Structural population	Worksite records	• Total number of employees • Numbers of employees by category (management, production, support) • Skill levels required for different jobs • Age—distribution of ages of employees • Gender—distribution by gender • Ethnicity—distribution by ethnicity • Other—languages spoken/written, work pattern

(continued)

TABLE 4.1. (Continued)

Information Type	Information Source(s)	Information to be Collected
Functional population	Employees and their nonwork interactions	• Social networks—relationships among employees and between employees and the community • Family—family and work relationships • Church—role of churches at worksite • Recreation—relations with work • Schools (adult education and child) • Sources of health information
Health status indicators	Worksite records Local and regional health records Insurers' records	• Rates and chief causes of morbidity and mortality among employees • Seasonal variation in morbidity • Occupational illnesses and injuries • Reasons for health-related loss time occurrences • Medical claims
Health care delivery system	Worksite records, employee interviews	• Physician access system—injuries, acute illness, chronic illness, preventive care, counseling • Access to other providers • Health insurance system/cost • Disability coverage • Workman's compensation system

Worksite health promotion programs	Worksite records, interviews with health promotion personnel	• Currently active programs
		   objectives
		   methods
		   evaluation criteria and structure
		   interim results
		   management support
		• Past programs
		   objectives
		   methods
		   results
		   management perception of results

(continued)

TABLE 4.1. (Continued)

Information Type	Information Source(s)	Information to be Collected
Additional useful information about the community		• Incentives for healthy living in place smoking seat belts
Community environment	Climate data on local area	Seasonal variations in temperature and rainfall; other climatic conditions affecting health
	Observation, agricultural data	Terrain, agricultural potential, natural resources
	Observation, inspection of local maps	Proximity to metropolitan area; relationships to surrounding communities, towns, and neighborhoods
	Business and economic statistics	Extent of industrial development, types of industry, major employers, status of local economy, relationship between industry and the economy
Community demographics	U.S. Census, regional or state estimates	Total number of residents in the community
		Breakdown of population into age, sex, and racial characteristics
		Percentage of change in population by age and sex over the past five years
		Percentages, by age and sex, of predominant racial and ethnic groups
		Distribution of educational levels (percentages with elementary, high school, college, and professional training)
		Median family income; extent of poverty

(continued)

TABLE 4.1. (Continued)

Information Type	Information Source(s)	Information to be Collected
Social and political structure	County or municipal summaries	Structure of local government; selection process for public officials
	Key informant interviews with school, municipal officials	Description of educational system; how leadership is selected; quality and resources within the educational system, schools, school enrollment, health-related activities
	County or municipal information	Parks and recreation facilities
		Predominant religious groups; relationship between religious practice and local decision making, number of churches
	Key informant interviews with news media personnel	Racial tension, labor unrest, economic struggle, political upheaval, community accomplishments
Mortality	Health department	$\dfrac{\text{Number of deaths}}{\text{Population of area}} \times 1000$
		Leading causes of death by age, sex, race, occupation
Morbidity		Incidence and prevalence of leading infectious diseases by age, sex, race, occupation
		Incidence and prevalence of leading chronic diseases by age, sex, race, occupation
		Incidence and prevalence of leading occupational illnesses by age, sex, race, and duration of exposure; classified by causative agent
Risk factors		Occurrence of predominant behaviors (health risk behaviors) associated with causes of death, disability, and illness
		Frequency or occurrence of nonbehavioral risk factors associated with causes of death, illness, and disability

types of information that should be collected for a particular situation should be based on the goal of being able to envision the circumstances of the individuals in the intended audience for the program, and the experiences that they are likely to encounter as they respond to the information about the program.

As table 4.1 shows, the information required to carry out a thorough needs assessment is considerable. In addition, the range of information requirements means that several different methods of collecting such information are needed. In the next section we describe and discuss several different techniques that can be used to collect needs assessment information.

TECHNIQUES FOR COLLECTING INFORMATION FOR NEEDS ASSESSMENT

In this section, we present the most common techniques that can be used for collecting information for needs assessments. It is important to realize that more than one approach is usually required to collect needs assessment information, and that various combinations of methods are often needed to fill specific gaps in information. The information collection techniques that will be presented are as follows:

1. Observation of the structural population to develop an awareness of the characteristics of the physical environment
2. Collection and review of numerical information
3. Key informant interviews
4. Intercept interviews
5. Focus groups
6. Community forum
7. Surveys of the worksite population

Observation

Although it may appear to be a trivial and obvious technique for collecting needs assessment information, there is no substitute for learning about a worksite and its population by direct, firsthand observation. The ordinary working conditions that exist, the rhythms and daily practices of the workplace, and the everyday behaviors of employees can best be learned by observation. If any health promotion activities are ongoing, it is critical to observe such programs and to learn as much as possible about how they are organized; their strengths, weaknesses, and the resources available to them; and the limitations that are imposed on them by the worksite environment. For example, observation of a textile plant where T-shirts were manufactured revealed a setting with formidable challenges to health promotion program development. The employees in this setting functioned on a piece-work basis. That is, income depended on the speed and quality of production. Workers who were able to produce T-shirts quickly without defects made extra money. This arrangement meant that time away from the workstation reduced productivity. The management of the plant was supportive of health promotion in general, particularly if it would reduce lost time and medical claims. They were quick to point out, however, that any programs would need to fit in with the ongoing production system. An example cited by management was an employee fitness program that was supported by the plant and offered exercise classes before or after shifts.

It is important to maintain a detailed record of worksite observations. Detailed notes are a minimum requirement. Photographs are a valuable resource that can be reviewed and shared with others if necessary. Copies of newsletters, notices, and information about informal means of communication used in the population should be collected as part of observation. For example, routine meetings and social activities that occur at the worksite should be noted as these may present opportunities for reaching employees at times that do not compete with work.

Collection and Review of Numerical Information

Collecting and reviewing information about the worksite population is an essential part of needs assessment. Records of the number of employees, their classifications, duration of employment, medical claims, and other related information are not likely to be available from sources other than the company. In most cases, such records are maintained by the human resources (personnel) department. Additionally, information on the health care and health insurance coverage status of the company is helpful in planning health promotion programs. Finally, in reviewing information on the company, it is particularly important to note changes over time. Such inspections can provide valuable clues about the effects of business cycles on the number of employees, and their classifications. For example, it is common for companies to hire temporary personnel to address specific needs and to let such employees go when the need is met. It would be important to understand this practice in planning a health promotion program, particularly if the program was to include a focus on achieving long-term behavior changes.

Key Informant Interviews

Key informants are individuals with specific knowledge about a population (Rossi, Freeman, and Wright, 1979). Key informants for worksite health promotion program development are likely to include human resources department personnel, owners and managers, union representatives, and other senior-level employees. In cases where the health promotion program is to focus on a specific condition, physical fitness, for example, other employees with relevant experience would also be considered as potential key informants. In cases where health services are involved, physicians or their staff personnel could also be key informants. The main desirable characteristic of a key informant is possession of information about the worksite that is not available elsewhere. In conducting key informant interviews, the same information is collected from each individual and the results are compared. It is believed that the key informants will have varying points of view that, when combined, will provide a well-balanced picture of the issues of interest to the needs assessment.

To illustrate how key informant interviews can be used in a needs assessment, consider the experience of a breast cancer prevention project for a rural worksite population. Key informant interviews were conducted with individuals from three different categories: local community leaders, employees, and health care professionals who provided care to the employees. Local community leaders were identified and selected to be interviewed based on their interactions with the worksite population. The group of local leaders included elected officials and owners of small businesses. The employee group was selected to represent the two main categories at the worksite and included skilled, experienced production workers and clerical workers. Health professionals were included as key informants if they had contracts with the worksite to provide care to employees. The procedures used in developing the key informant process included the following steps:

1. Characteristics of key informants were specified.
2. Strategies to recruit key informants and arrange interviews were developed.
3. Interview questions were developed and pretested.
4. Interviewers were recruited and trained.
5. Key informant interviews were scheduled and conducted.
6. Results from the interviews were summarized.
7. Arrangements were made for additional interviews to be conducted if necessary.

Sample items from the interview included the following:

1. General questions about the value of health (designed to get the interview started smoothly)
2. Questions about the main types of health concerns among employees
3. Experience, attitudes, and general feelings about cancer and breast cancer
4. Knowledge and beliefs about breast cancer and its causes
5. Interest in information about cancer prevention
6. Interest in participating in screening

The results from the interviews were summarized, leading to the following conclusions:

1. Employees value health and often rely more on family and friends than health care providers for advice on health matters.
2. Health care providers are consulted when symptoms appear, only rarely for prevention.
3. Cancer is not a primary health concern among employees.
4. Cancer has occurred among employee families, but usually in retired individuals.
5. Employees believe that breast cancer is increasing in the community.
6. Employees are interested in learning what can be done to prevent and cure breast cancer.
7. Employees would probably participate in screening if the cost was not too high and if scheduling did not conflict with responsibilities at home.
8. Results from screening must remain confidential to have trust of employees.

As the results from the example indicate, the information from the key informant interviews provided insights into the worksite population that would probably not have been available from other sources.

Intercept Interviews

These interviews are commonly used in marketing research as a low-cost, quick and easy means of collecting information. The process of conducting intercept interviews is quite simple. Individuals appearing to fit predetermined criteria are approached, often in public places, and asked to answer a brief set of questions. Common places for such interviews to be conducted are worksites when employees are entering or leaving, grocery stores, shopping malls and sporting events. The principal limitations of intercept interviews have to do with sampling and the effects of time constraints. Those who agree to be interviewed should not be assumed representative of a population, and they usually resist answering more than a few questions. For planning worksite health promotion programs, intercept interviews can be used for such purposes as gauging employees' general interest in programs and their awareness of health-related issues.

Focus Groups

Focus groups are planned discussion groups that are designed to collect information and opinions in a controlled setting (Morgan, 1992). They are commonly used in marketing research and have been widely used in health promotion program development. Two types of focus groups are in common use for health promotion program planning: those that are designed to assist with development of the basic concepts of programs; and those that are intended to review plans, educational materials, and presentations.

Concept development focus groups are used to verify the basic premise behind a health promotion program. As such, they can be very useful in revealing situations where there are differences in beliefs and/or opinions about issues. For example, focus groups convened to learn about screening for breast cancer revealed that employees were interested in screening but were even more concerned that their health care benefits would not be adequate for breast cancer treatment. They were supportive of the screening program but viewed it as incomplete if it did not address treatment issues.

Product review focus groups are the second type of focus group and are most commonly designed to collect reactions to education programs. Product review groups are typically conducted after concept development groups, and their primary task is to react to the image and content used in educational materials. For example, a product review focus group might be asked to react to the reading level, type of illustrations, and length of educational materials, and to tell the program developers whether they are appropriate for the intended audience. It is usually wise for product review focus groups to consider different versions of program materials and give their opinions about the strengths and weaknesses of each.

Conducting focus groups is deceptively easy. The groups require carefully planned recruitment, a trained moderator to lead the discussion, a thoughtfully prepared guide for the moderator, and a facility where the groups can be conducted comfortably.

A Community Forum

A community forum is a public meeting approach intended to collect a wide variety of opinions about issues, in this case related to worksite health promotion (Ross and Mico, 1980). Structuring such meetings can be tricky; the goal is to ensure that issues are raised but not to stifle discussion. A useful technique is to develop different ways to address an issue and ask the group to rank the versions in terms of desirability, feasibility, acceptability to the employees, and so on. For example, a program to increase fitness could be carried out in a number of ways, ranging from building a facility at the worksite to arranging for memberships at a local health club to providing "low-tech" fitness activities at the worksite. Asking the group to rate each option would be a good technique to generate discussion of pros and cons, as well as to generate new options. Fundamentally, however, the discussion could inform the program planners about the level of knowledge and interest in the idea at a point in time where plans can be changed.

Surveys of the Worksite Population

Surveys are easily the most complex and costly ways to collect information for needs assessment. On the other hand, well-designed surveys can produce a considerable amount of information that is representative of the population with a known degree of precision. Design of surveys is complicated and includes developing a definition of the population about which information is to be collected, selecting a process for identifying those who will be asked to respond, collecting and analyzing the responses, and developing estimates that apply to the population. For most situations the cost of collecting needs assessment information by a rigorous survey is excessive. However, the opportunity to obtain information with a known level of precision, and that can serve as a good evaluation tool, is very valuable to needs assessment.

THE NEEDS ASSESSMENT PROCESS

Now that we have introduced the types of information that can be collected for needs assessment and methods for collection, the structure of the collection process and the next steps will be discussed. Needs assessment for planning worksite health promotion can be presented as a brief series of steps, as summarized in table 4.2.

As depicted in table 4.2, the first three steps in the needs assessment process deal with collecting and reviewing the information collected for needs assessment. Step 4 is critical to program planning, as it identifies the intended audience(s) for the health promotion program. Steps 5 and 6 take the information collected and apply what has been learned to development of the basic building blocks for the program plan: goals, objectives, and evaluation criteria.

This is a good point to reemphasize the notion of needs assessment as a "never-ending" process. It is important that health promotion professionals continuously monitor the workplace environment and be able to detect changes that should be integrated into programs.

Let's consider an example of a back injury prevention program to illustrate how the steps in needs assessment would be used.

Step 1: Observation. As table 4.2 indicates, the objective of the first step in needs assessment is to visualize the environment where the health promotion program will be implemented. Although this is a relatively simple task, it is very important because there are many subtle facets of the work environment that are rarely, if ever, included in documents. Observation of the rhythms and customs of the workplace will provide insight into how a health promotion program could be integrated into the environment.

TABLE 4.2. Steps in the Needs Assessment Process

Step	Objective	Methods	Use(s) of Information Collected
1	Become able to visualize the environment where the health promotion program will be implemented	Participant observation of worksite and, if relevant, health services used for referral	Provides a foundation for anticipating resource needs and barriers to behavior change
2	Learn objective, factual information about the work environment and the health issue(s) to be addressed	Collect and review relevant quantitative information on worksite Interview key informants	Provides a data-based context for the program, identifies deficits in information, identifies possible evaluation criteria
3	Fill gaps in information about the issue(s) to be addressed and the environment	Collect subjective information through key informant interviews, employee forum	Provides an in-depth understanding of the barriers to be overcome in planning the program
4	Identify the intended audience(s) for the program	Review conclusions from step 3, identify intended audience(s) and verify with program sponsors	Confirms that the program planners and program sponsors agree about the intended audience(s)
5	Identify program goals and objectives	Review information from steps 1–4, develop goal and objective statements	Goals and objectives provide the basic foundation for program planning and evaluation
6	Identify tentative evaluation criteria	Negotiate process, impact, and outcome evaluation criteria with program sponsors	Evaluation criteria specify the information that will be needed for evaluation instruments and the evaluation model to be used

The environment for the program in our back injury prevention example is a warehouse that stores printed documents. As you enter the warehouse, you are met by the supervisor's assistant who will serve as your escort and guide. You quickly notice that nearly every employee is wearing a back support appliance. The appliance is made of cloth and foam rubber and has velcro closures. About half of the appliances appear to be dangling around the shoulders of employees rather than being tightly secured. You ask the supervisor's assistant about the back support appliance and you are told that they are an insurance requirement. As your tour of the warehouse continues, you are told that the primary duty is to process file boxes. The boxes must be numbered and placed in a numbered location. You notice that file boxes are piled on pallets and moved to the storage areas with a forklift. When the forklift arrives at the storage location, workers manually stack the file boxes onto shelves. The locations for storage of the file boxes vary from ground level to a third-level shelf that is about twenty feet up from the floor. Work in the warehouse is parceled out by a dispatcher. This individual assigns employees to specific tasks in the warehouse. When there are no boxes to be shelved or retrieved, the dispatcher assigns the employees to maintenance duties.

Your observation of the employees in action is very interesting. Each employee seems to have a unique approach to lifting and stacking boxes. Some are careful and appear to be well schooled in ways to prevent back injuries, while others appear to have no awareness of proper lifting techniques. As your observation continues, you notice that there are posters illustrating proper lifting techniques in the employee breakroom. The posters are clean and neat, the language is clear, and the illustrations are easy to follow.

Step 2: Collection of objective information. Objective information about the work environment and the health issues to be addressed usually requires extensive collection and review of printed information. Often coming in the form of annual reports, claims data, and other "company" information, this information will usually provide the planners with the program sponsors' point of view. It is important to recognize that in many cases documents on health-related issues are considered confidential by the employer and will not be released without proper clearance. It is wise to make efforts early in the needs assessment process to secure access to such documents.

Continuing with the example of the back injury prevention program initiated in step 1, you begin collection of objective needs assessment information by asking the warehouse manager about documents. She informs you that you will need to have clearance from the owner before you can view any documents in the warehouse. You visit the owner's office and learn that the warehouse is one of many business that are managed centrally. The annual report includes information on all of the businesses, and the section dealing with the warehouse is very general. The owner's assistant informs you that the human resources department has the employee records for the warehouse personnel. You visit the human resources department and learn that they will be willing to help you find information for the needs assessment, but that no documents may be copied or may leave the office area. They also request that you provide them with a list of items and information that you will need. You provide the human resources staff with a list of the information that you need. For the warehouse operation, you request

- total number of employees,
- number of employees who handle file boxes,
- ages of employees,
- back injury-related health claims over the past two years,
- disposition of all back injury-related claims, and
- names of health professionals who have provided care for employees with back injuries.

Finally, you ask the human resources staff about the back support appliances that you noticed in the warehouse. You are told that they were recommended by the insurance carrier and that the owner decided to purchase them for every employee. No on in human resources recalls any education program provided with the appliances.

Step 3: Collection of subjective information. In addition to objective information, it is important to collect other data that include personal appraisals. Such information is best collected through interviews, key informant interviews.

Now that you have observed the environment and obtained some objective information, it is time to focus on filling in gaps. The objective information shows that there have been several back injuries, and the health claim data indicate that they have required extensive treatment and periods of disability. You decide to use key informant interviews to learn more for the needs assessment. You identify the warehouse manager, the owner of the company, the head of human resources, and a sample of three individuals who work in the warehouse to be your key informants. To collect information from the health care point of view, you also include two physicians who provided care to injured employees.

The results of the key informant interviews help to fill in gaps. As you suspected, the back support appliances are not well understood by those at highest risk of back injury. Interestingly, they seem to direct employees' attention to their backs, however, and they are concerned about the risk of back injury. As one individual in the warehouse says, "They wouldn't make us wear these things if they weren't worried about us hurting our backs." The interview with the owner reveals that she is concerned with controlling health care costs, and the interview with the warehouse manager indicates little concern about back injuries. The interviews with the physicians indicate that the treatments provided for the back-injured employees were successful and that there was no lasting disability.

Step 4: Identify intended audience(s). The fourth step in needs assessment represents the beginning of the transition from information collection to synthesis and planning. The insight into the situation that has been gleaned from the combination of observations, objective information, and interviews sets the stage for identifying who should be considered in the intended audience for the health promotion program. At this point, it is useful to return to the concept of structural and functional populations and ensure that the needs assessment has been sufficiently broad to capture information from a functional population point of view.

The analysis of information collected for the back injury program needs assessment revealed that the intended audience should include the employees who are at highest risk, those who work in the warehouse and lift boxes to be specific, as well as their supervisors and the warehouse manager. In fact, the entire warehouse staff could benefit from the program. However, the most intensive attention should be directed toward the employees who lift heavy objects regularly.

Step 5: Develop goals and objectives. Goals and objectives are the fundamental components of program plans. *Goals* are broad statements that describe what the program should accomplish. *Objectives,* on the other hand, can be thought of as detailed, descriptive statements that specify how the goals are to be reached. Objectives include three fundamental components: they identify a subject, identify the action that is to occur, and specify how effects should be measured.

The goals and objectives for the back injury prevention program were developed and presented to the company owner. The goal for the program was simple and straightforward, while the objectives were divided into those for supervisory personnel and other employees

Goal: To reduce back injuries among the warehouse employees

Objectives: By the end of the program, participants will be able to

1. list three common work habits that increase the risk of back injury,
2. discuss how back injury prevention fits with overall safety awareness,
3. demonstrate proper lifting techniques to reduce risk of back injury, and
4. list two early warning symptoms of back injury.

By the end of the program, warehouse supervisory personnel will be able to

1. describe the role of back injury prevention in maintaining employee health,
2. demonstrate effective teaching of proper lifting techniques,
3. list three ways that employee behaviors can be monitored,
4. identify two incentives that can be offered to employees who learn and maintain proper lifting techniques, and
5. demonstrate procedures for providing first aid for employees with back injuries.

The goal and objectives were presented to the company owner, human resource department, and warehouse manager. The primary result of the ensuing discussion was general endorsement of the objectives and a "go-ahead" to finish program planning.

Step 6: Identify criteria for evaluation. Evaluation criteria are the indicators that will be used in assessment of the program's accomplishments. Evaluation can be focused on processes, impact, and/or outcomes. Recall from chapter 2 that the term *process* refers to the actual operation of the program, *impact* refers to the short-term (immediate) effects, and *outcomes* are longer-term effects. Regardless of the relative degree of emphasis, evaluation criteria for processes, impact, or outcomes associated with the program are needed.

Profiles in Health Promotion
When Needs Assessment Uncovers Hidden Agendas

One of the challenges for those who conduct thorough needs assessments is the situation where the results of the assessment reveal hidden agendas. Sometimes the unspoken goals are the results of internal company politics and don't have much impact on health promotion programs. In other cases, however, hidden agendas can put the program planner in an ethical bind. Consider the following example. A medium-size construction company comes to you asking your help in planning a health promotion program. The head of human resources, the individual who contacted you, agrees when you suggest that a needs assessment should be the first step in planning. You carry out the expected needs assessment activities beginning with observations and review of numerical information about the company. During key informant interviews you learn that the company has previously hired a health insurance analyst who reviewed records and worked on the negotiations with managed care providers. The result of the analyst's work, you learn, was to recommend that the risk profile for the company be improved by focusing on employees with significant risks of heart disease. Such individuals would be the focus of an intensive health promotion program. If the risk status of these high-risk individuals could be improved, then the program would be very successful. The health insurance analyst also recommended that employees with unchangeable risk factors, genetic predisposition, for example, be removed from the workforce (fired) to strengthen the company's hand in the negotiations.

At this point, you face the prospect of continuing to complete the needs assessment and plan the program, knowing that part of the program will identify those with unchangeable risk factors.

What ethical dilemmas are raised by this situation? How could you resolve them?

The most straightforward method for establishing evaluation criteria is to focus on the objectives for the program. If the objectives have been carefully developed, the evaluation criteria will be pretty obvious. When objectives are vague, however, evaluation criteria are more difficult to derive. Consider the example cited earlier to develop the back injury prevention program. This program has objectives for employees whose jobs increase their risk, as well as supervisors who are responsible for ensuring that the work is accomplished in a safe environment. Revisiting the objectives, the evaluation criteria can be derived. Table 4.3 illustrates evaluation criteria that could be used with the back injury program objectives. Note that the evaluation criteria are limited to objectives that are quantifiable.

TABLE 4.3. Objectives and Program Evaluation Criteria

Objective	Evaluation Criteria
Employees at risk of back injury should be able to do the following:	
1. List three common work habits that increase the risk of back injury	At least 75% of the employees completing the program correctly identify the three common work habits on a multiple-choice test
2. Discuss how back injury prevention fits with overall safety awareness	
3. Demonstrate proper lifting techniques to reduce risk of back injury	100% of the employees completing the program demonstrate proper lifting techniques in a simulation of warehouse operations
4. List two early warning symptoms of back injury	At least 75% of employees completing the program correctly identify two symptoms of back injury
By the end of the program, warehouse **supervisory personnel** will be able to do the following:	
1. Describe the role of back injury prevention in maintaining employee health	
2. Demonstrate effective teaching of proper lifting techniques	In simulations, supervisory personnel will cover 100% of the components included in a safe lifting practices module
3. List three ways that employee behaviors can be monitored	On a written test, supervisory personnel will list at least three techniques for monitoring employee back injury prevention behaviors that were discussed in the training program
4. Identify two incentives that can be offered to employees who learn and maintain proper lifting techniques	On a written test, supervisory personnel will list at least two incentives that were discussed in the training program
5. Demonstrate procedures for providing first aid for employees with back injuries	In simulated back injury scenarios, supervisory personnel will correctly provide emergency care, achieving a score of at least 80%

Check It Out

In this chapter we introduced several different techniques that can be used for collecting needs assessment information. Each technique has strengths and limitations, and deciding when each should be used can be challenging. Explore this concept by considering the following situations and deciding which needs assessment information collection technique from the following list would be appropriate:

- Key informant interviews
- Intercept interviews
- Focus groups
- Community forum
- Employee survey

1. A local foundation wants to offer free mammograms to the women age 40 and older who work in a local furniture manufacturing plant. How can you learn whether this screening service would be accepted by the company? What technique(s) could you use to learn how to introduce the screening program to the women?
2. The owner of a small company wants to "do something" to improve physical fitness among his employees. The company provides telephone answering services for physicians, a sedentary but high-stress job. The company has fifteen employees working three shifts. What techniques could be used to learn what health promotion activities would be likely to be successful?
3. A large utility company has initiated a survey as part of a needs assessment. The response to the mailed survey has been disappointing, however, as only 10 percent have sent the surveys back. How can the program planners learn why the response to the survey has been so poor? How can they learn the information needed if the survey doesn't work?

Summary

- Needs assessment is the process of collecting and analyzing information that is used to form the foundation for planning. The primary objective of needs assessment is to provide planners with information that will allow them to anticipate how program activities will be received by the intended audience.
- For planning purposes, populations can be considered structural or functional. A structural population is a community, a worksite, or other well-defined entity. A functional population focuses on interactions and may extend beyond a structural population.
- Areas of interest for needs assessment include structural and functional population characteristics, health status indicators, descriptors of the health care delivery system, worksite programs, community environmental descriptors, community demographic information, social and political structure descriptors, and vital statistics such as mortality, morbidity, and risk factors.

- Techniques for collecting needs assessment information include observation, review of official documents, key informant interviews, intercept interviews, focus groups, the community forum approach, and surveys.
- There are six steps in needs assessment; visualizing the environment, learning objective information, filling in gaps in information, identifying intended audiences for programs, developing program goals and objectives, and identifying evaluation criteria.

Bibliography

DIGNAN, M. B., and CARR, P. A. 1992. *Program planning for health education and health promotion.* Philadelphia: Lea & Febiger.

McKENZIE, J. F., and SMELTZER, J. L. 1997. *Planning, implementing, and evaluating health promotion programs: A primer* (2nd ed.). Boston: Allyn & Bacon.

MORGAN, D. L. 1992. Designing focus group research. In M. Stewart et al., (Eds.), *Tools for primary care research.* Newbury Park, CA: Sage.

ROSS, H., and MICO, P. 1980. *Theory and practice in health education.* Mountain View, CA: Mayfield.

ROSSI, P. H., FREEMAN, H. E., and WRIGHT, S. R. 1979. *Evaluation: A systematic approach.* Newbury Park, CA: Sage.

WINDSOR, R., BARANOWSKI, T., CLARK, N., and CUTTER, G. 1994. *Evaluation of health promotion health education and disease prevention programs* (2nd ed.). Mountain View, CA: Mayfield.

CHAPTER 5

Formulating Plans for Health Promotion Programs

OBJECTIVES

Developing a Framework for Planning

A Format for Developing Individual Health Promotion Programs

Selecting Appropriate Programming

Financial Impact

Company Policies

The Scope and Sequence of Health Promotion Programs

Levels of Intervention

Levels of Prevention

Personalizing Information for Change

Strategies for Facilitating Change

New Forms of Health Management Technology Used in Health Promotion Programming

Determining Educational Equipment Needs

Fitness Equipment Needs

Facility Needs

Marketing Strategy

Enrollment Procedures

Utilizing Outside Vendors

Legal Considerations for Health Promotion Programs

Profiles in Health Promotion

Check It Out

Summary

CHAPTER OBJECTIVES

After reading this chapter, you should be able to

- discuss effective planning procedures.
- describe the levels of intervention in health promotion.
- determine strategies for interventions.
- select an appropriate program mix in a comprehensive health promotion effort.
- analyze equipment needs for a comprehensive health promotion effort.
- develop screening and enrollment procedures for a health promotion facility.
- discuss potential legal considerations when conducting health promotion activities.

The evolution of a health promotion program is continuous. Before initiating a program, a great deal of effort must be spent designing it. This process starts after the needs assessment and data gathering, discussed in the previous chapter, and culminates prior to actual implementation of the program. Incipient planning efforts of this process should focus on selection of an employee wellness committee and establishment of priorities and time lines for the program. This chapter introduces the steps in the process. Issues such as program planning, program selection, equipment selection, enrollment procedures, and potential legal concerns are reviewed.

DEVELOPING A FRAMEWORK FOR PLANNING

Having a framework for planning provides a systematic method for deciding which strategies will be best for developing a successful health promotion effort. To be successful, a health promotion manager must know the current status of the program, the direction the program needs to pursue, and how to achieve the goals/destination of the program. Good planning does not need to be difficult, but it does require effort to ensure that the information necessary to effectively plan has been secured. Developing a workable, realistic plan for health promotion helps build confidence in the leadership, saves time, lowers stress, provides clear direction for the program, and furnishes reference points to evaluate effectiveness. Bensky and Hietbrink (1994) recommend utilizing a process called *The Five I's of Planning*. This framework establishes a format for decision making and seeks to answer a series of questions pertinent to developing successful health promotion programs (see figure 5.1).

In this process, the five I's of the model form a loop that summarizes information, clarifies assumptions, revises assumptions, provides direction, and determines what action(s) should be taken. The **Issues** component requires planners to identify questions/issues that affect the program mission, stated values, program mix, actual users, cost, and management of the program. This information has been gathered during the needs assessment. Obviously, the information about the users of the program must be accurate. Careful blending of company leadership goals for health promotion with the identified goals of the employees must be accomplished. Some of the important issues to be discussed include: (1) who the clients are; (2) what senior management and employees expect; (3) when potential clients expect to utilize program offerings; (4) where clients expect to use the services; and (5) what/why is motivating to them.

FIGURE 5.1. The Five I's of Planning

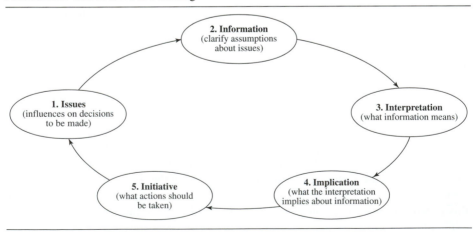

The second step, the **Information** component, seeks to clarify issues through collection of objective evidence to support or reject assumptions that will influence strategies and tactics used during the planning process. The information component is carried out via collection of the statements obtained in surveys/interviews with clients and management, facts from the health risk appraisals, knowledge derived from company data bases, and/or guidelines obtained from company policies. Once this information has been assimilated, **Interpretation** of what it means in relationship to health promotion programing can begin. The strengths and weaknesses of the program should be addressed at this time. Strengths might entail such things as the talents and skills of the staff and the support of the company employees. Weaknesses might include poor participation rates, poor evaluation of existing programs, or, perhaps, inadequate funding. Other questions investigated during this phase of the process include: (1) What opportunities are there for new programs that serve to enhance the adoption of wellness by the clients?; (2) What are the major gaps in existing services/programs?; and (3) What are the identified needs of the clients? Budget *alone* (or the lack thereof) should not be used as an excuse for not doing a program nor be viewed as the reason a program failed. Although all budgetary concerns cannot be overlooked, creativity can overcome many problems. For instance, if an advanced exercise program is a company and employee goal, yet the organization lacks funds for expensive equipment, alternatives can be developed. These alternatives may range from programs that incorporate a small collection of free weights to using elastic bands to seeking individuals willing to contribute used equipment that can be repaired. If potential or real weaknesses are identified, overcoming those barriers can actually enhance the possibility of success. Obtaining used exercise equipment and getting employees to participate in the "cleaning up" process can encourage a sense of ownership in the program.

After analysis of the data, the **Implications** concerning the information need to be considered. During this stage, goals are determined that should result in the strategies and tactics used to meet the health promotion needs of the clients and management. The implications process determines (1) what needs to be done first before other activities/planning can occur; (2) what equipment and supplies will be needed; (3) what personnel requirements will be; (4) whether experts outside the health promotion program should be included; (5) whether legal considerations will influence activity; (6) budgetary constraints; (7) what marketing procedures are to be used; (8) development of the coordinating, supervision, and reporting systems; and (9) what evaluation procedures will be most effective.

The final step in the procedure is the **Initiative** phase. The initiative phase is when final decisions are made and a report is written to determine how the plan(s) will be carried out, time lines for the activities are established, the budget is finalized, equipment is selected, employees or vendors are hired, marketing strategies are developed, goals/objectives are finalized, and evaluation procedures are established. The report is the blueprint for achieving the desired goals. Figure 5.2 provides an overview of the entire health promotion process from needs assessment through evaluation.

FIGURE 5.2. An Outline for Planning Comprehensive Health Promotion Programs

  I. Title of program
     A. Creates visibility for the program
     B. Provides creative marketing opportunities
 II. Needs assessment
     A. Surveys, interviews, HRAs, health data, focus groups, policies, etc.
     B. Description of target clients
     C. Internal assessment
     D. Resources available/needed
     E. Policies/regulations
     F. Evaluate the importance of information obtained
III. Mission statement for the comprehensive program*
     A. Reflection of program's philosophy
     B. Based upon needs assessment
     C. Leads to the development of the goals/objectives
 IV. Goals for the comprehensive program*
     A. Long-term
     B. Short-term
  V. Objectives for the comprehensive program*
     A. Long-term
     B. Short-term
 VI. Program offerings
     A. Improving of existing programs
     B. Development of new program offerings
VII. Strategies for behavioral change
     A. Strategies of personal change
     B. Strategies for cultural change
     C. Strategies for developing support—individual/groups
VIII. Strategies for marketing the program
     A. Center around goals/objectives of programs
     B. Selecting marketing activities
 IX. Timetable for implementing the program
     A. Develop time lines for marketing activities
     B. Developing time lines for program(s) implementation
  X. Evaluation plan
     A. Finalize for comprehensive program
     B. Finalize for individual programs

*When planning individual programs, these should be a reflection of the comprehensive program's mission statement, goals, and objectives.
Adapted from Dignan and Carr, 1992. *Program Planning for Health Education and Health Promotion,* Philadelphia: Lea & Febiger, p. 103.

A FORMAT FOR DEVELOPING INDIVIDUAL HEALTH PROMOTION PROGRAMS

Once the comprehensive plan has been outlined, the various identified programs must be developed. To develop effective health promotion programs, it is important to have a workable format for the planning committee to follow. Figure 5.3 demonstrates a format overview that can be utilized to develop individual health

FIGURE 5.3. A Planning Format for Individual Health Promotion Programs

I.   Program Name
II.   Company Mission Statement
III. Goals for the Individual Health Promotion Program

1.

2.

3. etc.

IV.   Objectives for Individual Health Promotion Program

1.

2.

3. etc.

V.   Evaluation Strategies for Individual Program Objectives

1.

2.

3. etc.

VI.   Session Outline (one for each session to be conducted)

    A. Objective(s) for session

    B. Session Warm-up Suggestions

    C. Transition to Main Focus of Session

    D. Session Content   E. Strategies for Personalizing   F. Evaluation

    G. Closure for Session

VII. Activities for Project Development—Time line

A. Activity	B. Start Time	C. Completion Time	D. Responsible Person	E. Resources
Develop module				
Plan marketing				
Print/purchase materials				
Assign instructors				
Begin marketing				
Registration for class				
Begin class				
Evaluation complete				

promotion programs. Some of the categories are self-evident while others need explanation, as provided in the following:

Program Name (title). The name selected for a comprehensive company health program should create identity. Program titles for various individual health promotion programs should key in to the overall program name. This helps potential clients identify with the comprehensive program, helps establish ownership of the program, and aids in marketing the individual program. In addition, the title should seek to motivate clients to find out more concerning the program.

Mission Statement. The mission statement is part of the planning document. The purpose is to help provide focus and aid planners in tying new programs to the mission of the comprehensive program.

Goals of Program. Goals are general statements of desired outcomes. Goal statements should reflect the desired outcomes for clients participating in health promotion activities. Stated goals should be tied to fulfillment of the mission statement of the comprehensive health promotion program. (See figure 5.4 and table 5.1.)

FIGURE 5.4. Conducting an Effective Health Promotion Meeting

If committees are to be effective, an agenda must be prepared and provided to all members prior to the meeting. Some suggestions for keeping a meeting productive and committee members happy and on-task are:

1. **Allow everyone to express their opinion.** Even if the suggestions may seem to be unpopular. Don't allow a small group or an individual to monopolize the meeting.

2. **Keep the meeting on target.** Don't stray too far from the agenda; stay focused.

3. **Move to agreement.** Once the topic/item has been discussed, move toward consensus and determine what activities should be next.

4. **Delegate responsibility.** Committee members will be more productive if they are assigned meaningful tasks/activities.

5. **Follow-up.** It is the responsibility of the health promotion chairperson to ensure the tasks/activities are moving toward completion.

6. **Give credit.** When someone does a good job, he or she should be acknowledged. Committee members will become tired very quickly of someone else taking credit for their good work or of working very hard and not being appreciated.

7. **Create enthusiasm.** Keep members excited about wellness by passing out articles or information concerning wellness topics. Invite vendors and agencies to demonstrate products or activities.

8. **Have fun.** Enjoy one another. Make it fun to attend meetings by serving good-tasting healthful snacks.

Adapted from Healthy, Wealthy and Wise—Fundamentals of Workplace Health Promotion, pp. 121–22. Used with permission.

TABLE 5.1. Sample Agenda of a Planning Committee Meeting

University Products Wellness Committee

April 12, 1999

Agenda Item	Time Allotment	Person Responsible
1. Introductory remarks	5 min.	Connor McHann, Chair
2. Approval of minutes	5 min.	Connor McHann, Chair
Old Business		
3. Women's health issues	15 min.	Aimee Andrews
4. Smoking cessation planning	20 min.	Jack Avery
5. Exercise club	10 min.	Catherine Coble
New Business		
6. Fall health fair	15 min.	Jay Beyers
7. Other business	10 min.	Connor McHann
8. Adjournment		

Objectives of Program. Objectives are precise, measurable statements of intended outcomes for clients participating in individual programs. Objectives may be developed concerning knowledge, values, behaviors, participation rates, or workplace changes as a result of programing. Objectives for programs should contribute to achievement of the goals of the comprehensive program.

Evaluation Procedures. The purpose of evaluation is to determine if program goals and objectives have been achieved. The evaluation section should indicate *how* the objectives are to be evaluated. For instance, an objective may have been achieved when 60 percent of employees attend a health fair or 95 percent complete a HRA or 33 percent of participants in a program complete an activity that occurs over a period of three months. Evaluation procedures will include a summary of techniques/strategies employed to measure success in accomplishing the proposed objectives.

Session Outline. To ensure positive outcomes with health promotion activities, each session must be carefully planned. Sessions are designed to meet the needs of intended clients. A detailed outline for each of the sessions should be developed. The following headings listed reflect information to be used in laying the groundwork for a favorable client experience. More than six sessions is probably stretching the ability of the client to find time to participate and maintain interest. A more realistic plan would be two to four sessions.

Program Objective(s): These objectives should reflect what the client should know, value, or feel at the conclusion of the session. More than two objectives per session where time is limited to forty-five to sixty minutes is probably unrealistic. An example of an objective for a session on Healthy Eating might be: At the conclusion of the program, the clients will be able to define the term "carbohydrate" and recognize foods that are carbohydrates.

Warm-up: A *warm-up* is any type of activity a facilitator chooses to establish the psychological "set" or tone of the session. A warm-up may be a series of questions to help the clients focus on what is to occur later, or it may be a brief demonstration or some exhibit that attracts attention. The warm-up should only last about two to five minutes.

Transition: The transition moves the focus from the warm-up to the actual material to be covered during the session. A transition is usually a statement concerning the material intended for the actual session.

Content: The main ideas or important points that will be emphasized during the session make up the content. An outline format can be used as a guide for the facilitator to follow. Information should be brief, yet sufficiently detailed to provide insight into the nature of the session from a content perspective.

Strategies: Strategies are techniques used to help clients personalize information. Strategies stimulate interaction among participants and help them assess their personal feelings about the information. Opportunities are provided for clients to weigh the possible advantages/disadvantages of decisions they might make concerning the material.

Evaluation: This section lists strategies for evaluating the effectiveness of each session. The amount or level of knowledge acquired, the attitude affected, or possible behavioral change attempted as a result of exposure to the session are evaluated.

Closure: Closure consists of summative/motivative statement(s) designed to encourage attendance at future sessions or for instituting lifestyle change.

Activities for Program Development. This is a time line that outlines the events and the tasks that must be accomplished if the program is to come to fruition. It provides for a due date and names the person responsible for each task.

SELECTING APPROPRIATE PROGRAMMING

If the needs assessment has been well done, a clear mission statement developed, accompanied by concise measurable goals/objectives, the actual programs will become clear and the planning thereof much easier than if the initial steps are lacking or poorly done.

Planning itself must consider such concerns as marketing strategy, staffing, facilities, equipment needs, company policies, as well as the budgetary implications of staffing, equipment, supplies, and facilities (Association for Fitness in Business, 1992). The budget process will be discussed in the next chapter. Components will vary from worksite to worksite, but all must be considered as programs are selected.

FINANCIAL IMPACT

Consideration of the financial/budgetary impact of potential programs on the health care costs of the company are always a concern. Considerations include: (1) What conditions and factors cost the company employees and their families the most money?; (2) What programs will have the highest employee participation rates, thus influencing cost per employee?; (3) Can the proposed program reduce short- and long-term health care costs?; (4) Will the program require additional staff, new staff training, or the employment of an outside vender (outsourcing) for program delivery?; (5) Will the program require additional equipment or space?; and (6) Does the program provide maximum visibility within the company through the most efficient use of resources? When selecting how funds will be allocated, the program that holds the greatest potential for greatest benefit to the company should be chosen.

COMPANY POLICIES

Policies are formal guidelines of procedures and expected behaviors. Policies can take many forms, ranging from purchasing supplies to charges for classes or facility use to how clients are to be enrolled in activities. In health promotion programing, policies may be the outgrowth of the assessment phase. For example, information gathered from the needs assessment may indicate that a smoke-free environment is desired. As a result of this information, the health advisory committee may be charged with formulating a policy to serve as the guideline(s) for establishing a smoke-free environment. Due to this policy, there may be a need for smoking cessation classes. Thus, the formulation of new policy (or enactment of an old one) impacts program planning. When considering possible programs, there should be an extensive review of any company/governmental policies that might have implications for health promotion.

THE SCOPE AND SEQUENCE OF HEALTH PROMOTION PROGRAMS

Program mix refers to the total program opportunities offered in a health promotion program (Association for Fitness in Business, 1992). Several concepts are vital to understanding the best program mix to be offered. One of the first program decisions is the scope. **Scope** refers to the depth or difficulty of the material to be presented (Foder and Dalis, 1989). Knowing the educational level and the current knowledge base of potential clients provides insight into the program content to be covered. A group of highly trained managers may have very little information in the nutritional area. As a result, beginning programs in the area of nutrition may need to be rather basic. If the clientele has considerable background in nutrition, more in-depth material needs to be offered. **Sequence** refers to the order in which information is to be presented. Understanding the abilities of potential clients influences when programs will be offered. For example, a group experiencing a high-stress work environment may need an introductory program explaining the short- and long-term effects of stress before they are ready to progress to a program of stress reduction techniques designed to evoke the relaxation response.

Some health promotion programs will offer a wide range of health and wellness programs while others will have limited options. Newer health promotion programs may use a more narrow approach to activities while programs that have been in operation for a while may require a broader variety of programs. Programs can be successful either way. Trade-offs may occasionally be necessary when selecting activities, but these decisions can be resolved if the mission statement expressing the desires of the management and employees is kept in mind. The key to selection is to address the most pressing priorities through appropriate activities, to allocate resources wisely, to properly utilize personnel, and to select programs within the mission created for serving the needs of the clients.

LEVELS OF INTERVENTION

In determining the types of program interventions, O'Donnell (1995) has identified the following three levels of intervention:

Level I: Awareness. Programs that increase clients' knowledge or interest in a health-related area are considered to be awareness-level programs. Most often, these types of efforts must be accompanied by additional strategies in order to impact individuals' lifestyles. Examples of awareness programs/strategies include newsletters, health fairs, health screenings (cancer, body fat, cholesterol, nutritional, HRAs), E-mail, posters, fliers, games, and classes or seminars held without providing follow-up or feedback to the clients.

Level II: Lifestyle Change. Programs that seek to change lifestyle patterns and personal behaviors are considered to be level II intervention programs. These types of programs seek to promote change through a combination of health education, behavior modification, personalizing of experiences, and feedback opportunities. Clients require sufficient time to institute change. They must be allowed the opportunity to weigh the merits of the change as well as the problems. Examples of lifestyle change programs include smoking cessation, time management, exercise and nutrition education, weight loss, and communication enhancement skills.

Level III: Supportive Environment. Supportive environment programs seek to create a worksite culture that encourages individuals to adopt or continue a healthy lifestyle. A critical aspect to long-term behavioral change is a good support system. Support can take the form of corporate policy, self-help groups, one-to-one counseling, or fostering a sense of employee ownership. One example of supportive environment programs includes the company developing a smoke-free environment after offering lifestyle change programs for smoking cessation as well as accessibility to various stop-smoking aids, such as over-the-counter drugs that reduce nicotine cravings. Another example of a supportive environment is allowing an extra ten minutes before returning to work after participation in an exercise program. The formation of in-house support groups for weight control, alcohol/drugs, parent support, or divorce recovery indicates a supportive environment. A growing trend in health promotion is development of individualized programs designed to personalize behavioral change. These programs usually involve contact with a trainer/support person/counselor to help maintain and provide motivation for change. Finally, a supportive environment is when employees perceive that programs are offered because the health promotion program desires to meet employee/client needs.

LEVELS OF PREVENTION

In addition to the levels of intervention, three levels of prevention influence health promotion program development. The levels of prevention determine if interventions will focus on preventing, treating, or managing an existing condition. **Primary prevention** is programs or activities designed to avert/prevent diseases, conditions, illness, or deterioration of health before they occur. Examples of primary prevention programs are an exercise class to help people decrease the risk of developing cardiovascular disease or cooking classes aimed at reducing the use of sodium. **Secondary prevention** is programs designed to limit the consequences, severity, or prevalence of a disease, condition, or illness. An example of secondary prevention would be conducting a screening program for early detection of breast cancer. The third type of prevention is tertiary. **Tertiary prevention** prescribes specific interventions to assist the disabled or diseased in limiting the effects of their condition. Tertiary prevention is illustrated by a company that provides a cardiac rehabilitation program for employees who have suffered a cardiovascular event of some type and want to limit further health problems. Obviously primary prevention is the most desirable, but in the health promotion business, all three types of prevention must be addressed. Table 5.2 provides some prevention targets and possible choices of intervention.

PERSONALIZING INFORMATION FOR CHANGE

Whatever health promotion seeks to do, it must incorporate strategies developed for the express purpose of allowing participants to assess their personal belief systems. People engage in behaviors they consider important or *valuable*. *Values* are the attitudes people have concerning everything from ethical beliefs to whether exercise is worthwhile. What is important varies from person to person, but what people truly value is what they tend to do. *Attitudes* are defined as predispositions toward action. For this reason, every effort must be made to help participants personalize information so positive health attitudes will be formulated and negative health attitudes modified. Only through personalizing information, making it real and applicable to each individual, will positive health behaviors result (chapter 3 provides information on the adult learner and behavioral change theories).

TABLE 5.2. Prevention Targets and Possible Intervention Strategies

Prevention Targets	Possible Intervention Strategies				
	Workshop	HRA and Personal Feedback	Printed Materials	Self-directed Change Materials	Personal Coaching
Smoking cessation (1)	X			X	X
CVD prevention (1)		X	X		X
Stress management (1)	X		X	X	
Physical activity (1)				X	X
Walking program (1)				X	X
Blood sugar testing (2)		X			X
Cholesterol testing (2)		X		X	
Blood pressure screening (2)	X		X		
Mammography (2)			X		
High-risk intervention (3)			X	X	X
Medical self-care (3)	X		X		X
Diabetes management (3)	X		X	X	X
Asthma management (3)	X		X	X	X
High-risk pregnancy (3)	X	X	X		X

1 = Primary prevention; 2 = Secondary prevention; 3 = Tertiary prevention.
Source: The Art of Health Promotion, p. 4. Used with permission.

Attempts to facilitate behavioral change must be accompanied by a variety of strategies that appeal to various learning styles. Strategies must be planned to provide opportunities for clients to personalize information. "Personalizing" means information has been assessed to determine if a specific behavior is worth the reward(s) or sacrifice(s) resulting from making a lifestyle change. If clients come to value certain behavior (view it as beneficial to their well-being and worth the difficulty), they will be more likely to initiate and maintain change. This doesn't mean they will exercise or eat nutritionally every day, but, for most days, these positive behaviors will be followed.

STRATEGIES FOR FACILITATING CHANGE

Multiple strategies should be employed to successfully facilitate behavioral change. Clients require a variety of opportunities to assimilate and assess their personal values. Some of the strategies that might be selected are found in table 5.3.

TABLE 5.3. Strategies for Creating Lifestyle Change

Strategies	Examples	Nature of Strategies
Audiovisual aids	Cassette tapes, charts, posters, textbooks, filmstrips, slides, videocassettes, overheads.	Used as a supplement to other strategies. Must be appropriate for age group. May need expensive equipment.
Behavior modification	Smoking cessation, stress reduction, weight management, exercise, time management.	Highly interactive, helps client assess personal behavioral and develop insight into how to facilitate personal change.
Television/CD-ROM/videotape	Self-contained instructional programs usually focusing on a specific topic or area.	Can stimulate discussion, good for cognitive information. Combined with other strategies, provide excellent learning tools. Costly.
Individual counseling/peer helpers	Individual counseling for exercise or nutritional needs, cardiac rehabilitation, alcohol rehabilitation.	Provide for individual needs. Help accommodate poorly motivated. No group interaction. Highly interactive between counselor and client.
Inquiry learning/skill development	Techniques include values clarifications, case studies, brainstorming, games, self-appraisals, peer group discussion, dramatizations, demonstration, role playing.	Can deal with complex issues. Help clients personalize information. May require a great deal of time. Difficult to evaluate. Can be used to demonstrate skill or simulate an action.
Lecture/discussion	Imparting information in a lecture or discussion environment.	Provide a great deal of information. Promote critical thinking. Passive learners. Not everyone a good lecturer. Can provide modeling.
Computers	CD-ROMs, telephone tag-lines, self-appraisals, exercise/nutritional analysis, health risk appraisals (HRAs).	Provide information in a self-paced environment. Programs can be very expensive. May be difficult to develop and expensive to purchase.

NEW FORMS OF HEALTH MANAGEMENT TECHNOLOGY USED IN HEALTH PROMOTION PROGRAMMING

Health promotion professionals are constantly searching for better, more creative ways to help clients live healthier lives. Some of the following creative strategies are now being implemented to facilitate change (*The Art of Health Promotion,* 1997):

Transtheoretical Applications. Using the transtheoretical model of behavior change (Prochaska, 1997; see chapter 3) as the framework, a questionnaire assessment is administered to determine which "stage of change" employees are currently experiencing. Information concerning the stages gained from the questionnaire is then used to develop communications and strategies customized to the clients' current "levels of readiness" to change. This model is designed to move people toward positive behavior change and to find methods to prevent relapse (return to a previous behavior that is unhealthy).

Dietary Supplementation. The use of "natural" supplements to achieve improved health status is a growing U.S. phenomenon. Increased interest in dietary supplementation and use of nutraceuticals for health enhancement is resulting in clients seeking advice and counseling about the merits and disadvantages of this behavior. As information continues to become available concerning recommendations for age, gender, eating patterns, and individual risk variables, providing information and developing methods for clientele to consistently engage in specific health-enhancing dietary supplement regimens needs to be integrated into current health promotion programming.

High-Risk/At-Risk Intervention. Using a proactive format, trained interventionists contact identified "high-risk/at-risk" individuals to discuss these risk factors. Conversations between the interventionist and client would include identifying the "stage" of readiness for the individual and the type of intervention(s) most appropriate for him/her. Clients have the opportunity to receive ongoing information through a "no-risk" format of phone, mail, or E-mail contact, providing individuals greater opportunity to manage their own health.

On-Line Telephonic Support. This format involves the provision of a toll-free number where a client has the opportunity to speak with a health professional about specific health issues. The service can consist of "symptom" education, advice about treatment or the need to seek medical attention, discussion of treatment alternatives, identification of resources for interventions, referral to network providers, and definitions of medical terminology/disease conditions. Services may be limited, depending on the company handling the health line. Informational, printed materials may be requested by users.

Self-Directed Change Modules. Self-directed modules provide written/computerized materials that allow individuals to manage their own behavior change. Materials are requested through a health advice line, survey, or incentive program. Booklets are arranged with step-by-step behavior change processes, offering options for personal choice while providing practical information. The time frame for change is usually an eight- to sixteen-week period.

Virtual Wellness. Rather than requiring individuals to physically visit wellness centers, information is collected via surveys that are optically scanned. Highly individualized reports are generated that can track behavior over time. Proactive interventions with phone access for questions, video materials, Internet and electronic communications, and suggestions on how to incorporate exercise, nutrition, and stress management into daily life along with periodic screenings, tailored health information, and personalized prevention priorities are provided.

Wellness Financial Incentives. Using financial incentive rewards (optimally in the $500–$1,000 range) such as merchandise, cash, nontaxable employee benefits, special privileges, flight coupons, time off, or special discounts, personnel are rewarded when they make new or maintain old health-enhancing behaviors (e.g., exercise moderately thirty minutes, five days a week; reduce cholesterol 10% from previous scores; participate in a fitness assessment; less than $250 of health claims in previous year).

Internet-Provided Health Support. For the growing majority of the U.S. population with access to the Internet, on-line health support primarily takes the forms of (1) health information, (2) support groups for specific problems, and (3) long-term involvement with information and experience sharing communities.

DETERMINING EDUCATIONAL EQUIPMENT NEEDS

Programs frequently need logistical support in a variety of areas, such as appropriate equipment to effectively conduct education activities. During the planning of any health promotion effort, it is essential that equipment needs be addressed. This is particularly true in new programs, where large amounts of monies may not be available for purchasing high-priced equipment or technology. Some basic types of equipment are needed to begin any program, although actual needs will vary somewhat with the types of programs offered. Budgets can be planned for additional purchases of equipment and technology as the scope of the programs increases.

Assessing equipment needs begins by asking, *What are the basic needs for making the various health promotion programs successful?* Some programs will require expensive initial investment while others will be rather low in capital outlay. Purchase of computer programs, nutritional assessments, booklets, and audiovisuals can increase costs quickly. Some possible educational aids, equipment, and technology are listed in table 5.4. It is assumed that basic office equipment—such as desks, chairs, tables, copiers, fax machines, telephones, and answering machines—is available. Beginning programs must budget for any items if they are unavailable.

TABLE 5.4. Educational Aids, Equipment, and Technology Needed for Conducting Health Promotion Programs

Equipment/Aid/Technology	Types of Items
Audiovisual equipment	Overhead projector Slide projector Audiocassette player VCR Camcorder Bulletin boards Chalk or marker boards

Computer equipment	Computers*
	Laser color printer
	Software
	    Word processing, spreadsheet
	    Graphics software
	    Basic statistics program (i.e., SPSS or SAS)
	    Health risk appraisals
	    Nutritional assessments
	    Desktop publishing
	    Fitness assessment
	    Electronic mail

Health assessment equipment	Blood pressure cuffs Sphygmonanometer Body fat assessment equipment Fitness testing bikes or treadmill Finger-prick blood drawing Scales Height/weight charts Flexibility equipment Strength testing equipment Biofeedback equipment
Cooking equipment**	Microwave Plastic food models Electric work Cooking/eating utensils Refrigerator Stove

*IBM-compatible hardware seems best suited for health promotion because of the potential variety of equipment and software programs from which to choose.
**Some programs may not have cooking equipment/facilities.
Source: Modified from *Guidelines for Employee Health Promotion Programs,* 1992. Used with permission.

FITNESS EQUIPMENT NEEDS

If an on-site fitness facility is available or will be developed, equipment selection for the facility will be a high priority. Equipment needs in the fitness area will depend on the size of the company employee program and the size of the facility available. In today's market, innumerable exercise equipment lines are available from which to select. In making a decision about what to purchase for a fitness facility, the most important considerations are the safety and durability of the equipment. Equipment that is easy to use by employees, the logistical support of the equipment company, the ascetic appeal of the equipment, the reputation of the company from whom the equipment is to be purchased, and the cost of the equipment are all significant considerations. When selecting the types of equipment to be purchased, care should be taken to include machines that develop and improve cardiovascular capacity as well as muscular strength and endurance. Cardiovascular equipment includes treadmills, stepmills, stairclimbers, stationary bikes, recumbent bikes, cross-country skiers, and rowing ergometers. Strength equipment may be a variety of machine formats or as free weights. For most worksite settings, when costs allow, strength training is best accomplished through the use of machines. The probability of injury is much less than with free weights. Most novices can safely operate various types of machines while more careful supervision and training is required to use free weights.

When purchasing equipment, the obvious question is "price." Research has shown that, if products are of high quality, useful, and fulfill the needs of the facility clients, purchasers are willing to pay more. Several questions concerning price and possible purchase include:

1. How does the product fit into the overall plan for the program?
2. Is purchasing this product based on the business plan?
3. Does purchasing this product meet the budget requirements for this year?
4. Will the product make a significant difference in the direction the program is going?

It is important to remember that a low-priced product is not necessarily "bad" nor a high-priced one "good," but "bells and whistles" cost money. More elaborate types of equipment will usually cost more. Is it more important to purchase more equipment or fewer pieces that offer more options? Again, the clientele, goals of the program, and budget should be used to determine the answer. Before any equipment is purchased it is vital to know how the equipment was developed, how long the company has been in business, what kind of service/technical support is available, and what the machine warranties are (Colacinao; 1995).

FACILITY NEEDS

The facility(s) available will strongly influence options concerning programming. Facilities are generally of two kinds: those used for exercise purposes and those used for educational/office purposes. Exercise facilities are a major proposition. While an architect will provide guidelines and suggestions if building a new facility or remodeling an existing one, health promotion specialists need to be aware of some basic requirements.

In an ideal world, the fitness area and the educational area will be part of the same facility. Unfortunately, not all health promotion programs have the advantage of a comprehensive facility on-site. In an educational facility, actual needs will depend on the nature of the educational components offered. The need for administrative/office space, health/physical assessment areas, resource rooms, storage areas, and classroom requirements should be seriously evaluated. Considerations for the various areas include:

Administrative/office area. The administrative and office areas should be functional and ascetically pleasing. Administrative offices should be large enough to allow staff to move comfortably through the area. A central check-in or "greeting area" for clientele and employees should accommodate peak traffic flow. Although actual size will vary, administrative areas should be a minimum of 800 square feet. This area is the best location for staff offices. Offices should be 100 to 150 square feet. All full-time personnel should have their own office, enabling them to counsel, plan, write, and perform other routine matters of their jobs more effectively. Additional office space should be planned for part-time or outside vendors (Athletic Institute and American Alliance for Health, Physical Education, Recreation, and Dance, 1985). Two people per office usually works well in the case of part-time personnel. The central administrative area should be allotted at least two storage places, 200 to 400 square feet, and planned for storing portable equipment, printed materials, and supplies. If an exercise facility is associated with the unit, the central area should be arranged so the majority of the exercise area can be supervised from it.

The central administration area should have a conference room large enough to hold staff meetings, wellness committee meetings, self-help groups, and small discussion groups. Two hundred to 600 square feet is usually sufficient.

Health/physical assessment area. The assessment area should allow for maximum privacy for clients. At the worksite, the assessment area should be

Well-maintained and properly used equipment are essential to minimize risks of litigation.

between 200 and 600 square feet. Room for taking blood pressure and to do height/weight, body composition, and fitness testing are the basic functions of such an area. Adequate storage space must be allocated for equipment, forms, and supplies. It is recommended the assessment area be near the central administrative area in case an emergency occurs that requires the attention of several staff.

Storage areas. One thing that always seems to be lacking is adequate storage space. For every classroom, assessment area, conference room, office, and the central administration area, additional storage space is desirable.

Resource room. A resource room can be utilized to hold books, pamphlets, videos, self-help, and other educational materials. The minimum square footage should be 200 to 600 square feet. The area should allow two to three people to browse, read, or view various educational materials comfortably.

Classroom space. The classroom should be environmentally pleasing, with bulletin boards and other visual display areas. Square footage should be sufficient to comfortably seat twenty-five to fifty people. The actual room should be no less than 1,200 square feet. Easily movable tables and chairs should be available to provide a variety of learning environments. If cooking classes are to be taught, a microwave and hot/cold water outlets are necessary. One or two storage closets and at least one electric outlet on each wall should be provided.

MARKETING STRATEGY

Throughout the planning of comprehensive health promotion programs, strategies for marketing to clients should be considered. Marketing strategies need to be considered early in the planning process, not as an afterthought on "how do we get people to

Health promotion programs must have successful marketing components.

become part of the health promotion effort." Chapter 7 contains information that will be helpful in planning a viable marketing plan for both comprehensive health promotion programs and individual health promotion efforts within the total program.

ENROLLMENT PROCEDURES

An often forgotten consideration is how to enroll clients in actual programs. Planned procedures need to be established on how clients can become part of program offerings, whether exercise classes or other activities.

Enrolling clients in an educational program can be a simple process, if adequately planned. If no screenings or assessments are necessary prior to the program, participants can simply fill out a registration form that provides staff with their name, phone number or E-mail address, and other information deemed necessary. Figure 5.5 illustrates a sample educational registration form. The registration process can be accomplished in a variety of ways, including E-mail, a mail-in form, or visiting the health promotion facility. Enrollment cards/forms should be placed at convenient locations throughout the facilities and included as part of regularly distributed marketing materials. The process can be more complicated if screening or assessments must be done prior to the beginning of an educational program. Assessments and procedures need to be scheduled and, in some cases,

FIGURE 5.5. Sample Educational Registration Form

Jayco Corporation
Registration Form
WELL NOW! FITNESS AND WELLNESS CENTER

Health Promotion Program_____Date_____

Name_____   Social Security Number_____

Work Address_____

Work Phone_____   E-Mail Address_____

Work FAX_____

Home Address_____   Home Phone_____

For Office Use Only (used only if necessary for the health promotion program)
- -

Health Risk Appraisal Yes___ No___   Date Taken_____

Appointment Date for HRA_____

Blood Pressure_____ Height_____ Weight_____

Nutritional Analysis Yes_____ No_____   Date Taken_____

Appointment for Nutritional Counseling_____

FIGURE 5.6. The Educational Enrollment Process

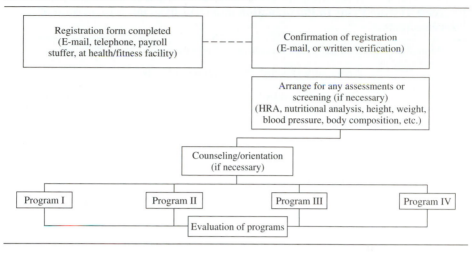

followed by individual counseling. An example of the enrollment process is shown in figure 5.6.

Enrolling clients into exercise programs requires serious forethought both for legal reasons and the well-being of the individual. The actual registration process can be the same as for educational programs, screening, and assessments. However, prior to participating in the exercise program, a series of steps must be taken to ensure safety. Before engaging in an exercise program, some type of risk assessment and a health history should be completed by the potential client. Typically, this will range from some sort of self-administered questionnaire, such as a health risk appraisal, to a more-sophisticated diagnostic test (American College of Sports Medicine [ACSM], 1998). The Physical Activity Readiness Questionnaire (PAR-Q) has been recommended as an entry-level exercise program assessment (Reading and Shephard, 1992). A copy of the PAR-Q can be found in appendix C.

The American College of Sports Medicine has provided several guidelines for determining the extent a client should be screened prior to beginning an exercise program. ACSM designates the following three initial risk stratifications (ACSM, 1998):

1. Apparently healthy individuals: These are apparently healthy individuals with no more than one major coronary risk factor.
2. Increased risk: These persons have signs or symptoms that are suggestive of cardiopulmonary or metabolic disease and/or two or more cardiovascular risk factors.
3. Known disease: Individuals with identified cardiac, pulmonary, or metabolic disease.

TABLE 5.5. ACSM Recommendations for (A) Medical Examination and Exercise Testing Prior to Participation and (B) Physician Supervision of Exercise Tests

A. Medical examination and clinical exercise test recommended prior to:

	Apparently Healthy		Increased Risk*		
	Younger[‡]	Older	No Symptoms	Symptoms	Known Disease[†]
Moderate exercise[§]	No[‖]	No	No	Yes	Yes
Vigorous exercise[¶]	No	Yes[#]	Yes	Yes	Yes

B. Physician supervision recommended during exercise test:

	Apparently Healthy		Increased Risk*		
	Younger[‡]	Older	No Symptoms	Symptoms	Known Disease[†]
Submaximal testing	No[‖]	No	No	Yes	Yes
Maximal testing	No	Yes[#]	Yes	Yes	Yes

*Persons with two or more risk factors or one or more signs or symptoms.

[†] Persons with known cardiac, pulmonary, or metabolic disease.

[‡] Younger implies ≤ 40 years for men, ≤ 50 years for women.

[§] Moderate exercise as defined by an intensity of 40% to 60% $\dot{V}O_{2max}$; if intensity is uncertain, moderate exercise may alternately be defined as an intensity well within the individual's current capacity, one which can be comfortably sustained for a prolonged period of time, that is, 60 minutes, which has a gradual initiation and progression, and is generally noncompetitive.

[‖] A "No" response means that an item is deemed "not necessary." The "No" response does **not** mean that the item should not be done.

[¶] Vigorous exercise is defined by an exercise intensity > 60% $\dot{V}O_{2max}$; if intensity is uncertain, moderate exercise may alternately be defined as exercise intense enough to represent a substantial cardiorespiratory challenge or if it results in fatigue within 20 minutes.

[#] A "Yes" response means that an item is recommended. For physician supervision, this suggests that a physician is in close proximity and readily available should there be an emergent need.

Source: Table used with permission of The American College of Sports Medicine.

Table 5.5 contains the recommendations of the American College of Sports Medicine. Based on these recommendations, the schematic of enrollment procedures in figure 5.7 has been developed.

UTILIZING OUTSIDE VENDORS

An outside vendor is any individual, group, organization, or company that provides a service that can be purchased or used free. The use of outside vendors for specific health promotion activities is often referred to as "outsourcing." Vendors can perform a variety of functions from supplying office supplies, computer programs, exercise equipment, and laundry services to conducting programs and classes. The use of outside vendors will be determined by the business policies of the organization and will dictate how purchases are to be made, if bids are necessary and for what items, as well as what decisions can be made directly by the health promotion director or staff.

Vendors with specified expertise who come in to teach or facilitate a health promotion program must be carefully screened and overseen by regular staff to ensure

FIGURE 5.7. Enrollment Procedures for Participation in an Exercise Program

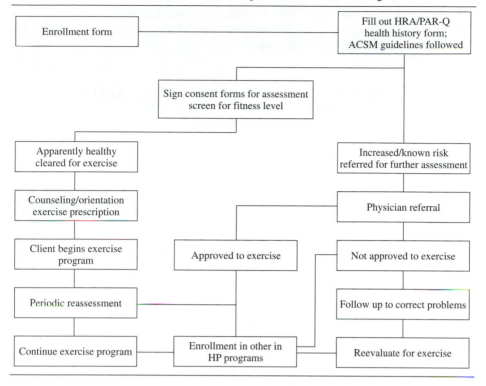

a professional presentation. If the vendor is to conduct a program, it is imperative that careful consideration be given to the "fit" of that person (or organization) to the clients within the company. Just because the vendor has developed a particular program or has taught similar classes elsewhere is no assurance that the philosophy, strategies, or personality of the instructor is appropriate for the company. Any vendors outside the full-time health promotion staff should be interviewed and their program materials carefully reviewed. The evaluation of the vendor and the program should be as carefully completed as any program conducted by regular staff. Whenever a vendor is used, it is in the best interest of the company to have a member of the legal staff check the contract to avoid misunderstanding and make sure all parties are in agreement as to intent and expectations for services. Any vendor providing services is a reflection of the total company health promotion program and the total quality of that program. One poorly planned, presented, and evaluated program can negatively impact health promotion goals for months or even years. Whenever possible, the regular health promotion staff should institute and operate programs. A reliable, competent staff guarantees quality, results in better employee ownership of programs, and allows for improved evaluation of staff and programs.

Outside vendors may also supply organizations with prepackaged graphic, audio, video, or computer programs or materials. As with outside people, groups, and organizations, purchased materials require rigorous assessment to determine the quality of the program(s). Materials should be appropriate for the intended audience and meet the requirements of the group(s) utilizing them. The background, personality, and qualifications of the teacher/facilitators using them also need to be considered so they are not using materials with which they are unfamiliar or are unsure how to incorporate into their program(s).

LEGAL CONSIDERATIONS FOR HEALTH PROMOTION PROGRAMS

The potential for litigation in health promotion is real. Although undue worry should not overpower decisions and programs offered, litigation should be of concern to everyone working within the profession and care should be taken to avoid it. Most cases in the legal arena center around some type of civil wrong called a *tort*. Most tort claims affecting exercise area are based on allegations of either negligence or malpractice (Herbert and Herbert, 1988). *Negligence* is regarded as a failure to conform one's conduct to a generally accepted standard. Negligence claims tend to center around accusations that a person (teacher, exercise leader, etc.) failed

 ## *Profiles in Health Promotion*

The FastTrack Racing Company manufactures auto racing transmissions, cam shafts, and quick-change rear differentials. The company employs six hundred people located at three sites within a five-mile radius of one another. The average age of the employees is 35 years, and the workforce is 65 percent men and 35 percent women. The company CEO decided several months ago to institute a health promotion program. He hired a health promotion consultant to do a needs assessment and a study of the management/workers concerning their receptiveness to health promotion activities. The needs survey indicated a high level of stress within the management, while the manufacturing segment experienced an inordinate number of injuries associated with the low back area. Seventy-five percent of the workforce (management and manufacturing) were found to be smokers. However, the needs survey did not indicate any appreciable interest in smoking cessation. The interest survey indicated that management personnel would be most interested in some type of stress reduction program. The manufacturing employees indicated a desire to have weight lifting equipment for exercise purposes.

After receiving the needs assessment and related research, the CEO did nothing with the information for six months and then decided to hire a health promotion director to plan and implement a program. A master's degree person was hired to manage and design the program. A six-month time framework was established before beginning the first programs. The new manager was given a secretary and told that, once everything was ready to begin, two new employees would be hired to help conduct the activities, if necessary. Assuming you are the new manager, what would be your plan for bringing the program(s) to fruition? What programs would you want to implement first? How would you go about the developmental process? What additional information you would like? What pitfalls do you foresee?

to provide due care to protect another person (client, participant) to whom the former owed some duty or responsibility (Herbert and Herbert, 1988).

Malpractice is a specific type of negligence involving claims against professionals for alleged breach of professional duties/responsibilities (Herbert and Herbert, 1988). The term malpractice is most often thought of as "medical malpractice," and includes all health-related professions. In health promotion, this would include personal trainers and those rendering rehabilitative services (Van der Smissen, 1990). "Educational malpractice" has traditionally been associated with failure to educate within the school system. However, efforts have been made to apply educational malpractice to failure to instruct or the learning of inappropriate methodology in the health promotion setting. "In a technical definition sense, educational malpractice can be applied to those persons in the educational (public and private) settings who perform negligently their instructional responsibility" (Van der Smissen, 1990, p. 210, part C). To avoid this type of legal consideration, all participants in any program should receive a written document containing: (1) a description of what is to occur in the health education/promotion class; (2) a disclaimer of responsibility for harm (a statement proclaiming the company is not responsible for any accidents, problems, etc. occurring in the class or resulting from it); and (3) the client's right to desist from further participation in the program. Further, the document should be examined by the company legal staff as to wording and legal requirements.

To protect against negligence and malpractice litigation in the exercise area, all participants must sign an informed consent/assumption of risk form (see appendix D). Some experts believe such consent should be obtained from the

---

✓ *Check It Out*

Listed below is a group of terms/activities that might be part of planning a health promotion program. Describe why each of the terms/activity is important in the planning process.

Term/Activity	Importance of Activity in Planning
Marketing Strategy	
Evaluation Plan	
Timetable	
Malpractice	
Module Format	
Enrollment Procedures	
Education Equipment	
Educational Facilities	
Sequence	
Scope	
Breadth	
Program Mix	

FIGURE 5.8. Areas of Potential Liability in Exercise Assessment, Administration, and Supervision

---

1. Failure to monitor an exercise test properly and/or to stop an exercise test in application of competent professional judgment.

2. Failure to evaluate the participant's physical capabilities or impairments competently, factors that would proscribe or limit certain types of exercise.

3. Failure to prescribe a safe exercise intensity in terms of cardiovascular, metabolic, and musculoskeletal demands.

4. Failure to instruct participants adequately as to safe performance of the recommended physical activities or as to the proper use of exercise equipment.

5. Failure to supervise properly the participant's exercise during program sessions or to advise individuals regarding any restrictions or modifications that should be imposed in performing conditioning activities during unsupervised periods.

6. Failure to assign specific participants to an exercise setting with a level of physiologic monitoring, supervision, and emergency medical support commensurate with their health status.

7. Failure to perform or to render performance in a negligent manner in a variety of other situations.

8. Rendition of advice to a participant that is later construed to represent diagnosis of a medical condition or is deemed tantamount to medical prescription to relieve disease conditions and that subsequently and/or proximately causes injury and/or deterioration of health and/or death.

9. Failure to refer a participant to a physician or other appropriately licensed professional in response to the appearance of signs or symptoms suggestive of health problems requiring medical or other professional attention.

10. Failure to maintain proper and confidential records documenting the informed consent process, the adequacy of participant instructions with regard to performance of program activities, and the adequacy of their physical responses to physical activity regimens.

From Herbert and Herbert, 1998. *Legal aspects of preventive and rehabilitative exercise programs.* Canton, OH: Professional and Executive Reports and Publications. Used with permission.

participant as well as the spouse (Herbert and Herbert, 1988). Even if consent forms are signed by the participant and spouse, it does not relieve an exercise leader/instructor from the responsibly of performing in a competent and professional manner. For some or all participants, a release from a physician indicating that the individual is healthy enough to participate may be needed. Any professional working in the exercise or health promotion area should carry liability insurance. Further, the standards developed by the American College of Sports Medicine and other organizations providing guidelines of professional conduct for people leading or supervising exercise programs should be closely followed. Several areas of potential liability have been identified. Figure 5.8 provides a summary of those areas.

Summary

- Establishing a systematic method of planning helps ensure a successful health promotion effort.
- The five I's of planning provide a framework for successful planning. The five I's are information, interpretation, implication, initiative, and issues.
- When selecting programs, one potentially valuable objective is the financial impact on the health care costs of the company.
- Policies are formal guidelines explaining how procedures are to occur or what behaviors groups are to exhibit.
- "Program mix" is the total of all program opportunities offered to employees in a health promotion campaign.
- Scope (depth or difficulty), sequence (order), and breadth (comprehensiveness) are all considerations when planning health promotion offerings.
- Three levels of program intervention—awareness, lifestyle change, and supportive environment—are utilized to facilitate behavioral change.
- For behavior change to occur, opportunities within the health promotion setting must be created that help clients personalize information about the potential impact on their lives.
- To successfully accomplish the personalizing process, a variety of learning strategies should be employed.
- Successful programs must have minimum equipment/technology that includes audiovisual equipment, computer hardware/software, health assessment equipment, and, perhaps, cooking equipment.
- How to market educational/exercise programs should be considered from the initiation of the health promotion process.
- Educational and administrative areas should be well planned, efficient, and utilized for maximum benefit of the clients if health promotion programs are to operate effectively.
- Enrollment procedures should be easy for clients and should include E-mail and mail-in registration for all educational programs.
- Enrollment in exercise programs requires special consideration due to the safety of the client and legal concerns of the health promotion staff/facility.
- Outside vendors can be used to carry out various health promotion programs, but careful consideration of expectations and evaluation of programs must be done prior to forming a contractual relationship.
- Malpractice is a special type of negligence involving claims against professionals for alleged breach of duties/responsibilities.
- Educational malpractice is associated with the failure to perform instruction responsibly or utilizing inappropriate methodology.
- All participants should sign a disclaimer of responsibility for harm before participating in any instructional process. The disclaimer form should be approved by the company legal department or adviser prior to participant use.
- To avoid exercise malpractice, all guidelines of the American College of Sports Medicine and other supervising organizations should be carefully followed.
- All exercise participants should sign a consent/assumption of risk form prior to participation in an exercise class.

Bibliography

American College of Sports Medicine (ACSM). 1998. *ACSM's guidelines for exercise testing and prescription* (3rd ed.). Baltimore: Williams and Wilkins.

American Journal of Health Promotion (AJHP). 1997. What newer forms of health management technology can be used in programming? *The Art of Health Promotion* 1(4): 1–6.

Athletic Institute and American Alliance for Health, Physical Education, Recreation, and Dance. 1985. *Planning facilities for athletics physical education and recreation,* edited by Richard B. Flynn. North Palm Beach, FL: The Athletic Institute.

Association for Fitness in Business. 1992. *Guidelines for employee health promotion programs.* Champaign, IL: Human Kinetics.

BENSKY, J., and HIETBRINK, R. 1994. Getting down to business. *Worksite Health* 1(1): 25–28.

BUTLER, J. T. 1994. *Principles of health education and health promotion.* Englewood, CO: Morton.

COLACINO, D. 1995. How to select equipment that fits your facility. *AWHP's Worksite Health* 2(4): 46–47.

DIGNAN, M. B., and CARR, P. A. 1992. *Program planning for health education and health promotion.* Philadelphia: Lea & Febiger.

FODER, J. T., and DALIS, G. T. 1989. *Health instruction: Theory and application* (4th ed.). Philadelphia: Lea & Febiger.

HERBERT, D. L., and HERBERT, W. G. 1998. *Legal aspects of preventive and rehabilitative exercise programs.* Canton, OH: Professional and Executive Reports & Publications.

HERBERT, W. G., and HERBERT, D. L. 1988. *Legal considerations. Resource manual for guidelines for exercise testing and prescription,* edited by Steven N. Blair and others. American College of Sports Medicine. Philadelphia: Lea & Febiger.

O'Donnell, M. 1995. Design of workplace health promotion programs. Rochester Hills, MI: American Journal of Health Promotion.

Prochaska, J. O., and Velicer, W. F. 1997. The Transtheoretical Model. American Journal Health Promotion, 12(1): 6–7.

Reading, T. S., and Shephard, R. J. 1992. Revision of the physical activity readiness questionnaire (PAR-Q). *Canadian Journal of Sports Science* 17: 338–345.

Van der Smissen, B. 1990. *Legal liability and risk management for public and private entities.* Cincinnati: Anderson.

Management Issues in Health Promotion Programs

OBJECTIVES

The Importance of Management

Communication and Management

The Art and Science of Management

Understanding the Budget Process

Types of Budgets

Developing a Budget

Types of Costs

Guidelines for Budget Development

Selection and Hiring of Staff

Conducting an Interview

Supervision of Employees

Developing Policy and Procedure Manuals

Ethics and Health Promotion

Profiles in Health Promotion

Check It Out

Summary

CHAPTER OBJECTIVES

After reading this chapter, you should be able to

- describe the management process.
- understand the impact of leadership on successful programs.
- identify administrative issues.
- understand the budgetary process.
- determine criteria for hiring and training staff.
- identify procedures for supervising health promotion staff.
- develop guidelines for procedure manuals.

The efficient, satisfactory management of a health promotion program is vital to its long-term success. Managing a comprehensive health promotion program can be an overwhelming task. Health promotion management requires planning, organizing, leading, motivating, and controlling the various components of an overall program. Effective health promotion management demands talent, ability, diligence, and hard work. More than that, good management mandates quality leadership.

Being a good leader (demonstrating leadership) is the key to managing a health promotion program that achieves its stated goals. Good leaders have the ability to create a vision for the future that motivates and directs others. Demonstrating leadership means the ability to interact with personnel so they can achieve their personal best and move the program forward while continuously reinventing and strengthening themselves. Leadership is the "hands-on" component of management. Even though the purpose of this chapter is to provide an overview of some of the technical aspects of management in a health promotion facility, it is hoped that the reader does not lose sight of the importance of successful relationships with people. Human relationship skills are not necessarily learned in textbooks or by in-service training, but require sensitivity, concern, and the desire to treat others as one would like to be treated.

THE IMPORTANCE OF MANAGEMENT

Management is "the process of planning, organizing, leading, and controlling an organization's human, financial, physical, and information resources to achieve organizational goals in an efficient and effective manner" (Horine, 1991, p. 3). Just as the body follows the head, so does the staff and quality of programming follow the manager's leadership. The following elements are part of the successful management process (Frost, Lockhart, and Marshall, 1988):

1. Establishing and achieving goals
2. Supervising personnel
3. Acquiring and utilizing resources
4. Facilitating group solidarity/commitment
5. Clarifying responsibility and accountability
6. Motivating personnel
7. Facilitating personal advancement of staff
8. Encouraging efficiency of operation

The actual practical functions of management are planning, organizing, implementing, and controlling (Trewatha and Newport, 1992). In reality, these functions are performed by all members of the health promotion staff and should not be considered only the function of one person with a certain title. If goals are to be achieved, all members of an organization must be involved in the management process; however, the responsibility of management falls upon the designated manager. Briefly, the functions considered part of management can be defined in the following fashion:

Planning. Involves the development of policies and programs; hiring, training, and evaluating of staff; budget development; assigning of duties; and, planning for future needs.

Organizing. Involves combining humans and material resources into a meaningful framework for achieving organizational goals. May involve dividing activities, delegating authority, and establishing protocols.

Implementing. Includes such functions as initiating and directing current and new programs as well as implementing the marketing for the various programs. Additional functions such as training, motivating, and communicating with the staff would be contained under "implementing."

Controlling. Involves the evaluation of programs as well as the personnel responsible for those programs. Controlling functions could be repair of malfunctioning equipment, changing behavior of an employee, or revising a policy or program.

Effective management is the result of both art and science. The *art,* or ability to work with staff and clients, communicate, and motivate, includes essential, less tangible skills. The *science* involves the technical components of how to effectively plan, develop budgets, establish protocol, and allocate resources. However, having

FIGURE 6.1. The Management Process

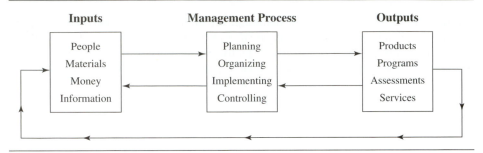

one ability without the other will almost certainly restrict the effectiveness of the health promotion effort. The management process may be viewed as depicted in figure 6.1.

COMMUNICATION AND MANAGEMENT

The key to successful leadership is good communications with all employees. Communication skills are necessary to fulfill the many roles of planner, supervisor, educator, motivator, counselor, marketer, and evaluator (Gettman, 1988). Good communicators have the ability to manage a team of individuals—each with their own personality, ideas, personal goals, and ambitions—harmoniously. Positive interactions with personnel via written and oral communication and professional interaction with staff and clients ultimately determine the successful manager. Beneficial communication ties together all facets of the management process and enables a group to function productively and with minimum confusion. Managers spend a great deal of their time and energy communicating with staff and clients. To be effective in this process, managers must be aware of the syntax, semantics, and context of the language they are using. Recognizing that people have widely varying perceptions about language and words and may interpret the same information quite differently, predicated upon their background and personal perceptions, is vital to open and rewarding communications. Choosing what words to use (vocabulary), understanding how to say them (voice tone), and knowing the situation where they will have the most beneficial impact are most important. The communication process can be facilitated by asking for constructive feedback, giving feedback in return, and developing the skill of being a good listener. To fully understand what is occurring, a manager must first listen carefully to what is being said.

Effective managers must be able to observe and comprehend body language. A good manager is sensitive to the nonverbal component (body language) of any communication. For example, even though an employee may *say* they agree with their manager, their body language may be portraying an individual who is angry, misunderstands what is being said, or is simply shy.

Effective communications are achieved with patience, sensitivity, and calmness. When a manager approaches an employee with anger, the employee tends to be defensive and to respond in an angry fashion. The employee is then placed in the position of defending him/herself or the position taken on the issue rather than participating in the process of communicating to find a solution to a problem. Good communication requires planning, understanding of human behavior, and seeking to comprehend another point of view.

THE ART AND SCIENCE OF MANAGEMENT

To facilitate the desired results in a health promotion program, three skills need to be considered. These skills are sometimes referred to as the *science* of management. These skills are (1) *technical*—the knowledge of health promotion program development, implementation, and evaluation, (2) *human*—the ability to work with people versus the technical skill of working with things and processes, and (3) *conceptual*—the ability to recognize the interrelationship between the parts of an organization and the overall goals (Trewatha and Newport, 1992). These are the skills that should be taught by educators. The attainment of these skills, theoretically, is reflected in the achievement of a degree or a certification.

How managers apply management skills and abilities may be referred to as the *art* of management. How to motivate, gain cooperation, and facilitate a sense of teamwork and ownership on the part of the health promotion staff and employees is perhaps the real challenge—the art of putting everything together and making it "work."

Fostering prestige and self-esteem of employees through inspirational talks or positive feedback on training or job performance are part of the art of management. Other factors include a working environment that is positive for employees—empowering them to make the decisions necessary to successfully accomplish their jobs. For this to happen, managers need to establish and clearly communicate the

Good leaders have the ability to create a vision and motivate others.

FIGURE 6.2. Components of the Art and Science of the Management Process

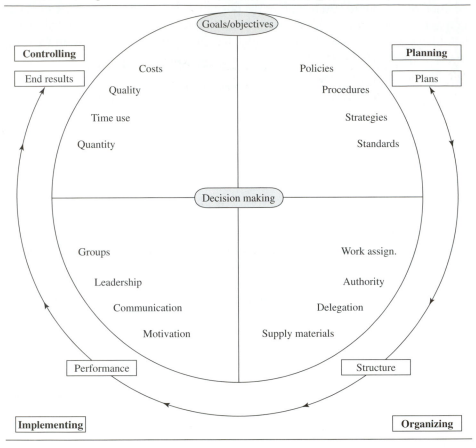

short- and long-term plans and goals of the program, to articulate the policies of the organization within which decisions should be made, and to take appropriate corrective actions when a problem is identified. Employees and staff need to perceive the manager as approachable, but not a pushover. Staff need to be able to talk to their manager about legitimate concerns. Management needs to know how to work with personnel who seem less inclined to perform satisfactorily in a way that moves them toward better fulfillment of their duties as opposed to developing an attitude of anger that spills over into their professional work. The artful practice of management is just as important as the actual knowledge of the science of the technical, human, and conceptual capabilities. The art and science of management must go hand in hand if a manager is to be successful. One factor without the other is of little use in the achievement of the health promotion objectives. Figure 6.2 provides a conceptual overview of the components that must be dealt with in both a science and art approach.

UNDERSTANDING THE BUDGET PROCESS

Budgeting is a systematic process that allows managers to plan and control resources for the purpose of achieving objectives (Trewatha and Newport, 1992). The budget describes the amount of money to be spent in a variety of accounts. The budget indicates the activities to be carried out, the number of personnel to be employed, the amount of equipment to be purchased and maintained, and other essential ingredients that serve to envision how dollars are to be appropriated. The budget process should aid the manager in controlling purchases, implementing programs, and planning functions. Budgets may be developed for subunits, departments, divisions, and/or whole organizations. The process of budget development may take up to a year and requires frequent feedback and review as to the status of the various budget projections. This review may be on a weekly, monthly, or quarterly basis. The usual time period for a budget is one year, although the budget is frequently broken down by the quarter or month. Budgets basically serve four functions: (1) They help managers coordinate resources and projects by determining the amounts of monies available; (2) they help define the standards needed by setting limits on costs and expenditures; (3) they provide clear guidelines about the organizations's resources and expectations; and (4) they facilitate performance evaluations of managers and units (Griffin, 1984) by using costs/costs containment versus attendance/results.

TYPES OF BUDGETS

Devising a budget can take many directions and utilize several formats. In the case of the health promotion professional, two formats are used most frequently. These formats are the line item budget and the functional budget. In the **line item** format, each category of spending is itemized according to its anticipated expenditure for the fiscal year (Kraus and Curtis, 1986). Typical line items are labor, materials, supplies, travel, purchases (other than supplies), shipping/freight, telephones/Internet, rent/leases, overhead, and the monetary allocations for various programs. Most of the preceding categories are broken down into further subcategories such as full-time employees and part-time employees or travel to conventions and travel to obtain certifications. Each heading will then be further subdivided into positions, numbers, or codes for each of the full-time and/or part-time employees or travel expenses and percentages toward reimbursement. (See table 6.1.)

The **functional budget** is based on the specific function each department provides. One common approach is to divide the budget into three major functional areas: administration, facilities/equipment, and special services. The strength of a functional budget for the health promotion facility is that it allows direct application to annual programs conducted in the health promotion program. Some examples of the functions that might be included in this type of budget are health screenings,

TABLE 6.1. Example of a Line Item Budget

Item	Projected Costs, 1997
Full-Time Staff Salaries and Fringe	
Director	$60,000
Nutritionist	35,000
Exercise specialist	35,000
Health educator	35,000
Secretary/clerical	23,000
Services Contractual—Part-Time Employees	
Exercise leader I	10,000
Exercise leader II	10,000
Smoking cessation specialist	5,000
Receptionist, front desk	7,500
Supplies and Printing	
Educational programs	4,000
Exercise program supplies	2,000
Testing and assessment	1,000
Office supplies	1,500
Marketing	
Materials	4,000
Printing	3,000
Postage (Based on 32 cents—first class)	1,500
Equipment	
Maintenance	2,500
Exercise—cardiovascular and resistant	10,000
Exercise assessment equipment	7,500
Computer hardware	10,000
Computer software	5,000
Miscellaneous	
Travel	5,000
Certification costs	1,500
Telephones	1,500
Licenses and permits	1,000
Training and development	1,500

marketing, programs, fitness center, educational materials, labor, and travel. (See table 6.2) Obviously, any line item mentioned earlier could be included in a functional budget also.

Most budgets will have a taxonomy or classification system that is used to break down costs into logical delivery systems or functions. Table 6.3 provides an example of the taxonomy system of object classification.

TABLE 6.2. Example of Functional Budget

Item	Projected Costs, 1997
Program Management	
Program planning	$8,500
Staff training	5,000
Consultant(s)	4,000
Program evaluation	500
Staff time	9,000
Program Promotion	
Marketing	8,000
Materials	3,500
Staff time	6,000
Services	
Exercise preassessment	2,000
Educational classes	6,000
Counseling	3,000
Evaluation	1,000
Staff time	16,000
Equipment	
Exercise assessment	2,000
Educational	4,000

TABLE 6.3. Classification System of Costs and Functions

Class	Description	Example
1000	Services, personal	Involves salaries and wages paid to persons employed by the company
2000	Services, contractual	Work, services, and materials supplied by contract; might include printing, binding, telephone, postage, freight, Internet service, travel expenses, advertising expense
3000	Commodities	Supplies and materials that are worn out, consumed, or impaired within a reasonable time; supplies that may be combined or converted to other uses such as cleaning, painting, or computer paper
4000	Current charges	Rents, insurances, computer licenses
5000	Current obligations	Fixed expenses—interests, taxes, loans, etc.
6000	Properties	Equipment, buildings, or land
7000	Debt payment	Borrowing or bonding—short and long term

(continued)

TABLE 6.3. (Continued)

Class Description	Example
Object Codes	
10–90	(2-digit codes—9 classes and 99 codes—used in small businesses)
100–900	(3-digit codes—9 classes and 999 codes—used in small to medium businesses)
1000–9000	(4-digit codes—9 classes and 9999 codes—used in medium to large businesses)
Objective Code Characteristics	
Fixed	Funds are earmarked and locked for a fiscal year; Cannot be revised. Example: service personnel
Fluid	Funds can be revised; ingress or egress
Floating	An object code is solvent as long as there is a free balance in its class. Example: commodities

DEVELOPING A BUDGET

How a budget is developed varies from organization to organization. Two commonly used corporate approaches are to build the budget from the top administrators down or from lower-level managers to the top. The former is referred to as top-down budgeting. **Top-down budgeting** is utilized when upper management determines an amount of dollars each unit/department is to receive. In health promotion, this would translate to the manager making decisions for the entire program budget. Undoubtedly, this is the most expedient method to accomplish the budgetary process, but it is the least accurate way to budget. While the initial budget proposal is usually open to further negotiation for additional funds by staff and other employees, there is less commitment (or involvement or sense of ownership) from them (Wilson and Glaros, 1994).

The **bottom-up budgeting** is much more labor intensive, since it requires each submanager/department head/unit manager to submit a preliminary budget before the end of a fiscal year (such as the person who runs the aerobics program and the one responsible for ordering and maintaining equipment and the one who runs the office). The guidelines for developing the budget, as well as the monies allocated for overhead, personnel wage increases, new hiring, and percentages of increase/decrease for the various components of the budget, are provided by the financial agency within each company. Using these guidelines, individuals within the program can then suggest how their monies can best be spent. Multiple input into financial planning lengthens the budget process but gives employees a sense of ownership and control over their individual programs and plans. In theory, the people responsible for each department would be in the best position to determine where monies can best be used to accomplish the most.

Once completed, the preliminary budget is then submitted to senior management. Senior management reviews the budget, may request additional information, and then either accepts the budget as is or orders cuts in the proposal. This process can require several reviews before finally being accepted as the budget for the next fiscal year.

On occasion, the company may ask that three budgets be developed: (1) a budget that accepts a percent change in the cost of certain components such as salaries, supplies, programs, and/or travel at a reduced level from the previous year (a reduced-level budget); (2) a budget that accepts all current programs, sets certain assumptions concerning costs increases, and determines what it would take, given these assumptions, to run the same program again next year (sometimes referred to as a current-level budget); and (3) a budget built on the same assumptions concerning cost increases, but also requesting the manager to describe what it would take to fully meet their goals/objectives (an expansion budget).

The budgetary steps can be viewed as a four-phase process running linearly over a period of time. Figure 6.3 illustrates the linear perspective of a budget, using a process that requires a year to complete. Some organizations will spend six months; others will spend less time in the developmental process. Budgets are usually developed through a series of hearings or meetings, beginning at the bottom of the program with a review of associated problems, and activities (past and future). The four phases of this linear process are as follows:

1. *Preparation.* During this phase, the focus is on the function(s) or program(s). What work is to be performed or what programs to be developed are defined. Personnel, materials, supplies, equipment, and so on are estimated, as well as the costs for all identified functions or programs.
2. *Presentation.* The presentation phase of the budget is where the budget is presented for review to relevant personnel. Presentation may be informal within the various units or with immediate supervisors. As the process continues, the discussions become more formal with the proposed budget moving up the chain of command. There may be negotiations, recommendations, or even cuts made to the proposed budget during this time.
3. *Adoption.* During adoption the budget is finally approved with all changes agreed upon by all parties involved. Allotments and amendments are accepted for the next fiscal year.

FIGURE 6.3. The Linear Perspective of Budget Development

Beginning of Fiscal Year									End of Fiscal Year		
Months 1	2	3	4	5	6	7	8	9	10	11	12

Executing the Budget (12 months)..

Preparation of Next Year's Budget (6–8 months)...........

Presentation of Budget (2–3 months).......

Adoption (4–6 weeks).....

4. *Execution.* The execution of the budget involves putting into operation the approved budget developed over the previous months. All components of the budget are put into operation, including initiating payroll changes, routine/formal purchasing, reporting, and revisions to the budget. During the actual execution of the budget during the operating year, the approved budget may need to be modified due to unexpected situations. Managers should have the flexibility to make necessary adjustments to their budget, based on review and discussion with their supervisors.

Even after the budget has been approved there may be several restraints on the spending process (Pickett and Hanlon, 1992). For example, the chief budget director may not approve the planned salary positions for a new health educator or nutritionist. Because of this, availability of funds may be delayed. Budget directors can further retard expenditures by having to review all purchase requests above a certain amount of money. Company policies may necessitate that all purchases above a certain cost be bid on by vendors, these bids reviewed, negotiated (sometimes), and finally accepted or rejected. This policy can lead to long delays, and the power of utilizing the budget in an effective manner may actually be in the hands of the budget director rather than the program manager. In addition, most companies have either monthly, quarterly, or semiannual budgetary reports with only certain amounts of monies spendable during that period, prohibiting further activity within an account after the originally agreed upon allocations have been used.

Most companies will allow managers to move monies from certain accounts into others. For example, money was budgeted for a smoking cessation class during a particular quarter, but was canceled due to lack of interest among the employees. In this case, the budgetary officer will probably allow the intended funds from that account to be transferred into travel or some other account needing additional funds.

Most companies will also have policies that do not allow transferring of monies from certain account into others. Salary is an example of an account where it is unlikely that funds would be transferable.

TYPES OF COSTS

Most budgets must account for three kinds of costs. These are fixed, variable, and semivariable. **Fixed costs** are expenses that do not change as a result of the program. For example, some salaries are fixed for a fiscal year and are not subject to increase for that time period. Another example is the rent paid for an exercise facility. Regardless of the number of days open or the hours of operation, the rent remains the same for the budget period. **Variable costs** are costs that vary according to the number of participants or the number of items purchased. An example would be that as the number of clients increases, the cost to operate the facility per client rises due to increased use of equipment and the resulting need for more maintenance/upkeep. Another example is when utilizing a health risk appraisal (HRA), the cost per HRA goes down as the number purchased goes up. **Semivariable costs** are costs that vary depending on the type of activity. An example would be the amount of expenditure for hiring a part-time employee due to increased participation in educational classes. Factors that might influence the costs are level of expertise, the availability of a suitable pool of employees, or the degrees/certifications required for the job.

GUIDELINES FOR BUDGET DEVELOPMENT

In the process of developing the budget, it should not be assumed a ceiling figure has been imposed on a budget. The budget should reflect the legitimate needs of the health promotion program rather than merely listing items that can be afforded under an arbitrary budget ceiling. However, it is a mistake to inflate a budget request deliberately in the expectation that it will be reduced by a certain percentage. It *is* important to attempt to ensure that the established goals and objectives can be obtained with the allocations allotted.

The beginning of the budget process involves estimating the resource requirements (any factors needed to implement the health promotion program) necessary for successful program operation. An accurate estimation is achievable through a comprehensive understanding of program activities, how the programs are interrelated, and effective communication with the budgetary officers. Since staff costs are usually the largest portion of program costs, determining staffing needs is a high priority. Part of the staffing process is developing benefit packages and defining who is eligible for benefits. Once staffing concerns have been clarified, the next step is estimating supplies and equipment needs. Supplies may range from materials needed for functioning of the general office to materials required to conduct the various health promotion activities. During this phase it is necessary to obtain information on the various costs, while attempting to forecast any future cost of trends which hold implications for potential functions.

As the budgetary needs of individual programs are determined, issues like the cost of materials again become important. Additionally, budget developers should seek opportunities to "link" services from other programs or share equipment to help with cost savings. Making phone calls to inquire about possible travel, training courses, and professional memberships are all ways to produce accurate cost predictions. A rule of thumb for budgeting is: Do your homework on costs and be prepared to justify all costs and expenditures.

During the course of review, any budget will be carefully scrutinized. Each item needs strong justification for existence. Items should not be included simply because they were in previous budgets. All projects, programs, and costs should be examined carefully to determine if they are still part of the goals and objectives of the health promotion program, if they are necessary, or if they have ceased to generate the need for revenue. If programs or program costs are weak, of little value, or not contributing to the overall benefit of the employees and company, they should be eliminated. Like an individual's reputation for honesty, budget credibility can be difficult to recover if upper management perceives they have been exposed to budget fraud.

SELECTION AND HIRING OF STAFF

Staffing needs are predicated on the health promotion program. No matter what the program size, amount of funds available, whether conducted in-house or utilizing primarily outside vendors, over the long term, a successful worksite health promotion program will be determined by the effectiveness of its staff. The skills of the staff, both work related and interpersonal, will be the source of the quality of programs offered and the basis of relationships that develop with participants. For this reason, the ability to accurately assess and fill staffing needs strongly influences the long-range success of health promotion programming.

Personnel needs originate with program design and goals. Since personnel is such a large budget item, each position should be carefully justified, predicated on specific program goals and needs. For instance, a company with five hundred or more employees that is building its own exercise facility will have greater and different health staffing needs than a small company (less than fifty employees) whose focus is health-related programming in the workplace to decrease medical expenses through programs such as blood pressure/diabetes/cholesterol screenings, easy access to mammography, and cancer risk reduction. For this reason, staffing can only be realistically determined after program goals have been clearly defined. Budget resources sufficient to cover the expenses of hiring appropriately trained and credentialed individuals need to be established.

The number of staff will be determined by a variety of factors, including the size of the organization, the number of people in the target audience, the number and types of programs to be offered (i.e., Is there a fitness facility on-site or will exercise classes be brokered out? How many and what kinds of educational programs will be offered?), resource people already available in the company who bring specific skills to the program, and the budget accessible to accomplish program goals. One way to plan programming is to develop a visual diagram of desired activities/ health promotion goals. Table 6.4 demonstrates a program plan that divides company plans into manageable units.

Reviewing the types and variety of programs desired can contribute to staffing plans. For instance, if most of the company's goals are in the area of medical screenings, it might be advisable to have a nurse on staff or easily available as a consultant

TABLE 6.4. Program Planning Activities—Health Promotion Program

Fitness Center	Health Screenings	Nutrition
Fitness Testing	Health Risk Assessments	Weight Management
Supervision of Employees	Blood Pressure	Cooking Classes
Exercise Prescriptions	Cancer Screening	Grocery Tours
Exercise and Aging	Cholesterol Screening	Nutrition Education
Exercise and Disease Prevention	Diabetes Screening	Nutraceuticals
Exercise Leadership	Low Back Care	Eating Out Healthy
Exercise and Health	Disease Prevention	Nutrition and Health
Education	Education	Classes

to conduct certain screenings. If most of the plans are for smoking cessation programs, substance abuse education, or alcohol abuse prevention, then an individual with an education/background in these areas would be a desirable staff member. On the other hand, if the program emphasis is on dietary/nutritional components, a registered dietitian (RD) would be one of the most important employees to be hired, since not only is such a person needed for program purposes, but many states do not allow individuals other than RDs to dispense nutritional/dietary information.

Employees need to be appropriately trained with education and certification in the areas in which they are hired to work. Bachelor's and master's degrees should be required for most jobs, with the use of interns (when available) to assist in less rigorous programs and activities. Usual job descriptions in the health promotion area often emphasize the need for easily recognized certifications from organizations such as the American College of Sports Medicine (ACSM), American Council on Exercise (ACE), Certified Health Educational Specialist (CHES), and the American Red Cross (CPR). Typical health promotion positions include the following:

Exercise Program Director. The program director is the chief administrator of the program. The job of the program director is to run the program; depending on the size of the company and the funding available, this can include anything from overseeing personnel to cleaning the equipment and the locker rooms. Ideally, this position is fundamentally managerial in nature, but it requires the knowledge and ability to conduct testing, education programs, outreach activities, public relations, staff management, marketing, and budgeting.

Exercise Specialist. The person who actually conducts exercise programs and oversees the testing and training of participants in the exercise area is the exercise specialist. Depending on the clientele, an exercise specialist will need expertise designing exercise programs and classes for a variety of age groups, medical conditions, activity levels, and for both genders.

Exercise Technician. An exercise technician is primarily responsible for graded exercise testing and routine screenings. A technician may be involved in any lab work, including record keeping, and would probably be CPR and emergency trained.

Health Educator. The job of the health educator is to develop appropriate health education classes. These classes could include disease prevention, smoking cessation, stress management, recognizing symptoms of heart disease/stroke, healthy shopping, eating nutritiously, low-fat cooking, and any areas the fitness staff lacks the background to present. In a company that emphasizes a fitness program, the health educator might serve as an adjunct to "round out" the total program. Behavior change theory is an important area of expertise.

Registered Dietitian. Some states may require that nutritional/dietary information be dispensed only by certified Registered Dietitians (RDs). RDs have the professional expertise to plan nutritional and dietary classes, provide nutritional/dietary guidelines, and write nutrition prescriptions. It is beneficial for

RDs working in the corporate sector to have expertise in exercise, adult education, and behavioral change theory as part of their professional base of expertise.

In some circumstances, other professionals, such as recreation leaders/specialists, physicians, exercise physiologists, and nurses may be used as supplemental personnel. These professionals may be consultants who assist or oversee specific activities, or they may be retained full-time if the clientele require special medical needs or are involved in certain activities. Support staff may be used on part-time assignment, may be shared with another area, or may function as full-time personnel who also serve as assistants to the director and/or may be involved in inventory, supply ordering, record keeping, and receptionist duties.

Once personnel needs have been determined, detailed, accurate job descriptions should be written. A job description must be written for *every* job. A well-written job description will be specific and describe the duties and expectations of the company concerning the employee. A specific job description establishes a level of accountability for acceptable work and helps the employee understand his or her responsibilities. Clearly established, the job description will serve as the criterion for evaluation of job performance. Many companies use a standard format that includes the amount of physical activity required in the position. A job description is really dependent on the needs of the company. An example of a job description is contained in figure 6.4.

CONDUCTING AN INTERVIEW

Staff selection should be carefully conducted. Poor staffing decisions can negatively impact a program for a long time. Considerations in hiring include ensuring that individuals are well qualified for the job, that all personnel can work well with one another, and can interact easily with clientele. Interviews of prospective hires should always be conducted with the program director and, ideally, any other personnel with whom the employee will interact. Since it is unrealistic to include the

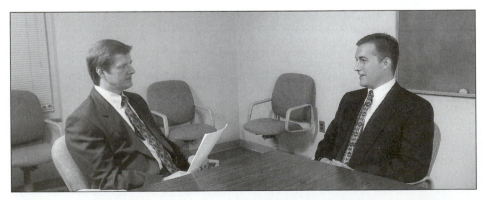

A carefully planned agenda and questions are needed before interviewing candidates.

FIGURE 6.4. Job Description: Exercise Specialist

Job Title: Exercise Specialist

Accountability: Reports to Program Director

Salary: $20,000 to $37,000 (depending on experience)

Summary Description: Assist the Program Director with daily supervision and operation of the fitness center; engage in client interaction; oversee fitness testing and other activities; and participate in developing and conducting health promotion programming.

Specific Job Functions:

1. Conduct fitness assessments; write appropriate exercise prescriptions; and engage in exercise counseling
2. Be the primary instructor for group exercise classes; ensure all classes are taught according to current exercise guidelines; and continuously implement evolving programs based on changes in exercise leadership organizations
3. Assist as needed in group and individualized wellness programs
4. Assist in equipment maintenance, including, as needed, cleaning and keeping in proper working order
5. Work with other fitness personnel in planning and conducting health promotion programming, including development of promotion and educational materials
6. Facilitate health education classes as needed
7. Maintain cutting-edge knowledge of industry trends/innovations and incorporate into work situation

Job Qualifications:

Education: Minimum Bachelor's degree, Master's degree preferred, in exercise physiology, health & fitness, or related field

Experience: Prefer two to three years in exercise leadership and design

Skills/Certifications: ACSM or ACE certification in exercise leadership; CPR certified: good interpersonal skills; group facilitation; leadership, organization, and program development skills.

Physical Requirements:

Standing/Walking	Routine	30%
Lifting	Routine	18%
Stooping/Reaching	Routine	20%
Climbing Ladders	Rarely	2%
Computers	Routine	25%
Driving a Car	Rarely	5%

---

entire company in the hiring process, an employee committee or representatives should be allowed the opportunity to meet and interact with prospective staff once selection has been narrowed to a few individuals. It is also advisable to let the rest of the staff meet and have the opportunity to interact with prospective employees. This allows the director opportunity to observe interactions between current and potential staff members. Other staff members may provide positive and negative feedback that can assist in making the best possible decision. Since, by necessity, staff must interact on a regular basis, they need to be able to work together cooperatively.

Involving employees and staff in the selection process provides them with a sense of ownership in the operation, contributing to overall positive morale and increased commitment to the program.

To ensure the best selection possible, a well-thought-out plan needs to be employed. The purpose of a resume or application form is simply to get an interview. Using the resume or application form as a guideline, it is important to select individuals who have sufficient training relevant to the duties defined in the job description. Education and certification are important. They are indications of personal motivation to learn and gain a solid knowledge base in one's field. On the other hand, education does not always ensure an individual's ability to successfully perform a particular job. The job interview provides an opportunity for the employer to learn more about potential employees and for potential employees to learn about the job requirements and the organization.

The job interview itself should be conducted by the immediate supervisor of a prospective employee. The interviewer should have a specific plan and purpose. Goals to be accomplished during an interview might include (1) discussing the program objectives from the candidate's point of view, (2) providing the applicant an opportunity to express his/her feelings/perceptions about the job, (3) validating information on the candidate's application form, and (4) describing the benefits of the organization. Planning for the interview should include determining the amount of time to be spent interviewing, the atmosphere to be communicated, the manager's perceptions of how the candidate can contribute to the total organization, and a description of what the organization can do for the candidate.

Some sample questions that might be asked in an interview are contained in figure 6.5. The questions asked should be predicated on the goals and purpose of the interview, so they will vary from interview to interview. Each applicant for a single position should be asked the same questions so an accurate comparison between interviewees can be established. Introductions to other pertinent personnel, such as the employee committee representative(s) and/or other staff can occur at some point during the initial interview, or, if there are a large number of applicants, upon a return interview. As stated previously, it is usually to the benefit of the company doing

FIGURE 6.5. Sample Questions for a Job Interview

1. What interests you about the job?
2. Why are you making a change from your current position?
3. What are some of your more recent accomplishments?
4. What part of you current job do you like and dislike?
5. What have you learned/do at your current job that would apply to this position?
6. Can you describe how you communicate and motivate others?
7. What are your strengths in relating to people?
8. How would you describe your temperament?
9. Can you describe one or two examples or new ideas, projects, or innovations of which you are particularly proud?
10. What are your future aspirations?

the hiring to include relevant people at some point before the actual hiring occurs. This guarantees a sense of ownership among all concerned and may be a decisive factor in selecting the best employee for the position.

SUPERVISION OF EMPLOYEES

Managing employees effectively may be the most challenging part of any job. Supervision of employees can occur at many levels, ranging from a staff person overseeing an intern's progress to the director of the program who is responsible for overseeing, training, ensuring effective accomplishment of tasks, and fostering a spirit of cooperation.

Supervision of staff will partially depend on the quality of the staff selected during the hiring process. If a good job of staff hiring has been done where each employee is qualified for his/her position, demonstrates motivation, is a self-starter, and cooperates with other personnel, then problems associated with supervising are minimized. Whenever personnel with positive attitudes, who are excited about doing their jobs, feel they are making a valuable contribution to the organization and the welfare of the employees, and are willing to work to achieve their goals are hired, actual time spent overseeing them is reduced. Of course, even highly motivated staff can become discouraged and have personal problems that can negatively affect their work.

Although there are a variety of leadership styles, experience suggests that the most effective managers know their business, facilitate the best working conditions possible, continually educate their staff, understand the personalities and working styles of their staff, foster opportunities for staff to appropriately provide input into the running of the program, and encourage the development of a sense of ownership. Most people want to feel good about their work. Finding ways to ensure staff are having positive experiences at work and are engaging in activities that contribute to their job satisfaction goes a long way toward achieving a productive work environment.

There are a variety of ways to positively influence staff. For example, adequate salary nearly always contributes to feelings of well-being. Careful, sensitive, encouraging evaluation of job performance, even if problems exist, can create a positive impact. Unnecessary harshness and criticism can result in decreased morale. Providing employees with positive feedback, encouraging them when they experience difficulties, and honestly complimenting them when they perform well or have an unusually successful program will, more times than not, result in a more positive attitude toward work and a deeper desire to perform well. Team building, over the long run, does lead to improved results. The health promotion program is a team effort, and all members of the team needs to pull their load to achieve success. Treating each employee as a valued employee and finding ways to encourage unity in work goals accomplishes more than a harsh or autocratic style where the supervisor demonstrates lack of trust in the employees, views the employee as serving the supervisor's needs, and seeks to constantly look for the negative.

TABLE 6.5. Sample Policy and Procedure Manual Contents

Section	Inclusions in Section
Personnel	Organization Chart
	Recruitment and Selection
	Job Descriptions
	In-Service Training
	Rules of Conduct
	Dress/Appearance
	Evaluation of Staff
	Certifications Desired
	Part-Time Employees
	Contract Employees
	Vacation Requests
	Sick Leave
	Insurance Benefits
	Travel Requests
	Grievances and Termination
Programming	Budget Procedures
	Planning Procedures
	Enrollment Procedures
	Emergency Procedures
	Hours of Operation
	Termination of Services
	Orientation of Members
	Exercise
	Educational
	Master Calendar
	Payment Procedures
	Market Procedures
	Exercise Testing/Screening
	Exercise Prescriptions
	Educational Programs
Members and Participants	Enrollment Procedures
	Orientation of Members/Participants
	Services Offered
	Guests
	Lockers and Laundry
Facility Management	Staff Opening and Closing Procedures
	Equipment Purchases
	Supply Purchases
	Facility Safety
	Equipment Inspection
	Cleaning and Maintenance
	Equipment
	Facilities
	Injury/Emergency Procedures
	Reporting of Injury/Emergencies
Educational Library	Hours of Operation
	Educational Materials
	Videos
	Purchases of Materials

DEVELOPING POLICY AND PROCEDURE MANUALS

For a health promotion program to continue to run efficiently as additional staff are hired or as personnel leave, a manual explicitly outlining the policies, procedures, and expectations of the program should be developed. The manual is an inherent part of the initial planning for the health promotion program. Development of the manual should occur as the process for planning the comprehensive program moves forward. The actual manual should be divided into the major areas of concern for effective program operation. The nature of the policy/procedure manual will vary from company to company, but there are major sections considered generic to any health promotion program (see table 6.5). An important aspect of the policy/procedure manual are the forms and protocols for various activities. Table 6.6 is a sample listing of some of the more common forms needed for smooth, effective operation.

TABLE 6.6. Common Forms for a Health Promotion Facility

Management Forms	Facility Management Forms
Purchase Requisition	Exercise Safety Equipment Inspection
Employee Performance Evaluation	Lost and Found
Time Sheets	Court Sign-up Sheet
Work Schedule	Daily Maintenance Log
Photo Copy	Equipment Checkout
Long Distance Phone Log	Exercise Equipment Repair
Budget Preparation	Employee Suggestions
Instructor Evaluation	
Participant Evaluation	
Inventory	
Educational Forms	**Exercise/Exercise Testing Forms**
Registration	Registration
Nutritional Analysis Logs	Informed Consent/Release
Behavioral Change Logs	Fitness Assessment
Body Weight Records	Exercise Prescription
Attendance Forms	Exercise Participation Logs
Evaluation Forms	Resistant Training
Library/Video Checkout	
Emergency Procedures Forms	
Procedures for Emergencies	
Injury Report	
Accident Report	
First Aid Inventory	

ETHICS AND HEALTH PROMOTION

Professionals from all facets of life are faced daily with ethical issues that have potential for influencing the lives of those they serve. Health promotion is certainly no exception and may have even more potential for ethical violations. The concept of **nonmalfeasance** or not causing harm or not doing evil (McKenzie and Smeltzer, 1997) has particular merit when interacting with individuals who are vulnerable to what they are told. Not causing harm or doing evil has several applicable areas of concern in the business of health promotion.

Business ethics is an area of potential concern for violating and misunderstanding of sound ethical functioning. Problems may revolve around the selection of vendors (relatives or friends), solicitation of bids for goods and services (using companies that charge more but give management a "kickback" or special service in exchange for business), special incentives offered for certain services, and benefits for friends or acquaintances (even if unqualified). When marketing and selling programs, dealing with employees, or engaging in client matters, business should be conducted in a truthful and honest fashion. Hopefully, every organization has formal guidelines and procedures regarding the appropriate way to handle a particular issue. It is the health professional's responsibility to maintain personal integrity and act in a fashion that will never tarnish the organization for which he or she works.

An area of paramount ethical concern is confidentiality between company members and the health promotion staff. Discussing a client's personal data with fellow employees must be done through proper protocol and in a way that promotes confidentiality. The only circumstance in which to discuss personal client information is professional. Gossiping about or making fun of a client, even if that client is nowhere around, is absolutely unethical. Releasing private information concerning a client without written consent is unethical, and, many times, illegal. Employees may reveal highly sensitive information to a trusted health promotion professional whom they regard as a confidante, such as a problem with depression or a struggle with drugs, or a sexually transmitted disease. In all these cases, not only has extremely personal information been shared, but potential harm to the individual, his/her family, and the company itself exists.

There is some concern that requiring people to stop smoking, wear back supports or seatbelts, or to use scare techniques to facilitate behaviors is unethical. To address these issues, several guidelines have been suggested. They are (Shirreffs et al., 1990):

1. Respect the goals and values of those in the target population.
2. Be aware of the *degrees* of autonomy related to health behavior.
   a. *Facilitation*—assisting in achieving objectives set by the target group (starting an exercise program or losing weight).
   b. *Persuasion*—arguing and reasoning with others (telling clients the importance of not smoking).
   c. *Manipulation*—modifying environment or psychic disposition (removing "junk food" from vending machines).
   d. *Coercion*—threating deprivation (face paying greater insurance costs if continuing to smoke).

3. Follow the necessary steps to provide informed consent to those in the target population. Clients should have explained to them the risks/benefits, alternative procedures, and be made aware they are free to discontinue program involvement at any time.
4. Be just and fair.
5. Protect the confidentiality and privacy of those in the target population.
6. Do not cause harm (nonmalfeasance). Do not omit something you should include (omission), and do not do something you should not (commission).
7. Work to bring about or do good (beneficence).

The framework of ethical behavior includes resisting the temptation to blame the client (victim blaming) for the health problems of the organization; for example, inferring or stating at any time that the prevalence of accidents within the company is the fault of employee behavior. To avoid this type of thinking, health promotion specialists must realize that behaviors are the result of a series of complex interacting factors and are not easily comprehended or modified. Those factors have been identified as (McElroy et al., 1988):

1. *Intrapersonal Factors.* Knowledge, attitudes, skills, and self-concept of the individual.
2. *Interpersonal Processes.* Impact of family, friends, coworkers, and other social support groups on health behavior.
3. *Institutional Factors.* Formal and informal rules and regulations by the company that affect health behavior.
4. *Community Factors.* Relationships between the organization and other institutions and networks in the community.
5. *Public Policy.* Local, state, and national laws/policies that affect health behaviors.

Health professionals need to consider: For whom do we work? Is the purpose of health promotion to improve the lives of employees, reduce health care costs for the employer, or promote high-level wellness for society? What happens when an employee's behavior is in conflict with the regulations of the company, or codes of ethical health promotion behavior seem to be in question? It is possible to be responsive to all sides of an argument, to understand the intentions of the corporate world versus employee desires, but there is a fine line in maintaining a sense of professional integrity, a sense of fairness, and ethical propriety. It is sometimes difficult to define the role of the health promotion specialist regarding their use of professional knowledge to influence clients' behavior. Health promotion specialists are neither caretakers nor dictators. Maintaining the position of one who facilitates, motivates, or empowers—allowing employees the opportunity to assume responsibility and ownership of their own lives—is often the most appropriate role.

Health promotion professionals must be prepared to deal with the aforementioned issues and other ethical concerns that may arise. Health promotion staff are in constant contact with employees throughout an organization, and, consequently, actions, statements, and behaviors must be considered carefully. To help determine ethical behavior, organizations such as the Association for the Advancement of Health Education (AAHE) and the Society for Public Health Education (SOPHE) have both published codes of ethics. These documents provide guidelines of what professionals should strive for in their behavior. Figure 6.6 provides the SOPHE code of ethics (abridged from 1993 revised version; complete code of ethics available on request from the SOPHE office).

FIGURE 6.6. SOPHE Code of Ethics

Health educators take on profound responsibilities in using educational processes to promote health and influence well being. Ethical precepts which guide these processes must respect the right of individuals and communities to make the decisions affecting their lives.

Responsibilities to Society

Health Educators:

- Affirm an egalitarian ethic, believing that health is a basic human right for all.
- Provide people with all relevant and accurate information and resources to make their choices freely and intelligently.
- Support change by freedom of choice and self-determination, as long as these decisions pose no threat to the health of others.
- Advocate for healthful change and legislation, and speak out on issues deleterious to public health.
- Are candid and truthful in dealings with the public, never misrepresenting or exaggerating the potential benefits of services or programs.
- Avoid and take appropriate action against unethical practices and conflict of interest situations.
- Respect the privacy, dignity, and culture of the individual and the community and use skills consistent with these values.

Responsibilities to the Profession

Health Educators:

- Share their skills, experience, and visions with their students and colleagues.
- Observe principles of informed consent and confidentiality of individuals.
- Maintain their highest levels of competence through continued study, training, and research.
- Further the art and science of health education through applied research and report findings honestly and without distortion.
- Accurately represent their capabilities, education, training, and experience and act within the boundaries of their professional competence.
- Ensure that no exclusionary practices are enacted against individuals on the basis of gender, marital status, age, social class, religion, sexual preference, or ethnic or cultural background.

Profiles in Health Promotion

The Maryweather Graphic Design Company has an on-site fitness and wellness facility. There are currently four employees plus a manager and assistant manager. It is the job of the two managers to develop budgets, plan purchases, develop/implement programs, evaluate the programs, and hire/train/supervise all employees. All four of the current employees have received in-service training prior to beginning their current assignment. However, one employee has recently begun to be late and refuses to follow the prescribed dress code for fitness and wellness employees. Several clients have expressed their displeasure with their attempts to have questions answered by the employee. Finally, two fellow employees have noted that, when answering the telephone for the facility, the employee in question has used inappropriate procedures. When hired, this person presented excellent credentials and the recommendations were exceptionally strong. During training the only comment made by the employee was that some of the points covered seemed unnecessary. Both the manager and assistant manager like the employee but realize that such behavior cannot continue. Assume that you are the manager of the Maryweather facility. What steps would you take to correct the situation? Describe the step-by-step procedures you would follow. Keep in mind that the employee has done a good job until recently, and you don't really want to fire the person.

Check It Out

In most corporate settings, if the facility is owned by the company, the largest expenses are those for the salaries of the staff. Other costs such as rent and utilities are absorbed in some area of the corporate budget. However, there are still many components of a budget that must be considered if the wellness facility is to operate effectively. Your job is to select categories, other than salaries, benefits, rent, and utilities, needed to keep your program functioning (such as telephones, supplies, equipment) and develop object codes for those components. Once the areas and object codes have been defined, research the potential cost for each of the identified areas. Determine a total amount of budgeted money for each category as well as the total amount of the projected budget minus the areas excluded in the mentioned parameter for this activity.

Category	Object Code	Budgeted Amount

Summary

- Management sets the standard for the entire health promotion program.
- Elements in the process of management include establishing and achieving goals, supervising personnel, acquiring and utilizing resources, facilitating group solidarity/commitment, clarifying responsibility and accountability, motivating personnel, facilitating personal advancement of staff, and encouraging efficiency of operation.
- Management is defined as "the process of planning, organizing, leading, and controlling an organization's human, financial, physical, and information resources to achieve organizational goals in an efficient and effective manner."
- Effective management is both an art and a science.
- Skills needed in the science of health promotion include technical, human, and conceptual skills.
- The art of management is the effective application of these skills.
- Budgeting is a systematic process that allows managers to plan and control resources for the purpose of achievement of objectives.
- Budgets serve four functions: They help managers coordinate resources and projects; they help define the standards needed; they provide clear guidelines about the organization's resources and expectations; and they facilitate performance evaluations of managers and units.
- A line item budget itemizes each category of spending with its anticipated expenditure for the fiscal year.
- A functional budget divides the budget into major functional areas, including administration, facilities/equipment, and services.
- Most budgets have a taxonomy that breaks down costs into logical functions.
- Top-down budgeting is when upper management determines the amount of monies each unit/department is to receive.
- Bottom-up budgeting is when managers submit their own budget for review and execution.
- The steps in bottom-up budgeting include preparation, presentation, adoption, and execution.
- Budgets account for three kinds of costs: fixed, variable, and semivariable.
- Fixed costs are expenses that do not change.
- Variable costs are those that change according to the number of participants or items purchased.
- Semivariable costs vary depending on the type of activity.
- When developing a budget, it must be assumed there is a ceiling figure. Items in a budget should legitimately reflect the needs of the program, and these items should be justifiable.
- It is not a good idea to arbitrarily inflate a budget in hopes of receiving more funds, since budgets should be carefully scrutinized by management.
- Personnel needs must be based on program design and program goals.
- Understanding program needs can facilitate determining staff needs.
- Typical health promotion positions include: exercise program director, exercise specialist, exercise technician, and health educator.
- Other staffing requirements might include recreation leaders, physicians, exercise physiologists, and nurses.

- Job descriptions must be written for every job. The descriptions should be specific and describe what the duties of the position will be.
- A well-written job description can provide the criterion for job evaluation.
- Selecting staff can positively or negatively affect the results of the entire health promotion program.
- A good staff selection process should include company employees and other staff members.
- Supervision of staff should include providing an atmosphere where personnel can provide input to the program, especially as it concerns their work and where staff work together cooperatively.
- A policy and procedures manual can help ensure the program will run efficiently even if personnel leave or must be replaced.
- A policy and procedures manual should include examples of commonly used forms.

Bibliography

Association for Fitness in Business, 1992. *Guidelines for employee health promotion programs.* Champaign, IL: Human Kinetics.

BELLINGHAM, R., and TAGER, M. J. 1986. *Designing effective health promotion programs: The 20 skills for success.* Chicago, IL: Great Performance.

CHENOWIETH, D. H. 1991. *Planning health promotion at the worksite* (2nd ed.). Dubuque, IA: WCB Brown & Benchmark.

FROST, R. B., LOCKHART, B. D., and MARSHALL, S. J. 1988. *Administration of physical education and athletics, concepts and practices* (3rd ed.). Dubuque IA: William C. Brown.

GETTMAN, L. R. 1988. *Management skills required for exercise programs. Resource manual for guidelines for exercise testing and prescription.* Philadelphia: Lea & Febiger.

GRIFFIN, R. W. 1984. *Management.* Boston: Houghton Mifflin.

HORINE, L. 1991. *Administration of physical education and sport.* Dubuque, IA: William C. Brown.

KRAUSE, R. G., and CURTIS, J. E. 1986. *Creative management in recreation, parks, and leisure services.* St. Louis: Times Mirror/Mosby College Publishing.

MCELORY, K., BIBEAU, D., STECKLER, A., and GLANZ, K. 1988. "An ecological approach to health promotion programs." *Health Education Quarterly* 15(4): 356–377.

MCKENZIE, J. F., and SMEITZER, J. 1997. *Planning, implementing, and evaluating Health Promotion Programs* (2nd ed.). Boston: Allyn & Bacon.

PICKETT, G., and HANLON, J. J. 1992. *Public health—administration and practice.* St. Louis: Times Mirror/Mosby College Publishing.

SCHIRREFFS, J., ODOM, J., MCLEROY, K., and FORS, S. 1990. *Incorporating ethics in the health education curriculum.* Paper presented at the Association for the Advancement of Health Education, April. New Orleans, LA.

STONE, W. J. 1987. *Adult fitness programs: Planning, designing, managing, and improving fitness programs.* Glenview, IL: Scott, Foresman.

TIMMRECK, T. C. 1995. *Planning, program development, and evaluation: A handbook for health promotion, aging and health services.* Boston: Jones and Bartlett.

TREWATHA, R. L., and NEWPORT, M. G. 1992. *Management* (6th ed.). Plano, TX: Business Publications.

WILSON, B. R. A., and GLAROS, T. E. 1994. *Managing health promotion programs.* Champaign, IL: Human Kinetics.

CHAPTER 7

Marketing and Maintaining Involvement

OBJECTIVES

Product Marketing and Social Marketing

Marketing Strategies

Launching a Marketing Program

Types of Marketing Strategies for Group Involvement

Targeting the Audience

Developing Informative/ Persuasive Messages

Keeping Clients Satisfied and Loyal

Common Difficulties Encountered in Long-Term Programming

Common Strategies to Encourage Long-Term Behavior Change/Program Participation

Profiles in Health Promotion

Check It Out

Summary

CHAPTER OBJECTIVES

After reading this chapter, you should be able to

- differentiate between product marketing and social marketing.
- develop marketing strategies appropriate for a variety of settings and social structures.
- describe methods to provide ongoing monitoring of marketing programs.
- list a variety of commonly used strategies to increase group involvement.
- write persuasive copy to promote group involvement in activities.
- identify ways to increase participation and adherence in established programs.

For any health promotion program to be successful, an effective marketing program is essential. Unfortunately, individuals in the health promotion field often know how to develop and manage programs, but until they can convince their potential participants of the need for their product and can ignite the desire within them to participate, health promotion efforts will fail. Marketing is frequently the key element that determines the difference between success and failure. Marketing is also the area most often overlooked by students and educators in the desire to ensure adequate knowledge about the benefits of living a healthy lifestyle.

Although marketing involves complex theories that frequently require years of study, this text discusses the basics ideas most frequently used in the area of health promotion. In reality, marketing is a fluid concept that necessitates constant updating and change to address a particular audience, specific circumstances, and evolving needs. The contribution of marketing to the success of any health promotion program and the future of health promotion itself cannot be underestimated.

PRODUCT MARKETING AND SOCIAL MARKETING

A **market** is the set of all people who have a real or potential interest in a product or a service (McKenzie and Smeltzer, 1997). **Marketing** involves the planned attempt to influence the market so there is a voluntary exchange of costs from that market with benefits from a provider. Marketing essentially offers benefits to an identified group of potential customers or participants who will pay some kind of price/prices (money, time, effort) to get those benefits (Pope, 1993). In health promotion, the exchange of costs and benefits is, at its most basic, the efforts (and possibly money) expended to achieve a longer life where individuals are healthier, are able to enjoy a higher quality of life, and/or feel better about themselves.

Product marketing can be defined as getting the right *product* to the right *place* at the right *price* (Eddy and Kahler, 1992) and letting the market know about it through *promotion.* Product, place, price, and promotion are also know as the **Four P's** of product marketing (figure 7.1). When using a product marketing concept, the health promotion specialist is looking for a way to balance the four P's so that a desirable outcome (a successful program) is achieved. To begin with, the right product (an unmet need among target clientele) must be identified. Next, the best place to conduct the program must be found. This includes sufficient space, lighting, and possibly acoustics; the appropriate level of comfort/attractiveness; and a time that will allow for the greatest number of participants. After determining these factors, the price must be established. While this may certainly include cost, special programs in the health promotion area are frequently either covered by the company or are already included in some other expense. In this case, the cost to the employee/participant/client is going to be primarily in time and effort. Time and effort are often at a premium for busy, working adults with families, so it will be nec-

FIGURE 7.1. The Four "P's" of Marketing

Product	Price
Actual product or program Name used Perceived need by target market	Effort Time of day/day of week Rewards for participating
Place	Promotion
Adequate facility Convenient for participants Comfort level	Advertising "Special deals" Rewards for participation

essary to "sell" individuals on the importance of the program. Last, an effective promotion campaign that includes all your advertising and "hooks" to encourage participation must be designed.

Each of the four P's in product marketing involves complex steps. Inadequate planning in any one of these steps may result in programs that are less successful than desired. Therefore, it is very important that the health promotion specialist clearly understands the target audience and is able to design programs that meet its needs.

Product marketing has its roots in manufacturing, where a tangible product is bought and sold. Because products are tangible, using this model would usually indicate a program or activity, although the product can also be conceived as "better health," "more energy," or some other less overtly tangible product. Because it is sometimes more complicated to define "products" in health promotion, an additional component pervasive throughout all lifestyle change programs is added to the concept of the four P's.

Health promotion, almost by its very nature, requires the additional component of **social marketing.** Social marketing may be called the marketing of ideas (Eddy and Kahler, 1992). Social marketing emphasizes the promotion of "nontangible" products, such as ideas, attitudes, and a healthier lifestyle—goals in health promotion. For health promotion to be effective, participants must not only attend programs, they must become convinced that the healthy behaviors espoused in those programs should be incorporated into their lives. Health promotion markets ideas, attitudes, and lifestyle change. Adapting new lifestyle behaviors requires making a lifestyle change and *lifestyle change usually is difficult to achieve.*

Social marketing is necessary to initiate lifestyle change. Sometimes individuals are willing to change their lifestyle because they have had a heart attack and recognize that if they don't change, they are likely to die prematurely. Most of the time, however, people either deny that they need to incorporate change into their lives until a cataclysmic event occurs or they put it off, planning on doing "it" (exercising, eating lower-fat foods, managing hypertension) until later, or they deny they need to make a change. Social marketing is used to persuade people that they *should* and that they *want* to make a change.

Social marketing theory delineates four basic types of programs or types of change. A *cognitive change* program is the most common. This type of change is knowledge based and is developed to help participants increase their information about specific health areas, such as the warning signs of a heart attack. An *action change* program focuses on a short-term activity, such as a blood pressure screening or female employees getting a mammogram. An action change program requires convincing clientele they need to have their blood pressure screened, even if they don't feel badly. This means they must have sufficient information to comprehend that how they feel is not a determinant of hypertension, and they must recognize that *hypertension is something that can happen to them without affecting how they feel on a daily basis.*

Behavior change programs are more difficult to achieve since the goal is to change behavior permanently. Getting an individual newly diagnosed with non-insulin-dependent diabetes mellitus (NIDDM) to exercise regularly, take his or her medicine on schedule, and incorporate new eating habits is an example of a behavior change program. Since most behavior is deeply ingrained, altering it requires a paradigm shift where the change is important enough to the individual to overcome a lifetime of doing things a certain way that is convenient, familiar, and enjoyed.

Value change programs are the most difficult. Values are sometimes defined as "predispositions toward an action." Values are qualities or an entity an individual considers desirable, useful, or important. They are feelings that are usually stable over time and not subject to capriciousness or change. Socioeconomic and cultural factors frequently come into play when dealing with values. If one's cultural or religious values state that specific degrees of undress are inappropriate, yet health promotion activity programs involve wearing fewer clothes than is considered allowable or health risk assessments involve exposing body parts, some employees will be unable to become involved. Concerns over privacy issues, particularly if employees have conditions about which they are extremely sensitive, may cause people to not participate. They may be afraid that if the company or their bosses learn of their disabilities, they will be treated differently (unfairly). Feeling pressured by the company to participate in activities they consider unacceptable or invasive, even if employees understand that participating would be beneficial, may place them in a discouraging position. Being able to address values-laden issues successfully is probably one of the most complex problems faced by health promotion professionals today.

In health promotion, the goal is always to improve the health and well-being of the target market. This can only be accomplished with the cooperation of the client. Proper understanding of the target population—what *they* think; what *they* want; how *they* feel; what *they* perceive—cannot be overlooked if programs are to achieve their goals. The target population's perspective may vary so widely from the viewpoint of the health promotion specialist that all marketing attempts can fall flat. It is often simply not sufficient to develop and advertise programs. Brilliant marketing strategies will fail if they do not touch the pulse of the people.

The way to learn what people think is to ask them (needs assessment) and then use what they say as the source for marketing planning. Social and cultural issues are of paramount concern, and any successful, long-term health promotion program requires sensitivity to the unique problems of various groups along with incorporation of perceptive social marketing concepts that specifically address the problems of the targeted group.

MARKETING STRATEGIES

The marketing strategies to be used are based on several factors. To begin with, the setting (see chapter 2) will be a primary factor in determining strategies. The clientele will differ according to the setting. For instance, the main offices of a bank will be composed mostly of adults with white-collar jobs who work at a desk or behind a counter or window while seated. On the other hand, a telephone company will consist of some office workers but will also include people who work outside and away from the office on telephone lines or who drive and make "house" calls,

Marketing strategies depend on many factors.

running new telephone wires into people's homes. The diversity of the types of work-related problems could vary significantly, altering the kinds of health promotion programs that would be most beneficial for each company.

The goals of management will affect strategies, since how management wants to spend its money will definitely influence what programs are developed (chapter 2). The clientele itself will be an important determinant of strategies because the health needs of people vary by age, ethnic group, socioeconomic status, and education. Since most health promotion specialists work with adult learners, it is important to understand their learning processes (see chapter 3).

The foundation for deciding what activities and programs to initiate or expand in a marketing plan include:

1. *What the clientele already knows.* There is no reason to use time and money on programs that provide information participants already know.
2. *What new kinds of information are needed.* If health care expenses indicate the population is at high risk for heart disease, including surgery, then prevention issues are probably suggested. This can include symptoms of a heart attack, the difference between angina and a myocardial infarction, and what to do if an infarction is a possibility.
3. *Based on the population, the types of "advertising" that will most likely affect the target audience.* If most of the population works outside the primary health promotion site, then different communication formats would be used than if all workers share common areas daily. Posters on a bulletin board will not be effective if the population does not pass by the bulletin board daily.
4. *Based on the population, the materials (preexisting if possible) that will work most effectively.* If the population is low literacy, there is no reason to develop workbooks or long, written explanations of a program. Alternative ways to ensure the message is understood and retained need to be developed.

5. *The cost of the event(s).* Is this particular idea worth the money needed to advertise and present? Will results and participation warrant the expense, considering your overall budget?

6. *The time period(s) that will be more accessible to the greatest number of people.* How many people will come back to work on a Saturday morning to attend a lecture or activity or stay after work for an hour? Is there "break" time during the day that can be used to foster health programming activities?

7. *The length of the program.* For the most part, health practitioners like to schedule exercise programs lasting an hour or longer. However, is this a time frame that would be effective or would more people attend and participate if a shorter time period was used?

8. *Deciding on a single or multiple event activity.* Onetime events are generally easier to stage, but recurring activities (e.g., exercise classes) may be more effective. If the amount of information to be disseminated is very large, more than one meeting should be held. It is better to provide smaller chunks of learnable, applicable information that can be personalized than to try to give too much information that is not understood.

9. *Ensuring that participants know how the information is applicable to their lives.* And, after completion of the program, will they know *how* to apply it to their lives?

10. *Keep it simple.* Life is complicated enough without presenting long, involved programs that only generate more confusion. Change usually occurs in tiny, manageable chunks.

The basis of almost all sales is to create a need in the customer. The salesperson then supplies the need. In marketing health promotion programs, the concept is the same. Marketing generates sales. To be successful, health promotion personnel must market and must market well. It is nice to share information with others, but professionals in the health promotion field tend to give away information too easily and at too low a price. It cannot be stressed enough that people engaged in health promotion need to first realize they have a valuable product, promote the fact that they have lifesaving information, and then not give that information away. If people want to know how to cook low-fat meals, let them come to a presentation about cooking low fat. If health professionals "give" information away (tell them how to incorporate low-fat cooking into everyday meals while talking at the water cooler), there is no need to attend programs. People will simply ask when they pass in the hall. This is unsatisfactory, because they are receiving information in a haphazard manner that may not really meet their needs and potential programs are being ruined. No one expects a lawyer to give legal advice over a soda in the breakroom, nor would the lawyer. Yet health professionals often think nothing of giving in-depth explanations about weight loss to any one who asks, even though this is information in which they invested time and money to obtain.

LAUNCHING A MARKETING PROGRAM

After determining what a successful health promotion event is going to be, it is time to pick the title. The title can make the difference between attendance and nonattendance. The title is what grabs the attention of the audience. The title can be a range of things, depending on the type of advertising being done and the targeted audience. The title is probably the primary component of the advertising plan.

Advertising is a component of marketing, falling under the category of *promotion*. Advertising is the use of any form of media or word of mouth to let people know about the product. Advertising itself may take one of two forms. **Internal advertising** is done within an organization. **External advertising** is marketing extended to a larger audience, such as the community. The exact types of advertising may vary and may include both types, depending on the target audience and where they will be addressed. Be sure the message (title) is being communicated effectively to the audience and that it arouses interest. A variety of channels (media) will need to be used.

Advertising designs should be kept simple but eye-catching. Usually, less is more. Graphic artists should be used when feasible and appropriate, but artists can be expensive. Costly art work should be used sparingly with more money put into programs than into advertising. With the growing accessibility of desktop graphics, this problem may be decreased or eliminated in some situations. An individual with excellent desktop programs and capabilities can produce very sensational materials with a minimum of cost. Increasing time for initial programming design work when necessay can reduce unexpected difficulties.

Implementing the program is where the actual activity begins. Long-range programs require more implementation than single session events. From the onset of planning, how to streamline implementation should be considered. This includes finding ways to share resources when feasible, prevent unnecessary duplication of effort, promote continuity of services, and set up central sources of information for clientele (Hudson Institute, 1987).

When new programs are being developed, especially large, long-term ones or ones introducing new concepts, it is often advisable to conduct pilot tests. These are smaller versions of a larger program that are only open to a small group of people. Using a pilot test allows time to refine a program through feedback and observation of what is occurring.

Health programs, whether long term or short term, are usually introduced in "phases." This process may be done in a variety of ways. A program may be phased in by offering a range of programs, so there is more than one program for everyone. This is necessary because it would be extremely rare to have a target audience homogenous enough to have one event satisfy everyone. Other ways to phase in programs are by offering them at different locations or at varying ability levels. Exercise classes are pretty standard fare in health promotion, yet not everyone can participate at the same level. Programs can also be phased in by limiting participation to various events.

Kick-off "events" are frequently good ways to initiate new programs, especially ones that will be a major portion of a total plan. Initial events can include ribbon cuttings, local celebrities, drawings, food tastings, or other activities.

Since a cornerstone of health promotion is successful marketing, everything done by health personnel in a related environment should be aimed at successfully marketing the product (an aerobics class for better health, a stress management program for a happier life, low-fat cooking classes for a slimmer body, etc.).

Marketing materials must be carefully planned and designed.

Opportunities should be actively sought out to promote events and programs. Encouragement should be offered to get people to attend. And health personnel need to listen as hard as they market. Listening to what people say is the best way to develop new programs that they will attend.

All programs and events should be the best they can. Shoddy, second-rate presentations or equipment will not encourage long-term or repeat participation. If a smoking cessation program is planned, it must be one that has demonstrated effectiveness and it must be presented by someone who knows her business. Time is needed to start new programs, but word of mouth is the best way to achieve ongoing success. Good, well-presented activities are the best advertisement available.

Monitoring a Marketing Program

Even single-event programs require monitoring. Monitoring programs provides valuable, immediate feedback as to the success or relevance of what was developed. It can also provide clues to what things should be emphasized in ongoing plans. Knowing what particular aspects the audience considers most relevant and useful leads to future successes. Health promotion is constantly evolving. The "hot" topic of today may not be of any interest to anyone tomorrow. By monitoring programs, it is possible for health promotion programs to remain current and address the needs of the participants.

Monitoring can be done in a variety of ways. Somebody in the health promotion segment should attend meetings, classes, and events to assess firsthand what is occurring. Is the program of high quality? Are members of the audience participating? Are they actively involved? Which portions of the program seem to arouse the most interest? What portions seem to result in the least interest or effect? Are the program objectives being met? Get feedback from participants via a brief questionnaire immediately following each event. Periodic questionnaires about overall programming can provide other means of monitoring current programs and develop new plans. This information may also be used for evaluation, a more formal method of determining progress toward achievement of program goals (more detailed information on evaluation will be presented in chapter 8).

TYPES OF MARKETING STRATEGIES FOR GROUP INVOLVEMENT

Some marketing strategies are common fare in the health promotion arena. Advertising promotions include newsletters, display boards, posters, brochures, tabletop tents, E-mail, and pay envelope stuffers. While each of these has benefits, over time people may become immune to their effect. In fact, they may not even read many advertising materials if they are not truly eye-catching. Graphics and variation (not using the same techniques continuously) may retain long-term advertising punch. Personal interaction can increase effectiveness of these types of advertisement. For instance, passing out one-sheet advertisements as people clock out or putting up posters during lunch or when the shift is changing or the most number of people are passing and then encouraging conversation about the event should increase participation and awareness rates. (See figure 7.2.)

Incentives may also be used to stimulate interest in new or ongoing programs. At one time, it was possible to get people to do almost anything for a free T-shirt. Unfortunately, free T-shirts are not usually as effective as they once were, but they will still work when used occasionally. Incentives can be divided into categories. Briefly, types of incentives include:

- *Corporate Policies and Procedures.* Demonstrating organizational support, options such as flextime or time off for achieved goals.
- *Personal Recognition.* Any public or private praise, such as certificates or parties, for having achieved health promotion goals.

FIGURE 7.2. Marketing Techniques for Promoting Health Programs

Tent cards	Telephone tag lines	Gift certificates
Flyers	Computer tag lines	Newsletters
Bulletin boards	Give-away prizes	Electronic mail
Payroll check stuffers	T-shirts	Brochures
Posters	Paper weights	Letters from VIPs
Health fair	Pencils/pens	Skits
Movie certificates	Cookbooks	
Restaurant certificates	Headbands	
	Gym bags	
	Shoelaces	

- *Tangible Rewards.* Free merchandise, rebates, and/or discounts either on-site or provided by outside businesses, for either participation or achieving specific results.
- *Teams and Competitions.* Any group activity that provides social support. Making a commitment to others on a "team" is often a powerful incentive, but the technique should be monitored carefully since unhealthy behaviors should not be used (e.g., starving or eating in an unhealthy manner to win a weight loss contest).
- *Health Care Benefits.* May include reduced health care cost or health "rebates" at the end of the fiscal year
  (Adapted from The Washington Business Group on Health).

Events such as an open house or a health fair can provide learning experiences, increase awareness of health problems, and be a means to advertise current programs. Generally, either type of event attracts a lot of walk-through traffic, some of which probably is not currently involved in health promotion activities. This may create interest in programs or provide information about issues people would like to know. Due to the amount of time required to organize major events, they are usually implemented only on an annual or semiannual basis. If held too frequently, they also lose their effectiveness. Health fairs and open houses should include a wide variety of participants, "freebies," "hands-on," experimental activities, and many types of information. A lot of "outsourcing" (the use of vendors and professionals outside the company from health-related organizations, such as the American Heart Association or a local fitness club) is usually necessary to put together a first-class event.

In the corporate environment, brown bag lunches and informal group meetings can be used. Both are convenient, because they can be held on-site during working hours. On the downside, people may use their lunch time to relax or take care of personal business. Meetings may be difficult to arrange due to scheduling problems or limited space. Lectures can be boring. Health professionals need a constantly changing variety of methodologies to attract the most people. One technique may work one day and fail terribly the next.

Every month, frequently every week or every day, is now some national day (World AIDS Day; Great American Smoke-Out) that can be used to promote health activities while keying in on the advertising already occurring in the media. For instance, February is Black History Month. This might be an excellent time to address health issues of particular concern (such as diabetes or hypertension) to people of color.

Seasonal/holiday events are also commonly used to design programs. Seasonal advertising should be approached cautiously since, depending on the population, special occasions may not be relevant for everyone. The seasonal/holiday promotion can overpower the actual program(s) being offered, especially with all the media promotion surrounding many holidays already. The type of programs advertised should address the issues of the season, however. People are already incredibly busy between Thanksgiving and Christmas. Their *lack* of time and frequent fatigue and overload can be tapped into and be used to increase participation. Quick tips for time management or providing easy ideas for holiday gifts for the whole family (such as roller blades or a gift certificate to the fitness facilities at work) can be invaluable. On the other hand, individuals who have no family may be feeling particularly lonely or isolated. Providing options for holiday activities, such as the names and phone numbers of orphanages or homeless institutions that need assistance gathering toys or feeding people who have no where to go, may initiate activity that would be beneficial to both the receiver and the giver.

TARGETING THE AUDIENCE

Today's market is multicultural and highly diverse. Data indicate that five out of every six people entering the job market now or soon will be nonwhite, female, or a recent immigrant (Hudson Institute, 1987). In 1990, official census figures demonstrated that 12.7 percent of the population was African-American; 11.4 percent was Hispanic; 3 percent was Asian, and 10 percent Native American. Growth rates for proportions of these populations include 110 percent among Asians; 53 percent among Hispanics; 13 percent among African-Americans; and 4 percent among non-Hispanic whites. Along with the cultural differences found within these populations, socioeconomic differences found between white- and blue-collar workers can be profound. Overall, the population is aging, and it is likely more and more workers will continue working past the age of 65. Two-income families and single parents will increase, with many stress-related problems directly associated with these circumstances.

Understanding the diverse needs of the audience can be overwhelming in some circumstances. Behaviors considered appropriate in one culture may be interpreted as rude or cruel by another. Developing programs that target the populations without causing offense and that will inspire participation in any given situation can be challenging.

Targeting the audience is based on really understanding the population. For this reason, health promotion personnel need as much information about the target audience as possible and they need to find ways to relate to them positively. In addition to the standard demographics usually obtainable through a business or organization, other types of data can help develop appropriate, viable programs that people will attend. These types of data include:

- Workstyles
- Lifestyle values
- Race (preferred category)
- Ethnic origin
- Primary language in the home
- Family values
- Regional influences
- Perceived needs
- Preferred method of learning
- Literacy level
- Interests
- Personal characteristics

When a program is not successful, it may be due to things not quickly understood by health promotion personnel. For instance, a contest that has as a reward a trip for two may not foster much interest in an environment that has a population

FIGURE 7.3. Characteristics of Programs That Effectively Target At-Risk* Populations

All information and work is kept confidential.
Mutual trust exists where participants feel supported but don't fear being made to feel
  guilty.
Behavioral approaches are carefully chosen to meet the learning style, level of readiness,
  and expectation of the individual. A variety of approaches are used.
One-on-one individualized programs are used.
"Excuses" are eliminated and neutralized by making access to programs simple without
  involved sign-up processes.
Continual reinforcement is provided via person-to-person feedback.
Programs are focused on specific issue.

*At-risk populations are ones with elevated blood glucose, blood pressure, blood cholesterol, triglyceride, body fat,
tobacco users, and diabetics.   (Adapted from Harris and West, 1994.)

that values large families. Being able to take only two family members on a trip may
be viewed as a problem. Highly competitive games may not be as successful among
a population that values the success of the group over individual achievement. An
environment where employees tend to view management with distrust may not feel
like the company is really concerned about their welfare and will resist attempts to
"force" them to cooperate or be involved in management-sponsored programs.

   In most culturally diverse environments, a "menu" of activities, learning
opportunities, and types of interaction are vital. Understanding the population as
individuals, their culture, and being able to interact effectively with them is basic.
Involving as many diverse individuals in planning as possible can be critical in
some situations. Collaboration with group leaders may be essential. In highly
homogenous environments, it should be easier for health promotion personnel to
ascertain needs and direct health promotion attempts toward them.

   People are always unique. What one person loves, another will hate. Even
among different cultural and ethnic groups there is great individual diversity. The
bottom line to successful health promotion planning is to know the audience really
well, design programs specifically geared toward their individual needs, and then
give the programs time to work. If the programs are not as successful as desired,
seek suggestions via personnel contact when possible. Asking people what they
want may not always yield the desired results from a program- or information-
perspective, but it should yield great dividends in creating personal, long-term
relationships. (See figure 7.3.)

DEVELOPING INFORMATIVE/PERSUASIVE MESSAGES

The primary purpose of most advertising messages is to get the attention of the
readers so they will read what is on the paper. Cluttered media, especially too many
words and pictures, can overpower messages. There is already paper overload in
society, at the office, and in the mail. How much of it does anyone actually read?
Most of it gets thrown away or ignored.

Designing effective marketing pieces can be done, and it can be done at moderate cost. Most advertising will be done in-house. Some rules to remember:

- *Be concise.* Much written information is accepted or rejected within seconds. What needs to be said should be said quickly and in a manner that will initiate action. Carefully chosen words that inspire are the best.
- *Keep graphics simple.* Pictures are rarely necessarily. Simple, eye-catching designs are usually more effective.
- *Mystery can arouse interest.* It's not necessary to give away the whole story with an advertising piece. Advertising should be the hook that pulls people in.
- *If something is working, keep using it.* This is analogous with, "if it's not broken, don't fix it." There is no reason to mess with success just because someone thinks more variety is needed or they are tired of a promotion.
- *Use the word* free *or offer something free when feasible.* Everyone likes a bargain or to get something for nothing. There really are very few things that are free, but offering special gifts as incentives is a help.
- *Use a friendly tone.* It attracts more attention.
- *Talk "one-to-one."* Make the audience feel like the advertising piece is really just for them. Make as personal a connection as possible.
- *Know the audience's "hot buttons."* Include words, graphics, and references that appeal specifically to the audience and to their culture, language, and interests.
- *Address the audience's wants and needs.* That is what they care about. They want to feel like someone cares about them.
- *Make the target population feel like they are getting a bargain.*

Not all of the preceding suggestions can be used in all marketing efforts, but they should be considered guidelines to keep in mind when any advertising piece is being developed. Know the population, keep advertising simple and to the point, and stay up-to-date with health promotion information. If something doesn't work, try something else.

KEEPING CLIENTS SATISFIED AND LOYAL

The ultimate goal of all health promotion efforts is behavior *change*. This means that people have to not only attend initial programs, but they have to take that information and change their behavior by permanently adapting a healthier lifestyle. One way to do this is by continuing to attend pertinent programs that can help them maintain a healthier way of life. Ongoing support of clientele can also contribute to future efforts through one of the most powerful advertising tools—word of mouth.

COMMON DIFFICULTIES ENCOUNTERED IN LONG-TERM PROGRAMMING

Unfortunately, many factors adversely affect both initial and ongoing participation. These include time constraints, inconvenience, lack of energy, failure to achieve personal goals (even if they are unreasonable), and lack of enjoyment in participation. Sometimes people fail to understand the need for permanent change. They lower their blood pressure through exercise and weight loss and then get sidetracked and do other things and lose what they achieved.

Often people look for easier ways to achieve their goals. Weight loss is a common concern, and "easy" weight loss products can be found everywhere. There are products that can be purchased that claim to cause weight loss while sleeping, by washing fat away, and while eating to one's heart's content. Low-fat and no-fat cookies and cakes abound, yet, as a nation, people weigh more and have a higher percent body fat than before such products were introduced. No safe, proven, effective, "easy" weight management system has yet been developed, yet people continue to invest money in one system after another. Some people may experience temporary decreases in weight using various systems, but continuous, long-term managed weight loss has not appeared.

People need to understand that, unfortunately, if they are offered a diamond ring for $1.50, the ring is probably not worth 50 cents. There are no real shortcuts that have demonstrated themselves successful at this time. Maintaining involvement in programs that are challenging when people are constantly being pulled in other, seemingly easier, directions is an ongoing dilemma. Developing and maximizing long-term programs and building loyalty among target populations can be accomplished but requires incorporating multiple strategies and approaches. To begin with, it is important to avoid using approaches that have demonstrated themselves to be unsuccessful over time.

Programs that are run with inadequate staff or resources or programs that are simply not of interest to the target population contribute to failure. It is better to offer fewer interventions that are well done than too many that are poorly done. It is unwise to put too much emphasis on extrinsic rewards. Rewards and incentives are good and they can jump-start people, but, ultimately, unless people are internally motivated, the rewards may not achieve what is wanted. Programs that emphasize rewards and incentives need to also find ways to develop intrinsic desire within their participants in order for them to maintain healthier behavior.

Over time, praising one or two or more highly successful participants can backfire. Building support groups and developing camaraderie among participants while focusing on results, however small, is necessary to make the kinds of long-term cultural and behavioral changes needed for successful projects. Social support can initiate change of its own by providing others to share similar difficulties with and finding inspiration in the acceptance and encouragement of friends.

COMMON STRATEGIES TO ENCOURAGE LONG-TERM BEHAVIOR CHANGE/PROGRAM PARTICIPATION

Situations change, people change, and strategies change. A long-term health promotion program needs to continuously incorporate the latest information, techniques, and strategies available. Information should be based on the latest research and should change according to new discoveries from credible sources. Before conducting massive new programs, it is wise for health promotions people to have "pilot" tests with smaller groups, allowing time for feedback and refinement. Staying abreast of new and changing activities can keep programs alive—as long as successful, familiar programs are not abandoned.

Although environment undoubtedly influences behavior, emphasizing personal responsibility is also a must. Not exercise leaders, educators, company administrators, nurses nor anyone else can do something for someone else. Individuals themselves have to make the change and incorporate new behaviors into their lives; this begins by taking one small step at a time. Health promotion specialists can present the program, but they cannot do the work, and potential and current participants need to understand that from the beginning. At the same time, clients must be empowered by their workplace and those in authority around them to realize they can achieve results.

Win-win approaches are more positive and achieve better results over the long run. This can be done by always emphasizing that participating is a form of winning. Not everyone will, or needs to, achieve world-class results to improve their health, well-being, outlook, and quality of life (DeJoy and Wilson, 1995).

Even though it is impossible to be all things to all people, it is imperative that the health promotion specialist work very hard to establish and maintain a positive, approachable image. Health promotion specialists must be able to develop marketing that pleases people or they will not participate or support programs, no matter how good or useful they are. It is important for health promotion personnel to remember *they* are the strongest form of advertising around. Building positive long-term relationships and personal loyalty takes time and can be difficult, but there are factors that can contribute to achieving this. Other factors that contribute to developing and maintaining loyalty are listed in table 7.1.

TABLE 7.1. Techniques to Assist in Developing Loyalty Among Clientele

1. Relate to clientele as individual people with individual concerns and needs.
2. Really try to help people, rather than just "sell" to them.
3. Reduce what newcomers may perceive as "risk" by making them as comfortable as possible in the circumstance. Going to an aerobics class with a bunch of young, fit people can be terrifying to older, less-fit individuals.
4. Be as honest and straightforward as possible. Don't promise changes that can't be delivered.
5. Believe in what you do and this will translate into the people who hear you.
6. Encourage involvement at every level—from planning to participating to cleaning up. Help potential clientele "own" the program so that it becomes something of themselves and more valuable to them.
7. Make your programs and events irresistible.
8. Never promise anything unless you can back it up.
9. Talk about what your people want and need. Encourage them to tell you what is on their minds, from a health perspective.
10. Actively seek out individuals who will lead and encourage others to participate. Every group has leaders. If the leaders become involved, many of the others will follow.

Profiles in Health Promotion

You are the newest member of a health promotion group that provides services to small companies who don't have in-house wellness programs. Currently this group offers annual HRAs, on-site exercise classes two days a week during lunch or immediately after work, blood pressure and diabetes screening, and one-on-one nutritional counseling as well as quarterly low-fat cooking events. Your health promotion group is looking for a new program that will have a noticeable impact on the various businesses they are currently servicing. You live in a large, metropolitan area where the population is predominantly African-American, with most of the remaining population categorized as white. However, there is a growing Hispanic and Asian population. The businesses are widely disparate in nature. What types of programs would you suggest? Choose one type of program and design the marketing concept for your program including preferred forms of advertising. Describe how you would advertise it (and why) and design a media piece to accompany your campaign.

Check It Out

The health promotion department of the McLaren Lawn Equipment Company is planning to offer a weight reduction program to its fifty-five employees. The program itself has already been developed, but the marketing needs work. As chairperson of the Employee Health Promotion Committee your charge is to develop the strategies to be used to market the program. The marketing campaign will begin in two weeks and will continue until after the program begins a month later. Use the following form to design your marketing scheme.

Timeline:	Week One	Week Two	Week Three	Week Four
Marketing Strategy:				
Techniques to be Used:				

Summary

- Marketing is the planned attempt to influence the market so a voluntary exchange of costs and benefits between the market and the provider occurs.
- Marketing is a powerful key to its success.
- Product marketing is composed of four P's: product, place, price, and promotion. Each of these components interacts with each other and will vary in importance with time and circumstances.
- Social marketing involves the promotion of "nontangibles," such as ideas, attitudes, and lifestyles.
- The focus of social marketing plans is to initiate some type of change.
- The types of change involved in health promotion social marketing attempts are cognitive change (a change in knowledge); action change (initiating a short-term activity); behavior change (permanently altering some form of behavior); and value change (a shift in a basic belief).
- Marketing strategies will vary.
- A program analysis (determining what programs to offer) is based on the needs of the population, the goals of management, and the personal goals of the health promotion program.
- Questions to be considered when designing marketing programs include: What does the population know?, What do they need to know?, What methods of marketing best suit this population?, Is there any material currently available that would be suitable?, What are the costs?, What is the best time period?, How long should the program be?, What is the best format?, Will participants consider the information applicable to them?, and How complicated will it be to accomplish?
- Actual implementation of a program may begin months before the event.
- Phasing in programs has proven the most successful way.
- Phasing in can be accomplished by offering a variety of programs, offering them at different locations, limiting participation, or offering them at different levels. For major programs, pilot testing may be advisable.
- Good programs are the best advertisement.
- Monitoring programs to ensure quality and merit is necessary.
- Common types of health promotion marketing strategies include newsletters, posters, brochures, E-mail, and envelope stuffers.
- Incentives and rewards are particularly effective at the beginning of programs.
- Incentives may take the form of corporate policies and procedures, personal recognition, tangible rewards, teams and competitions, and health care benefits. Seasonal programming and major events such as health fairs should be used carefully.
- Today's society is highly multicultural and what one cultural group will find interesting may be offensive to another.
- Media can be used effectively but is not always easy to develop.

- Guidelines for designing interesting media include: conciseness, simple graphics, using mystery, repetition, offering "free" stuff, using a friendly tone, addressing the audience, knowing the market's "hot buttons," knowing the needs of the market, and making the population feel like they are getting a bargain.
- Programs that last need core clientele who provide repeat business.
- Understanding the market, advertising and addressing their concerns, having good staff members, keeping abreast of the latest health information, and developing good personal relationships where the needs of the individuals are met can build a loyal following.

Bibliography

DeJoy, D. M., and Wilson, M. G. 1995. *Critical issues in worksite health promotion.* Boston: Allyn & Bacon.

Eddy, J. M., and Kahler, H. S., Jr. 1992. *Well now: A manager's guide to worksite health promotion.* Omaha, NE: WELCOA.

Gilbert, G. G., and Sawyer, R. G. 1995. *Health education: Creating strategies for school and community health.* Boston, MA: Jones and Bartlett.

Harris, J., and West, D. 1994. How to reach at-risk employees. *AWHP's Worksite Health* 2(2): 33–35.

Hudson Institute. 1987. *Workers 2000: Work and workers for the twenty-first century.* Indianapolis, IN: Hudson Institute.

Leutzinger, J., and Newman, I. 1995. Using social cognitive theory as a framework for designing medical self-care interventions. *AWHP's Worksite Health* 2(2): 44–47.

McKenzie, J. F., and Smeltzer, J. L. 1997. *Planning, implementing, and evaluating health promotion programs: A primer* (2nd ed.). Boston: Allyn & Bacon.

Pope, J. L. 1993. *Practical marketing research.* New York: American Management Association.

U.S. Bureau of the Census. 1990. Washington, DC: U.S. Department of Commerce Bureau of the Census.

Wunderman, L. 1996. *Being direct: Making advertising pay.* New York: Random House.

CHAPTER 8

Evaluation of Health Promotion Effectiveness

169

OBJECTIVES

Levels of Evaluation

Types of Evaluation: Process, Impact, and Outcome

Selection of an Evaluation Model

Sampling

Quantitative Evaluation

Validity and Evaluation

Qualitative Evaluation

Combining Quantitative and Qualitative Models of Evaluation

Profiles in Health Promotion

Check It Out

Summary

CHAPTER OBJECTIVES

After reading this chapter, you should be able to

- define evaluation and program evaluation.
- list reasons for conducting program evaluation.
- discuss four different levels of evaluation.
- define process, impact, and outcome evaluation.
- describe the steps in selecting an evaluation model.
- distinguish between quantitative and qualitative evaluation.
- describe the principles governing analysis and reporting of evaluation results.

This chapter focuses on evaluation of health promotion programs and how such evaluations are planned and carried out. Making decisions about the approach to take in designing program evaluation can be quite challenging because there are several approaches to choose from. All approaches to evaluation have strengths and weaknesses, advantages and disadvantages; in this chapter we discuss the relative merits of several ways that evaluation can be conducted. Following an introductory section, we present different approaches to thinking about health promotion program evaluation as well as discuss the basic concepts that underlie each. The remaining sections of the chapter cover selection of an evaluation model and design, analysis, and reporting of results.

A basic question that we should deal with right away in this chapter is what we mean by the term *evaluation*. In the context of this text, when we use evaluation we mean a planned sequence of steps or parts that all contribute to arriving at a judgment about the status or value of a program. More formally, evaluation can be defined as the process of collecting information about a health promotion program for the purpose of comparing what is learned with standards of achievement (Green and Kreuter, 1991). In essence, evaluation often consists of determining what has been achieved and comparing achievements with the goals and objectives used in planning the program.

The approach taken in carrying out evaluation depends to a great extent on the needs of the situation. The methods used depend on the nature of the program to be evaluated, as well as what is wanted from the evaluation. It is also important to recognize that evaluation can have many different purposes. For example, evaluation can be used to:

- assess accomplishments or diagnose shortcomings;
- determine the relationship between costs and benefits;
- blunt controversial issues by collecting "objective" data that help make decisions;
- justify promotion, retention, or termination of employees and/or programs;
- maintain, expand, or disband existing programs; and
- provide justification for new programs.

In spite of the fact that evaluation can be costly, it is valuable. The value in evaluation comes from the notion that "rational and objective" use of information is accepted as the best path to making good decisions. Decisions based on experience or intuition often seem less sound than those based on data—and data are collected through evaluation.

LEVELS OF EVALUATION

What should evaluation be focused upon? Are there specific aspects of programs that should be considered in designing evaluation? As it turns out, evaluation can focus on a wide array of targets. A useful way to think about this is to consider evaluation as a process that can be conducted at varying levels. Four different levels for evaluation of worksite health promotion programs, ranging from simple to complex (see figure 8.1), include **activity, standards, efficiency,** and **effectiveness** (Blum, 1974).

FIGURE 8.1. Four Levels of Evaluation as Applied to an Employee Fitness Program Adapted from Blum, 1974.

Level of Evaluation	Name	Task(s) for the level
Four	Effectiveness	Examine whether the program is achieving the goals and objectives formulated during planning.
Three	Efficiency	Analyze whether the number of participants served by the program is sufficient to justify costs (staff, facilities, supplied, etc.).
Two	Standards	Determine whether the program staff have the needed certification(s) ensuring that they are trained to provide the program.
One	Activity	Assess whether the program is functioning as planned.

Activity

Program activity is very general and means collecting information that reflects whether the program is going on as planned, in the most general sense. For example, if a program is intended to provide fitness classes for employees, are such classes offered under circumstances where employees can participate? Are the classes offered at convenient times? Are the facilities appropriate for employee needs?

Standards

Evaluation focusing on meeting minimum standards takes the activity level previously described and adds on an assessment of whether the activities are working in the right direction. For the fitness classes example, standards evaluation could focus on staff qualifications and could ask whether the staff have the necessary training to conduct classes safely.

Efficiency

Evaluation focused on efficiency inquires about the relative balance of outcomes from the program and the resources invested. An efficient employee fitness program, for example, would serve many employees with a relatively small staff.

Effectiveness

Effectiveness is probably the most familiar level of evaluation. Effectiveness evaluation asks if the program activities are producing the results promised. An employee fitness program could be considered effective if the proportion of overweight employees in the workforce was reduced.

The levels of evaluation just described give rise to an important concept. The level of evaluation should be closely matched with the type of information needed or required by those asking for evaluation. Evaluation that is carried out on levels one, two, and three is relatively simple compared with evaluation at level four. In many cases, those asking for evaluation of health promotion programs at the worksite want information that fits with levels one, two, and three, because these levels address common management issues such as cost, lost time, and absenteeism.

TYPES OF EVALUATION: PROCESS, IMPACT, AND OUTCOME

Process, impact, and outcome are variations on the basic theme that underlies evaluation. The basic theme is that evaluation should capture information that reflects how a health promotion program functions and what it produces. The term *process* is used to identify the activities that occur as routine parts of the program (how a health promotion program functions). *Impact* and *outcome,* on the other hand,

FIGURE 8.2. Process, Impact, and Outcome Evaluation of a Worksite Breast Cancer Education and Screening Program

Program Objectives	• To increase awareness and knowledge of breast cancer screening
	• To increase the proportion of women age 50 and older who have annual mammograms
	• To reduce health care costs associated with breast cancer
Program Activities	• Distribute breast cancer education materials for six month
	• Provide workshops for women during breaks and after hours
	• Publicize opportunities to phone health promotion program for additional information
Evaluation Measures	
Process	• Educational materials have been distributed to all women
	• Attendance at lunch and after-hour workshops are as anticipated
	• Requests for additional information average 12 per week
Impact	• Knowledge scores on breast cancer quiz given after the workshops
	• Over 83% of eligible women had mammograms in the past year
Outcome	• Health care costs for breast cancer treatment are reduced by 25%

identify two different products of the program. Impact denotes the immediate or short-term effects of the program, whereas outcomes are longer-term effects. It is important to realize that the three types of evaluation are usually used in combination, and not exclusively. Thus, a thorough evaluation of a program would include collection of information on the program and how it functions (process), the immediate changes that occur as individuals participate in the program (impact), and finally, the changes that may occur in the long run after participants have completed the program. Figure 8.2 illustrates how program objectives, activities, and evaluation measures could be related in evaluation of a worksite breast cancer education and screening program.

Process Evaluation

Process evaluation is designed to collect information that reflects on the program's functioning. In the purest sense, process evaluation is intended to find out whether the program was implemented as planned (Gielen and McDonald, 1997). However, process evaluation can also include information that focuses on program development; *formative evaluation,* in other words. Here, we will include formative and process evaluation under the phrase "process evaluation" because both types of evaluation reflect efforts to monitor program activities and not the results from the program.

Impact and Outcome Evaluation

Impact and outcome evaluation focus on the products of the program but differ in terms of degree. Impact is the term that we use here to denote immediate or short-term effects that are associated with the program. Outcomes are program effects that do not occur immediately but are observed, it is hoped, over time. For example, a health promotion program that provided information about screening rates for breast cancer might be able to produce increased awareness of the need for screening merely by publicity and distribution of educational materials. Increases in screening rates would probably require a longer period of time to develop, however, because women only require screening periodically. The information provided by the program would not be needed by all women immediately and might not appear relevant to those who had just received screening. Outcome evaluation criteria such as incidence, prevalence, and mortality from breast cancer, as well as health care costs and loss of work time would require even longer periods of time to observe.

To illustrate how process, impact, and outcome evaluation might be used, let's consider an example of a worksite health promotion program focusing on preventing repetitive motion injuries among sewing machine operators in a textile plant. Repetitive motion injuries include a spectrum of conditions that involve a common mechanism. As susceptible workers use certain joints in repetitive pattern, inflammation and swelling of tendons and muscles can occur. Certain areas of the body, particularly the upper extremities, are most commonly affected. Those afflicted develop stiffness and pain in all of the structures subjected to the stress from the repetitive motion. For sewing machine operators, the pain and stiffness results in loss of motion and a substantial reduction in ability to operate the machinery productively. The company management wanted to reduce lost time due to repetitive motion injuries, and a worksite health promotion program was suggested as a possible solution. The health promotion program provided education to workers about the risk factors and early warning signs of repetitive injuries. It also included ergonomic analysis of workstations and provided suggestions to workers and management to minimize risks through training. For example, workers new to the job were provided training that included modules designed to build skill, as well as muscle strength and endurance. Finally, the program included a component that suggested ways for managers to provide reduced workloads for workers with repetitive injury complaints. The information on repetitive motion injuries was conveyed to employees via printed leaflets inserted in paycheck envelopes, informal workshops, and individual consultation. For managers, continuing education was provided at staff meetings and included information on the mechanism of injury, activities that increased risk of injury, and risk reduction strategies. Evaluation of the health promotion program focused on processes, impact, and outcomes. Process evaluation measures included tracking of the printed materials to determine whether they were received by employees. Additional process evaluation included observation of the informal workshops and continuing education sessions and review of records on repetitive motion injuries maintained by the plant occupational health nurse. Impact evaluation included knowledge assessments of the managers following the continuing education sessions, and brief interviews with employees concerning their awareness and knowledge of repetitive motion injuries. Outcome evaluation focused on tracking medical claims and lost time due to repetitive motion injuries.

Now that we have introduced the levels and targets of evaluation, it is time to consider issues related to how these concepts are to be applied using models of evaluation.

SELECTION OF AN EVALUATION MODEL

What is an evaluation model? In a general sense, models provide guidance by illustrating a process or outcome. Evaluation models function in a similar way by providing a general structure that illustrates how the evaluation should be conducted. There are many different evaluation models, however, and the process of making a choice can be complicated. A useful way to approach the decision about an evaluation model is to consider the following questions:

1. Are there changes that occurred among *individuals* who were exposed to the program?
2. Are there changes that occurred among *groups* who were exposed to the program?
3. What changes in *population trends* over time can be observed?
4. What happened when specific program activities were implemented?
5. *Why* did change occur or not occur as planned?

It is important to recognize that all of the questions just listed are relevant to most program evaluations. Some questions may be more important than others, however, depending on the nature of the program and the reason(s) for conducting the evaluation. It is also important to recognize that although the questions imply different approaches to evaluation, they share at least one common thread. The common thread is the idea that there are expectations of what should have happened because of the program. The basic steps that should be considered in selecting an evaluation model are shown in figure 8.3.

Step 1: Orientation to the Task

The first step in selecting an evaluation model is getting oriented to the task. The program to be evaluated, those who are asking for the evaluation, the setting that the program operates within, the purpose of the program and reason(s) behind the evaluation, and the population that is served by the program are all topics that need to be explored in this initial step. It is important to understand as much as possible about these issues early in the process of selecting the evaluation model because the information collected is likely to rule out some approaches to evaluation and

FIGURE 8.3. Steps in Selecting an Evaluation Model

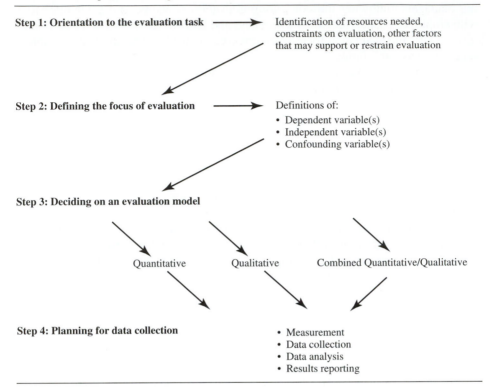

support others. In addition, the resources that are available for the evaluation will become apparent as well as the constraints. Some of the most important answers needed from this initial phase in selecting the evaluation model can be obtained from answers to the following questions:

1. What was expected from the program at the time it was planned?
2. Have expectations changed since the program began?
3. Are there processes or products of the program that can be observed?

Step 2: Defining the Focus of Evaluation

The second step in selecting an evaluation model is particularly important to making a good choice in an evaluation model, because it is the point where a decision about the part(s) of the program to be observed for evaluation will be made. Recall the earlier discussion about levels of evaluation. The information on levels is most useful in this step. It is common to find that the level of evaluation preferred by company managers is different from those who manage the health promotion program. Health promotion program managers' interests often focus on measures of program effectiveness, whereas those of the company may focus on other levels of evaluation. Another consideration in step 2 involves process, impact, and outcomes. For some situations, process evaluation may be emphasized over impact or outcome evaluation. Other situations will focus on impact and outcome and will minimize attention to process. For health promotion professionals, it is important to include process evaluation along with impact and outcomes. The information from process evaluation is needed to determine the strengths and weaknesses of the program activities. Limiting evaluation to impact or outcomes risks missing important information that could be obtained from process measures.

As the program to be evaluated and the general approach to be used become clearer, critical definitions can be considered. The following definitions are central to evaluation:

Independent variable(s)—the program including its component activities that are believed to have impact on participants

Dependent variable(s)—measures that will be used to assess the impact of the independent variable(s)

Confounding variable(s)—factors that could explain changes in the dependent variable(s) other than the program (independent variable)

Step 3: Deciding on the Evaluation Model

Once a clear picture of the program and the expectations of the evaluation have been developed, the decision about the evaluation model can be approached. As figure 8.3 shows, three general models can be adopted: quantitative, qualitative, or a combination of quantitative and qualitative methods. Choosing the quantitative model is perhaps the most traditional approach to evaluation. Quantitative evaluation is based on the idea that program accomplishments are best expressed in terms of **objective, numerical measurement.** The advantage of numerical measurement lies in the ability to use numbers to summarize a large amount of information in succinct, reproducible ways. Qualitative evaluation, on the other hand, focuses on information about the program that is not necessarily numerical. Importantly, the qualitative approach encourages the collection of **subjective information** about the program where there is no desire to summarize information numerically. Qualitative evaluation seeks to *describe* the program and its accomplishments and identify conclusions from assessment of the descriptions. The third model involves combining elements of the qualitative and quantitative approaches in the evaluation model. Choosing one of the paths can be made easier by asking the following questions:

1. *What are the goals and objectives of the program?* Are they expressed in numerical terms or are they "qualities"? For example, are participants expected to behave differently in observable ways or to think or feel differently? Thinking and feeling are qualitative terms; behaving differently in observable ways is more quantitative than qualitative in character.
2. *How are the goals and objectives to be assessed?* If assessment is expressed numerically, then quantitative evaluation is a good choice. If assessment is not expressed in numerical terms, qualitative methods may be the way to go. If the numerical or the qualitative approach fits, then a combination may be indicated.

3. *Does the assessment involve observation, measurement, or both?* Observation would suggest the qualitative approach, measurement the quantitative.

Let's consider an example of how these questions might be used. Recall the example described earlier of the health promotion program to prevent repetitive injuries. One of the main goals of management, and their reason for supporting the program in the first place, was to reduce medical claims (costs) associated with repetitive injuries. Management was clear in their opinion that medical claims data are an objective, measurable indicator of repetitive injuries. Furthermore, they felt that the claims data were sufficiently objective to be used as the means to express the success or failure of the program. This information would strongly suggest that a quantitative evaluation model should be used. Now let's take this example one step further. Suppose the quantitative evaluation using the claims data was completed as planned. Based on the analysis, management concluded that the program worked pretty well, but not as well as expected. At this juncture, they want to know *why* the program functioned as it apparently did. Such situations where evaluation issues are not *how much* but *why* or *how* indicate a need for qualitative evaluation or a combination of quantitative and qualitative evaluation.

In the final analysis, decisions about which evaluation model(s) to use can be influenced by a variety of forces. The needs of those who want the evaluation conducted are obviously important, but other sources of influence include factors such as the source(s) of evaluation data available, access to personnel with the skills needed to conduct the evaluation and, importantly, availability of funds to support evaluation.

Step 4: Planning for Data Collection

Selection of a quantitative, qualitative, or combination evaluation model provides the overall structure needed to plan for data collection. If the quantitative evaluation

Evaluation involves more than physical assessment.

model was selected, then the next steps involve review and selection of the best design for the specific situation. Likewise, for the qualitative evaluation model, there are many different options for data collection. If the combined quantitative and qualitative model is selected, the process of planning for data collection will be more complex than if one of the other models is chosen. Care must be taken to consider not only data collection using each model but also how the models may interact. Regardless of the evaluation model selected, the following questions should be asked and answered in planning for data collection:

1. How will the dependent variable be measured?
2. How will the results of measurement of the dependent variable be expressed?
3. What will be the plan for collecting data, and what resources will be needed?
4. What will be the plan for analyzing the data?
5. How should the results be presented? What resources will be needed to produce needed reports?

Now that we have examined the steps in selecting an evaluation model, we are almost ready to consider specific strategies for collecting the needed information. However, it is important that we first consider a fundamental issue: sampling.

SAMPLING

In a perfect world, the information wanted for program evaluation would be collected from each and every program participant. In other words, evaluation data would be collected from the *population*. In reality, it is rarely possible to collect information from all program participants. Thus, a sample of program participants is usually needed that can provide information about the program. The goal in **sampling** is to develop a plan to identify participants that can provide evaluation information that is closely representative of the information that would have been provided by all of the program participants (the population). The more closely the sample represents the population, the better the estimate of information about the program will be (Kish, 1965; Sarvela and McDermott, 1993).

Several different approaches can be used to select a sample for use in program evaluation. Fundamentally, sampling can be carried out at random or systematically. Within each of these basic categories, it is possible to use additional techniques to simplify the process and to improve the quality of the sample. The choice of sampling methods depends to a great extent on the program to be evaluated, but it also depends on resources available, the type of assessment that is to be carried out, and the population. The sections that follow discuss several different approaches to sampling.

Random Sampling

The word *random* implies that the only rule that predicts whether an individual will be selected from the population is chance. For a random sample, therefore, we can assume that each individual selected had an equal chance of being chosen. For situations where the individuals in the population are similar, a random sample can be assumed to be highly representative of that population.

Systematic Sampling

Systematic sampling means that the selection process is carried out according to a specific rule. In this case, the method is to use a list of all members of the population and to select every kth individual, where k is a whole number. For example, selecting every fifth name from a list would be a systematic sampling process.

Stratified Sampling

Stratified sampling addresses the problem of how to select a sample from a population that has subgroups that must be represented. For example, imagine a worksite where evaluation needs to include employees who work in different departments. If random or systematic sampling were used, we would risk not selecting the desired number of employees from all of the departments. Creating strata, groupings of individuals according to criteria that are of interest (such as departments), and then carrying out sampling within the groups would guarantee that we would select a sample that includes members of each strata.

Cluster Sampling

Cluster sampling is used when it is not possible to list each individual in the population, but it is possible to list groups or clusters. In this case, selecting clusters, at random or systematically, and then selecting individuals within each cluster, again at random or systematically, would provide a sample of the population.

To illustrate the various types of sampling and how they function, let's consider an example. A large industry developed and implemented a health promotion program to increase exercise among its employees. The industry had approximately thirty thousand employees working in fifteen plants. The program was directed at all employees, and each plant added exercise facilities for their employees to use at minimal cost. The task given to the evaluators was very broad: to estimate how well the program worked. Given the size of the employee population, it was not considered feasible to collect data from every employee. To ensure that those included in the evaluation would have been exposed to the program, sample selection was limited to employees who had been with the company for at least one year. The approaches to sampling considered were as follows:

> *Random sample.* Payroll records from all fifteen plants would be merged into a single list and a sample of fifteen hundred individuals would be selected at random. Payroll records were selected for sampling because they include all employees (the population) and the amount of time that each has been working. The probability of selection for each employee would be .05 (1,500/30,000).

Systematic sample. Payroll records from all fifteen plants would be merged into a single list and every twentieth individual on the list would be selected for the evaluation. Selecting every twentieth employee would yield a sample of 1,500 (30,000/20 = 1,500).

Stratified sample. To ensure that each of the fifteen plants would be represented adequately, each plant was considered as a stratum. Random samples of one hundred individuals were selected for the evaluation from each plant. (Note: A systematic sample could have been used within each plant.)

Cluster sample. Concerns about invasion of privacy could bar the use of payroll records to identify employees for the evaluation. In this case, each plant would be considered as a cluster. A random sample of the fifteen plants would be selected, and each employee in the selected plants would be asked to provide information for the evaluation.

In summary, sampling is a process that structures selection of participants for evaluation in situations when it is not possible or feasible to include everyone. In the best case, the sampling process is designed to increase the likelihood that the important subgroups in the population are represented in the sample. When the sample is representative, the conclusions from the evaluation are likely to apply to the population across the board. Now that we have introduced the basic concepts that underlie sampling, let's return to the task of making decisions about how to collect data for quantitative evaluation.

QUANTITATIVE EVALUATION

The quantitative model, as described earlier, uses numerical measurement and "traditional" research design to structure program evaluation. Here we review the basic concepts and designs that underlie quantitative evaluation. The reader should be aware that a huge literature is available on the topic of experimental design, however, and the readings mentioned at the end of this chapter should be consulted for additional information.

Two main concepts must be kept in mind with regard to quantitative evaluation designs. First, evaluation is intended to measure the effect of the **independent variable** (the program) through changes in the **dependent variable.** There can be multiple independent and dependent variables with any program, of course. Second, evaluation designs need to be selected to control for important **confounding factors** (variables). Simply stated, confounding factors get in the way of being able to say that the program was directly responsible for the results that were observed in the evaluation results. For example, evaluation of a worksite health promotion program designed to increase participation in fitness classes might be confounded by differences in levels of fitness-related activity of various groups of employees. If some groups were already exercising regularly, they might not participate in the worksite program. In this case, interpretation of the results of the evaluation would be confounded by the existing fitness activity levels of the workers. If the evaluation design included consideration of current fitness activity levels, then it would be possible to describe the gains produced by the program among workers who were *not* exercising.

Quantitative evaluation designs are based on classic experimentation (Campbell and Stanley, 1963; Cook and Campbell, 1979; Fisher, 1970). Based on the principles that guide the design of experiments, evaluation can be described as "true" experiments or "quasi experiments." The difference between true and quasi experiments rests with the use of random assignment of evaluation participants to various groups. In essence, when random assignment can be used, the evaluation design is stronger than when random assignment cannot be used. In practice, random assignment is often difficult to implement in worksites. As a result, most health promotion program evaluations use quasi-experimental evaluation designs. In the sections that follow, we discuss several of the most commonly used quantitative evaluation designs.

Before-and-After Designs

Perhaps the most commonly used approach to program evaluation is to ask the question "Did the program participants change as a consequence of participating in the program?" To answer this question, information will be needed that reflects their condition before and after they participate in the program. Figure 8.4 below illustrates the before-and-after design. As shown in figure 8.4, the program (X) takes place in the period between the premeasure (O1) and postmeasure (O2). Although the before-and-after approach can be used to demonstrate program effects, it has one overwhelming limitation—the lack of information from a comparison group. Without information from a comparison group, it could be argued that the effects measured could have occurred without the program.

Adding a comparison group (also known as a "control," "comparison," or "observation only" group), to the design (see figure 8.5) expands the scope and the power of the evaluation considerably. To begin with, there are now four groups instead of two, which increases the task of evaluation in general. Second, there is now a group that can reflect changes that occur with the passage of time (between O1

FIGURE 8.4. One Group Before-and-After Evaluation Design

O1 X O2

Note: The notation that will be used in illustrations of evaluation designs is as follows
O = information collection; in figure 8.4, information is collected at two points in time, O1 and O2.
X = program implementation; in figure 8.4, the program is implemented in the period of time between O1 and O2.

FIGURE 8.5. Before-and-After Design with a Control Group

Group 1 O1 X O2

Group 2 O3   O4

and O2) among those who do *not* receive the program. This group provides a standard for comparing the change that occurs in the group that receives the program.

In adding a group that is measured in the exact same way (O3 and O4) as the group that received the program, it is now possible to measure what would happen if no program was provided. The more that the two groups are similar, the better is the estimate of the effects of the program (X).

Evaluation of Trends

An extension of the concept of collecting evaluation information before and after the program is the notion of collecting such information at several points before, during, and after the program is implemented. This approach increases the cost and time requirements for evaluation, but it also provides much more information. Importantly, the added time periods before allow the evaluator to collect information that would otherwise be missed. Figure 8.6 illustrates the trend evaluation approach. As figure 8.6 shows, evaluation information is collected at one point in time before the program is implemented, twice during the period when the program is active, and twice after the program has ended.

A particularly useful aspect of the trend approach to evaluation is that the added information collection points provide opportunities to detect changes associated with the program with greater detail than designs that limit collection to one or two occasions. For example, if the program changes through time, or if the effects of the program do not occur immediately, the trend design would be able to detect such occurrences. It is important to realize that the trend evaluation approach is quite flexible and the timing and number of evaluation points can be tailored to the specific situation. Trend evaluation approaches can also be designed to include comparison groups. The addition of a comparison group provides strength to the evaluation, since it will provide more evaluation data describing changes through time in a group not exposed to the program.

Posttest-Only Designs

A concern with the before-and-after approach is the possibility that measurement carried out before the program could influence measurement that occurs after the program. This phenomenon is called "carryover." The result of this situation would be confusion about which effects detected in the measurement carried out after the program were due to the program, which were due to measurement carried out before the program, and which were a product of both the measurement and the program. The risk of such contamination is increased when the time between the before

FIGURE 8.6. Schematic of a Trend Evaluation Design Without a Comparison Group

Time 1	Program Initiation	Time 2	Time 3	Program Termination	Time 4	Time 5
O1	X==>	O2	O3	<==X	O4	O5

Note: X ==> <==X indicates the period when the program was active.

FIGURE 8.7. Posttest-Only Evaluation Design with Comparison Group

Group 1	X O1
Group 2	O2

and the after measurements is brief, or when the measurement process itself influences program participants.

To counteract these threats, the "posttest-only" designs have been proposed. Also known as "after-only" designs, this approach eliminates the need for measurement before the program is implemented. Of course, if there is no measurement before the program, evaluators must assume that such measurements are not needed for the evaluation. The posttest-only approach is best suited for situations where participants are assigned to groups at random. With random assignment, any characteristics that could influence the evaluation can be assumed to be distributed at random between the two groups. In other words, random assignment means that one can assume that factors that could influence the results of evaluation (confounding factors), including those that the evaluators are not aware of, are as likely to influence those receiving the program as those in the control group. Figure 8.7 illustrates a two-group, posttest-only design.

Before-and-after and posttest-only designs are only the tip of the iceberg when it comes to evaluation designs. A host of experimental designs can be used for program evaluation. However, the concepts that underlie the designs that we have included here are repeated over and over again in more complex designs. The fundamental ideas to remember are that evaluation designs are strengthened by the use of comparison groups and that measurement may influence the results of the evaluation. Without comparative information, evaluation is threatened. Measurement may also influence the evaluation process. It is important to consider the possible effects of measurement and to select an evaluation design that will allow such effects to be minimized—or measured if they cannot be minimized.

VALIDITY AND EVALUATION

An evaluation is valid to the extent that it measures the program's accomplishments in the manner intended. In other words, a valid evaluation collects information about the program with accuracy and in accordance with guidance from the evaluation design. Validity can refer to the activities of the program and their contribution to impact or outcomes, or it can refer to the generalizability of results. The former type of validity is referred to as **internal,** whereas generalizability is termed **external** validity.

Internal and external validity are critical aspects of evaluation, and it is important to consider factors that may influence them. A number of well-known factors influence internal and external validity. The following sections provide a review of these factors.

Factors That Influence Internal Validity

The factors that influence internal validity are characteristics of the components of the program and their interactions with those who participate. The factors include history and maturation, testing and/or the instruments used, selection bias, differential attrition among groups in the evaluation, and regression artifacts.

History

History refers to the unfortunate occurrence where an event or information outside the program is believed to cause effects that are similar to those that the program is supposed to produce. For example, suppose a very well known employee developed breast cancer during the time that a cancer education program was going on at a worksite. It would be difficult to know whether an increase in screening was due to the program, the knowledge of the coworker's disease, or both. If internal validity expresses the extent to which the program actually produced effects observed in the evaluation, then an event such as a coworker's breast cancer becoming known by the women at the worksite could be a potent threat. In summary, events or information that are not part of the program but that may function in the same way as the program are considered "historical" factors. Historical factors can reduce internal validity.

Maturation

Maturation refers to the phenomenon where evaluation information collected over time is affected by "natural" changes in participants. For example, in an evaluation of a health promotion program, workers were assessed immediately after they were hired and again after one year. In this case, the responses of the workers could be influenced by the changes in their understanding of their jobs and the company that develop over the year, in addition to changes associated with the program.

Testing and/or Instrumentation

As discussed previously, it is possible that the information collected during evaluation is due to the reactions to the method(s) used for measurement rather that the intervention. This phenomenon is sometimes referred to as "reactivity," when responses change as a reaction to measurement itself. The effect of this phenomenon is uncertain; it may change responses or it might not. For example, in a survey of alcohol use among workers, it would be likely that responses would be affected by the nature of the subject area and the fact that an employer was asking such questions as much as the content of the questions themselves.

Testing and instrumentation are two different threats to internal validity. *Testing* refers to the impact of collection of information related to evaluation. *Instrumentation* refers to the specific way that the information is collected. As it turns out, clever evaluators can develop ways to collect the information needed so that the threats to internal validity are minimized. For the questions about alcohol use among workers, collection of information by a third party—someone with no connection to the company—would be one way to reduce testing effects. Likewise, collecting information anonymously with assurance that the company would not be able to identify individual respondents would be one approach to reducing instrumentation effects.

Selection Bias (Self-Selection)

Selection bias, also known as "self-selection," occurs when decisions about participation in evaluation, or assignment to groups, are made by the subjects of evaluation. For example, suppose that a health promotion program is offered to employees in a large industry. If evaluation is limited to those who choose to participate, then there is a risk of selection bias. Those who choose to participate probably represent the healthier employees within the population. This type of selection bias has its own name, the "healthy worker effect." Ascribing the characteristics of those who volunteer for programs, or for evaluations, to the population is ignoring selection bias.

Differential Attrition

Attrition is defined as the loss of participants over time. In the context of this chapter, by attrition we mean loss of sources of evaluation information over time. In many instances, evaluation designs are used where participants are considered in groups, intervention or control, for example. When attrition occurs unevenly across groups (differentially), the estimates of program effects may be distorted. In general, any source of influence that distorts the comparison of groups works against internal validity. Losses of participants through attrition result in less information for the evaluation as a whole.

Regression Artifacts

In this context, regression artifacts refer to the general phenomenon called "regression to the mean." Regression to the mean occurs when one measurement results in values that are far different from what was expected. In this instance, what was expected is described as the "mean." When regression to the mean is suspected to have occurred, it is based on the presumption that if measurement was repeated, the result would be closer to what was expected (the mean). How does regression to the mean threaten the internal validity of evaluation of worksite health promotion programs? When results from evaluation are wildly different from what was expected, and there is no effort made to confirm that the measurement is accurate, the conclusions from the evaluation are likely to be inaccurate.

Factors That Influence External Validity

External validity is the extent to which the results of an evaluation can be generalized. It is important to realize that generalizability can be focused in specific directions, and that as a result, external validity can have "qualifiers." For example, an evaluation of a health promotion program focusing on fitness in a specific type of work setting may have considerable external validity. The external validity would come from the fact that the evaluation design was rigorous, participants were selected in a carefully thought-out sampling plan, data collection used standardized instruments, and so on. External validity would be established for the type of work setting and the methods used in the health promotion program, and the conclusion would be that similar results should be expected in other similar settings using the same types of methods.

Any force that threatens internal validity also threatens external validity. It makes sense that a program that has little internal validity (one cannot be certain that the program produced the effects observed in the evaluation) would also have little or no external validity. After all, if we can't be certain how the program results were produced, we should not expect to be able to repeat them. The main threats to external validity involve selection of those who participate in the evaluation and how the selection interacts with the program and the evaluation methods.

Randomness/Representativeness

External validity is strengthened when evaluation information is collected from a broad spectrum of program participants. It is strongest when all participants contribute information for evaluation, but such occurrences are quite rare. In most cases, we must use information from a sample of participants. When the sample is selected with care and planning, external validity is enhanced. Selection bias, notably the healthy worker effect, is one of the most common threats to external validity of evaluations of worksite health promotion programs.

Selection-Treatment Interaction

Interaction between selection of evaluation participants and the type of program (treatment) being evaluated means that individuals with specific characteristics may react differently to the program than would other participants. For example, a cancer prevention program may have dramatic effects among workers with a personal or family history of cancer. For those with no personal experience with the disease, the program may have much less effect. Selection of evaluation participants to include consideration of experience with the program's subject area may help to reduce bias of this type. On the other hand, using a random sampling approach would include the assumption that all participants have an equal chance of having factors in their lives that will color their reaction to the program.

Testing-Treatment Interaction

Interactions between the evaluation methods (testing) and the program (treatment) can seriously threaten external validity. Such interactions occur when the type of evaluation method used influences the way that the program is perceived. Consider how different the impact might be if we were to evaluate a fitness and weight loss program by physically weighing participants as opposed to having them complete written diet and exercise diaries. Selection of evaluation methods that are well established or even standardized helps to reduce threats to external validity due to measurement.

QUALITATIVE EVALUATION

The qualitative evaluation model is best described in contrast to the quantitative model. Where the quantitative model seeks to measure, the qualitative seeks to describe. Where the quantitative model aims toward assessing outcomes, the qualitative aims to describe the process of producing the outcomes. Finally, where the quantitative model is focused on testing whether the program produced the expected outcomes, the qualitative model asks *why* program outcomes were produced. With these differences in mind, let's review the types of activities that are involved with qualitative evaluation.

Qualitative Evaluation Methods

Several different types of methods are used in qualitative evaluation. For program evaluation, the following methods have great relevance: participant observation, interviews, group techniques, and review of program documents. Most evaluation efforts involve combinations of qualitative methods and are not limited to a single approach.

Participant Observation

Participant observation is perhaps the most commonly used technique for collection of information for qualitative evaluation. In participant observation, the evaluator receives the services of the program just as any other individual would. The evaluator may or may not inform others participating in the program that she or he is actually an observer. Participant observers will record their experiences, observations of other participants, the behaviors of those providing the program, and a review of any tasks that participants are asked to complete or program materials. The conclusion to the participant observation is to provide insightful (hopefully) descriptions of how the program operates and how it affects participants.

Interviews

Data collection through interviews (usually open-ended) with program participants is a second method for collecting qualitative information about programs. The purpose of the interviews is to capture information about the program that cannot be observed. In essence, the interviews are designed to collect the recollections, impressions, and informal evaluation of the program by participants.

In addition to participants, interviews are also commonly conducted with program managers and others who serve as staff. The results from these interviews can be compared with the responses from interviews with participants to compare different points of view about the program.

Group Techniques

Working with groups of program participants, with those providing the program (staff), and perhaps with program sponsors is another commonly used qualitative evaluation technique. Focus groups are probably the best-known technique used in qualitative evaluation. Focus groups are specifically designed to collect unrehearsed responses to predetermined questions. The focus group approach has been used for many years in commercial marketing, and in recent years has been applied to social marketing situations, program planning, and program evaluation. Focus groups are best conducted by an experienced moderator. The focus group participants should also be selected carefully, with the goal of identifying individuals who will be able to provide the needed information in a group setting.

Review of Program Documents

Collection and review of documents or records related to the program is another method of qualitative data collection. Most programs produce a substantial "paper trail" that includes planning documents, position descriptions, budgets, and so on. Documents such as these can provide valuable insight into the program, particularly as related to the goals of the program and decisions made regarding personnel.

COMBINING QUANTITATIVE AND QUALITATIVE MODELS OF EVALUATION

As was mentioned in the previous chapter, the apparent dichotomy in the approach to evaluation between the quantitative and qualitative actually goes to the very spirit and motivation for evaluation. Traditional (quantitative) evaluation is based on the tenets of the scientific method, where precision and consistency of measurement are paramount. These two qualities of measurement occupy their position of importance because perhaps the most basic precept of the scientific method is that good research withstands replication. This means that not only must the conclusions of the original research emerge from the replication but that the methods used must be as identical as possible. Precise, consistent measurement is born of standard methods that are subject to a minimum of interpretation. Adherence to such standards produces findings that are precise but—and this is the other side of the argument—often limited in scope to the point that the process that produced change is ignored

Profiles in Health Promotion

Evaluation can have many uses. Imagine that you are a health promotion manager of a manufacturing company. The company president instructs you to conduct an evaluation of claims for health care. She mentions that the insurance company wants to increase rates next year. You conduct a review of the previous year's claims and find that the most expensive claims were for costs associated with the treatment and rehabilitation of three employees who had heart attacks. All three individuals were men over the age of 50. Two of the men had been with the company for more than twenty-five years, and the third for eighteen years.

After learning the results of your quick investigation, the company president meets with representatives of the insurance company and medical consultants and learns that the population of employees is at high risk of heart attack, and that more of such events are expected. The reasons given are that the employees are mostly male, their average age is 41, about half are smokers, and many are overweight. The company president immediately calls for development of a program to reduce the risks of heart attack and asks you to evaluate its effectiveness. What process, impact, and outcome measures would you focus on in your evaluation? The insurance company carefully suggests that part of the evaluation should include identifying employees who are at greatest risk of having heart trouble. For such employees, they suggest that the company offer them early retirement. Such a strategy will reduce the risk to the company. Do you agree?

Check It Out

A small firm that manufactures laminated countertops was concerned with health risks associated with exposure to dust in the plant. Production of the countertops involves sawing wood and laminate countertop, sanding, and attaching the laminate to the wood with glue. The work produces quite a bit of wood dust, most of which is removed by a plantwide vacuum system. Most of the employees who produce the countertops have minimal education (did not complete the sixth grade), and several do not speak English. The objective of the program was to reduce exposure to dust by increasing use of face masks. The methods developed for use with the plant population included the following: (1) colorful, attractive posters to be displayed in the lunchroom showing a worker using a dust mask; (2) printed information included with paychecks describing the health risks associated with continuous dust exposure; and (3) informal workshops conducted during the first half-hour of the workday once a month. In addition, the employer made certain that approved protective devices (dust masks) were available in several locations throughout the plant. The program was initiated during the fall and was continued through midspring.

1. Describe the overall objective of the program.
2. Suggest ways that the success of the program could be measured.
3. Briefly suggest a quantitative approach to evaluating the program.
4. Describe any confounding variables that may influence the quantitative evaluation.
5. Briefly suggest qualitative methods that could be used to evaluate the program.
6. Do you think that this program would be best evaluated using a quantitative, qualitative, or combined approach? Why?

altogether. If the point of evaluation is to determine the usefulness of the process in producing change, then why change occurred is at least equally as important as how much change occurred. Out of this debate, which has ebbed and flowed for decades, qualitative evaluation has emerged as a legitimate option.

Summary

- Evaluation is the process of comparing program accomplishments with expectations.
- Evaluation can be used for several different purposes.
- There are four different levels of evaluation: activity, standards, efficiency, and effectiveness.
- Evaluation can focus on process, impact, and outcomes.
- Processes are the activities by which the program produces change.
- Impact is the short-term results from the program.
- Outcomes are long-term results.
- Evaluation models include quantitative, qualitative, and a combination of the two.
- The process of deciding on an evaluation model includes a series of steps.
- The basic questions that guide planning for data collection include the following:
    How will the dependent variable be measured?

How will the results of measurement be expressed?
What will be the plan for collecting data?
What will be the plan for data analysis?
How should results be presented?

- Random, systematic, stratified, and cluster sampling are methods of selection for evaluation.
- Quantitative evaluation involves the adaptation of experimental design for program evaluation.
- Quantitative evaluation focuses on collecting objective, measurable information.
- Qualitative evaluation focuses on capturing descriptive information about the program.

Bibliography

BLUM, H. L. 1974. *Planning for health: Development and application of social change theory*. New York: Human Sciences.

BORUS, M. E., BUNTZ, C. G., and TASH, W. R. 1982. *Evaluating the impact of health programs: A primer*. Cambridge, MA: MIT.

CAMPBELL, D. T., and STANLEY, J. C. 1963. *Experimental and quasi-experimental designs for research*. Chicago: Rand McNally.

COOK, T. D., and CAMPBELL, D. T. 1979. *Quasi-experimentation: design & analysis issues for field settings*. Boston: Houghton Mifflin.

DIGNAN, M. B., and CARR, P. A. 1992. *Program planning for health education and promotion* (2nd ed.). Philadelphia: Lea & Febiger.

FISHER, R. A. 1970. *Statistical methods for research workers* (14th ed.). New York: Hafner.

GIELEN, A. C., and McDONALD, E. M. 1997. The PRECEDE-PROCEED planning model. In K. GLANZ, F. M. LEWIS, and B. K. RIMER (Eds.), *Health behavior and health education: Theory, research, and practice* (2nd ed.). San Francisco: Jossey-Bass.

GREEN, L. W. 1977. Evaluation and measurement: Some dilemmas for health education. *AJPH* 67(2): 155–161.

GREEN, L. W., and KREUTER, M. W. 1991. *Health promotion planning: An educational and environmental approach*. Mountain View, CA: Mayfield.

KISH, L. 1965. *Survey sampling*. New York: Wiley.

KOSECOFF, J., and FINK, A. 1982. *Evaluation basics: A practitioner's manual*. Beverly Hills: Sage.

LEVY, P. S., and LEMESHOW, S. 1980. *Sampling for health professionals*. Belmont, CA: Lifetime Learning.

PATTON, M. Q. 1980. *Qualitative evaluation methods*. Beverly Hills: Sage.

PATTON, M. Q. 1982. *Practical evaluation*. Beverly Hills: Sage.

REICHARDT, C. S., and COOK, T. D. 1979. Beyond qualitative versus quantitative methods, in T. D. COOK and C. S. REICHART, *Qualitative and quantitative methods in evaluation research*. Beverly Hills: Sage.

ROSSI, P. H., FREEMAN, H. E., and WRIGHT, S. R. 1979. *Evaluation: A systematic approach*. Beverly Hills: Sage.

SARVELA, P. D., and McDERMOTT, R. J. 1993. *Health education evaluation and measurement: A practitioner's perspective*. Dubuque, IA: WCB Brown & Benchmark.

WEISS, C. H. 1972. *Evaluation research: Methods for assessing program effectiveness*. Englewood Cliffs: Prentice-Hall.

CHAPTER 9

Utilizing Assessment Instruments

<table>
<tr><td>

OBJECTIVES

Validity, Reliability, and Usability: Qualities of Assessment Instruments

Validity

Reliability

Usability

Assessment Instruments in Worksite Health Promotion Programs

Selecting an Assessment Instrument

Profiles in Health Promotion

Check It Out

Summary

</td><td>

CHAPTER OBJECTIVES

After reading this chapter, you should be able to:

- define validity, reliability, and usability of assessment instruments.
- distinguish between concurrent and predictive validity.
- identify characteristics of instruments that enhance validity and reliability.
- describe characteristics of assessment instruments used in worksite health promotion programs.
- list considerations for selecting assessment instruments.

</td></tr>
</table>

In this chapter we present and discuss basic concepts underlying assessment instruments and their application to worksite health promotion programs. The concepts that form the foundation for assessment are important for all phases of program development, but they are particularly relevant to evaluation. As it turns out, much of the worth of evaluation is directly traceable to assessment and to the decisions made about how it is carried out. Assessment instruments that are used in worksite health promotion programs are often paper-and-pencil forms that are designed to record important information about programs and how they function.

A wide array of assessment instruments are used in worksite health promotion programs. Perhaps the most common type of instruments are health risk appraisals (HRAs) that are completed by individuals and focus on providing a personalized assessment of risks to health. Other instruments focus on assessing general health status and more specific health behaviors such as diet. Finally, some instruments focus on very specific behaviors that are important to safety and health in the workplace, such as those assessing behaviors related to back injuries. In this chapter, we review fundamental characteristics of assessment instruments, including validity, reliability, and usability. In addition, we show examples of the most common types of instruments and discuss their use and their strengths and limitations. Finally, in this chapter we address the important task of selecting assessment instruments.

VALIDITY, RELIABILITY, AND USABILITY: QUALITIES OF ASSESSMENT INSTRUMENTS

If the results from an assessment are to be useful, they must have a known level of accuracy. Further, if we want to be able to communicate the results of assessment,

FIGURE 9.1. Characteristics of Valid, Reliable, and Usable Assessment Instruments

Characteristic	Qualities
Validity	Assessment captures the quantities and/or qualities wanted. • A valid instrument "assesses as intended."
Reliability	Assessment is consistent from one administration to the next. • A reliable instrument "measures consistently."
Usability	Process of collecting information with the instrument fits with the environment. • A usable instrument "produces results readily."

we need to be able to describe how the results were derived in such a way that they can be reproduced. In other words, for an assessment instrument to be valuable, it must be able to produce valid information, and do so in a reliable manner. In addition to validity and reliability, assessment instruments need to be usable by the intended audiences. Instruments that are overly complex or lengthy are of limited interest because they won't be used, even if they have the potential to produce valid assessments in a highly reliable fashion. Figure 9.1 summarizes the characteristics of valid, reliable, and usable assessment instruments.

To help focus on the "nitty-gritty" of validity, reliability, and usability of assessment instruments, let's consider an example. Suppose that you find yourself in the position of having to describe the health status of a group of employees. To be more specific, the company management wants to obtain a general sense of the current health status of the employees and the major threats to their future health (risk factors, in other words). The ultimate use of the information will be to identify opportunities for instituting health promotion programs at the worksite. One more thing: the company management wants to minimize the cost of collecting this information by having the employees complete a paper-and-pencil questionnaire— and they don't want to have the employees away from their stations very long. Learning of the company's agenda, you recognize that there are several existing assessment instruments that could be used to collect the needed information. The issue is choosing among them with the goal of selecting the assessment instrument that will collect the needed information accurately, reliably, and with a minimum of disruption to the workplace environment.

VALIDITY

The term *validity* is used to describe the extent to which an assessment instrument functions in the manner intended (Vogt, 1993). What does this mean? The phrase "assesses as intended" means that an underlying plan has guided the selection of information that is being collected by the instrument, and that the information that is collected will be useful. Consider the example of the paper-and-pencil assessment instrument mentioned earlier that is intended to assess the "health status" of the group of employees. What evidence would we require to determine the validity of the instrument? Answering such a question can be approached from several different vantage points. One approach would be to examine the instrument carefully, item by item, and decide whether the information that is collected by the items reflects the depth and breadth of the concept of "health status." Another approach would be to compare the results from the assessment instrument with other health-related information about the employees. If the instrument is valid, there should be a high degree of correspondence between the health-related information and the results from the assessment instrument. For example, employees who have ongoing health problems should have different results on the assessment instrument than employees without health problems. The concept of validity can be approached from several different points of view. That is, there are different types of validity: it can be estimated in terms of the specific content of an instrument, by comparing the instrument with standards, or by seeing how well the instrument discerns among people with different characteristics. In addition, validity can refer to the current situation or it can predict a future condition or conditions. In the sections that follow, we discuss different types of validity. Three concepts to keep in mind as you consider the different types of validity are, first, that validity is not a "yes or no" issue, but rather an issue of degree. Second, validity is an issue that is argued (arguments for and against validity can be made, in other words). Third, the validity of an assessment instrument can be approached from several points of view. The most common approaches to validity are to consider the content of the instrument, the results of the assessment in terms of predetermined criteria, and the extent to which the instrument captures important ideas. Such ideas are called "constructs."

Content Validity

An assessment instrument can be said to have a high degree of content validity when it represents the topic adequately. Content validity is often applied to situations where an assessment instrument is designed to focus on a well-defined area that can be broken down into components. For example, basing assessment on program objectives is a good way to work toward achieving content validity. An instrument that assesses each objective at an appropriate level of depth would have good content validity. For example, an instrument to assess health status might focus on specific components of health such as dietary practices, exercise, exposure to microorganisms, and safety issues. An instrument with good content validity would be one that covers each of these areas. On the other hand, an instrument that was supposed to assess health status but only tapped a few areas would be considered to have less content validity.

Criterion-Based Validity

Criterion-based validity is based on standards that are recognized as being meaningful to the topic that we are trying to assess. For an assessment instrument to have criterion-based validity, it must include items or other components that provide information that can be compared with the criterion. In many cases, the criteria for criterion-based validity are derived from professional organizations, government agencies, or even laws. For example, assessment of a worksite fitness program could have criterion-based validity if it included evaluation of the qualifications of personnel derived from a professional organization such as the American College of Sports Medicine (ACSM). ACSM stipulates training and experience needed for individuals to supervise exercise (Peterson, 1997).

Concurrent and Predictive Validity

Criterion-based validity can reference the present or the future. The terms that are used for these reference points are *concurrent* and *predictive*. Concurrent validity focuses on assessment related to the present, while predictive validity is concerned with the future. The need for concurrent and predictive validity derives from the purpose of assessment. In some cases, the assessment should be focused on performance that is occurring now—currently, in other words. For example, suppose we were concerned with evaluating a program designed to train employees to do cardiopulmonary resuscitation (CPR). Assessment focusing on knowledge of the CPR protocol, the rates of breathing, and ratios of breaths to chest compressions could be based on standards of the American Red Cross or American Heart Association, two organizations that provide standards for CPR training. The association of the assessment with the national organizations would indicate that the assessment had concurrent validity. However, it is clear that just knowing the facts about CPR does not mean that an individual can perform the skills when needed. Thus, a performance test that assesses ability to actually *do* CPR would be more likely to have predictive validity. Again, standards set forth by the American Red Cross or the American Heart Association would provide the basis for claiming predictive validity of the assessment.

Construct Validity

In many cases, assessment instruments focus on interactions among workers, their feelings, or attitudes. These targets of assessment are not qualities that fit within the structures of content or criterion-based validity. Rather, they reflect processes or themes that are complex and do not lend themselves to objective assessment. These qualities are referred to as *constructs* in the parlance of instrument validity. A construct is a theme or process that we can perceive but usually cannot observe directly (Vogt, 1993). Imagine a situation where the focus of assessment is "stress," for example. We can attribute people's behavior to stress, and we can recognize that situations are probably stressful, but we cannot observe stress itself. Stress, in this context, is something that happens within people. Constructs like stress are often the targets of assessment for worksite health promotion programs, however. Such programs may be designed to reduce stress, to "empower" employees through assertiveness training, or to "improve attitudes," and the assessment instruments used to evaluate these programs need to focus on constructs. Hence, the notion of construct validity is derived. Construct validity is the extent to which an instrument assesses a construct.

An assessment instrument can be said to have construct validity when it collects information that describes the theme or process being assessed. Construct validity can be demonstrated by comparing the results from the assessment instrument with a theory or concept that is already believed to be valid. For example, an instrument to assess stress would be considered to have construct validity if it were able to identify individuals who had sought counseling for stress-related conditions. When there is an acceptable definition of a construct that is already known, then a quality exists that can be used as a benchmark validating an assessment instrument.

In summary, the following basic concepts of validity have been presented:

1. A valid assessment instrument collects information that contributes to accurate description of predetermined targets.
2. The extent to which an instrument is valid can be assessed by collection of information that correlates with the target of the instrument.
3. When validity is established through comparison with standards, it is referred to as "criterion-based."
4. Content validity is based on coverage of specific information. An instrument with good content validity includes assessment that covers the information at the appropriate level of depth.
5. Criterion-based validity is based on assessing external components and can be concurrent or predictive. Concurrent validity is based on the here-and-now. Predictive validity focuses on future performance.
6. Validation of some tests cannot be attached to criteria that exist in the real world; rather, these tests are intended to measure a theme or idea. These themes or ideas are called constructs.

RELIABILITY

We have just completed discussing validity, the extent to which an instrument assesses in accordance with expectations. Assessment has another component, however—reliability. A reliable instrument assesses consistently; that is, it elicits responses in the same way in each situation. In other words, if the assessment is conducted with employees in several different departments in a large company, the way that the employees respond is consistent.

Reliability is expressed as the correlation among repeated administrations of the instrument (to the same individuals) or as the correlation of responses to each item in an instrument. Each of these methods expresses the extent to which responses to the instrument are consistent. The interpretation of reliability estimates depends on the context and purpose of assessment. If the instrument is to be used to make a decision where the cost of error will be great, then we would want an instrument with high reliability. Where the cost of error is not high, we may relax a bit about reliability. Consider a situation where employees at high risk of breast cancer are to be identified. If the assessment instrument has questionable reliability, then the errors may result in employees not being screened. In such a case, the reliability coefficient should be at least .80 (Cronbach, 1951, 1970). As a general rule, when reliability coefficients are less than .80, the instrument does not perform in a consistent manner. Such inconsistency may be associated with confusing language that requires interpretations, terminology that is not clear, or complicated directions that are difficult to follow. Any of these factors, or other similar factors, can result in changes in how the same individual might complete an assessment instrument at different points in time.

USABILITY

Usability is the ease with which an assessment instrument can be used in a particular setting. Instruments that have good usability have acceptable levels of validity and reliability, of course, and they are also attuned to the specific characteristics of the worksite population. Assessment instruments with good validity and reliability exist in great number, but usability is highly dependent on the setting. Factors such as the required reading level for an instrument or the complexity of the instrument (skip patterns, etc.) influence usability.

Usability can have a dramatic impact on the validity and reliability of assessment instruments. A lack of usability, one with directions that are too complicated for the worksite environment, for example, introduces error into the assessment process. Some guidelines to consider in evaluating the usability of assessment instruments include the following:

1. How much time will be required for workers to complete the instrument? Will it take so long that they are likely to get bored? Will it take so long that the environment will be disrupted?
2. Is the instrument practical for use in the worksite? Will it apply to all those who are involved with the worksite health promotion program? Is it realistic for this setting in terms of time and equipment needed?
3. Can the administration of the instrument be made standard? Do the directions require interpretation? Could people other than you administer the instrument?
4. Is the instrument appropriate for the setting and the employees? Is it written at the appropriate level of reading? Does it require reading, writing, calculation, or other skills that are beyond those of the average employee? Is it likely to hold the attention of workers?
5. Can the assessment instrument be processed easily to give the information that is wanted? Will the information be easy or difficult to summarize? Are there good reasons for asking each question?

These questions may help you to examine the usability of an assessment instrument. Clearly, usability is not a technical issue; rather, it is an issue of common sense. A usable assessment instrument is one that can collect the information needed in ways that are interesting and well matched to the employees.

ASSESSMENT INSTRUMENTS IN WORKSITE HEALTH PROMOTION PROGRAMS

Now that we have reviewed some of the basic information on assessment instruments, we have a foundation for discussing approaches to assessment used in worksite health promotion programs. Recall that in the evaluation chapter (chapter 8) we presented evaluation as being focused on processes, impact, or outcomes. As it turns out, we can use this same approach in discussing assessment instruments. Some instruments are focused clearly on assessing processes, while others focus on immediate or short-term effects, and still others are concerned with monitoring

One of the chief long-term goals of health promotion programs is to maintain participation.

longer-term outcomes. In rare cases, a single type of assessment instrument can address processes, impact, and/or outcomes. In most cases, however, assessment instruments are more limited in scope. In this text, we have selected several of the most common types of assessment situations that are encountered in worksite health promotion programs and have included representative instruments for each situation.

Health Risk Appraisal

The health risk appraisal (HRA) may be the most commonly used assessment instrument in worksite health promotion programs. As the phrase "health risk appraisal" implies, the HRA is basically designed to collect information about risks to health and provide an appraisal of health status in terms of those risks. The risks identified by an HRA fall into several broad categories, including medical history, lifestyle, stress, and safety and physiologic information. HRAs come in many forms, however, and all do not collect the same type of information. Regardless of the information collected, HRAs function in the same way. The data provided are compared with "standard values." These standard values are provided by National surveys, such as those presented in the U.S. Surgeon General's report, *Healthy People 2000* (Anderson and Staufacker, 1996; USPHS, 1991). By comparing the information that an individual provides, areas where the individual's status is better and worse than the average values can be detected. Using modern computers, messages can then be generated that either congratulate individuals on their health status, or provide information, education, and sources for help in improving areas where necessary.

HRAs can be used to appraise current health behaviors, assess the impact of behaviors on health status, and predict future outcomes as well. The validity and reliability of HRAs depend on the accuracy of information provided by individuals and the standard data that are used to compute health risks. When the standard data are up-to-date and appropriate for the individual, validity is quite high. Reliability is controlled by the consistency of data provided to the program. If a lot of change occurs in the data that individuals provide, the reliability will suffer and is mainly limited by the extent to which the individual reports her/his information accurately. Usability of HRAs is only moderate, however, because individuals are asked to report on a wide range of facts and behaviors. Recall of such information may be incomplete, inconsistent, or both.

An HRA instrument can be obtained from several different sources. The Centers for Disease Control and Prevention (CDC) produced one version for the public domain in 1980 (CDC, 1981), and in 1987 an updated version was released by the Carter Center (Amler et al., 1991). Several private companies also provide HRAs. The version of HRA provided by Action Steps Assessment Programs (ASAP!™) is presented in figure 9.2.

To find out more about the ASAP!™ contact the authors at 611 Ryan Plaza Drive, Suite 700, Arlington, Texas 76011. The E-mail address is ASAP!@hmhs.com.

FIGURE 9.2. **Health Risk Appraisal (HRA) provided by Action Steps Assessment Programs (ASAP!™)** The goals of ASAP™ are to support the individual in her/his efforts to prevent disease, promote productive interactions between the individual and health care providers around key issues of prevention, and to facilitate population-based prevention activities by health care providers, employers, and health plans

---

ASAP!
The next-step HRA

Adult Health Survey

Good Health. We all want it! This survey can help you get it.

1. Last Name, First Name, Middle Initial ....

2. Social Security Number ....

3. Health Plan Number ....

4. Date ....

5. Your Sex M? F? ....

6. Birthdate ....

Questions 7 & 8 are optional. If you answer them, we will give you feedback that is adjusted for your race/ethnic origin where appropriate.

7. Are you of Hispanic origin? ◯ Yes ◯ No

8. What is your race?
- ◯ African American or Black
- ◯ White
- ◯ American Indian or Alaska Native
- ◯ Asian or Pacific Islander
- ◯ Mexican American, Cuban, Puerto Rican or Latino.
- ◯ Other or Mixed Race

FIGURE 9.2. *(continued)*

9. Marital Status:

    ◯ Single (never married)   ◯ Separated or Divorced

    ◯ Married   ◯ Widowed

Questions about Your Medical History

10. Has a doctor ever told you that you have any of the following health problems?

Allergies	◯ Yes	◯ No	◯ Not sure
Arthritis	◯ Yes	◯ No	◯ Not sure
Asthma	◯ Yes	◯ No	◯ Not sure
Cancer (except skin cancer)	◯ Yes	◯ No	◯ Not sure
Diabetes	◯ Yes	◯ No	◯ Not sure
Heart Disease	◯ Yes	◯ No	◯ Not sure
High Blood Pressure	◯ Yes	◯ No	◯ Not sure
High Cholesterol	◯ Yes	◯ No	◯ Not sure
Lung Disease	◯ Yes	◯ No	◯ Not sure
Migraine Headaches	◯ Yes	◯ No	◯ Not sure
Osteoporosis	◯ Yes	◯ No	◯ Not sure
Any other serious illness?	◯ Yes	◯ No	◯ Not sure

(Please specify: _____)

11. Has your doctor given you medication or pills for any of the following health problems?

High Blood Pressure	◯ Yes	◯ No	High Cholesterol	◯ Yes	◯ No
Heart Disease	◯ Yes	◯ No	Diabetes	◯ Yes	◯ No
Lung Disease	◯ Yes	◯ No	Chronic Pain	◯ Yes	◯ No

12. Have you had your blood pressure checked in the past **two** years?

    ◯ Yes   ◯ No   ◯ Not sure

> If you answered yes above, please answer the next two questions. Your blood pressure is given as two numbers (for example, 140/80). Please mark the ovals that best match your systolic blood pressure (the top number) and your diastolic blood pressure (the bottom number).

Systolic Blood Pressure

    ◯ 160 or higher

    ◯ 140–159

    ◯ 121–139

    ◯ 120 or lower

    ◯ Don't know/Don't remember

Diastolic Blood Pressure

    ◯ 115 or higher

    ◯ 105–114

    ◯ 90–104

    ◯ 85–89

    ◯ 84 or lower

    ◯ Don't know/Don't remember

(continued)

FIGURE 9.2. (*continued*)

13. Has your cholesterol and HDL-cholesterol been checked within the past **five** years?

Cholesterol: ⬭ Yes ⬭ No ⬭ Not sure   **HDL:** ⬭ Yes ⬭ No ⬭ Not sure

If yes, please mark the statement that best describes your levels:

Total Cholesterol Level
- ⬭ 240 or higher
- ⬭ 200–239
- ⬭ 181–199
- ⬭ 180 or lower
- ⬭ Don't know/Don't remember

HDL-Cholesterol Level
- ⬭ 60 or higher
- ⬭ 46–59
- ⬭ 36–45
- ⬭ 35 or lower
- ⬭ Don't know/Don't remember

Questions 14 through 25 Are for Women Only:

14. At what age did you have your first menstrual period?
⬭ Before age 12   ⬭ 12–13 Years Old   ⬭ 14 Years or Older

15. How old were you when your first child was born?
⬭ I have never had children   ⬭ 20–24 Years Old   ⬭ 30 Years Old or older
⬭ Less than 20 Years Old   ⬭ 25–29 Years Old

16. How many women in your birth family (mother and sisters only) have had breast cancer?
⬭ 0   ⬭ 1   ⬭ 2 or more

17. How long has it been since your last mammogram (breast x-ray)?
⬭ I have never had one   ⬭ 1–2 years ago   ⬭ Don't know/Don't remember
⬭ Less than one year ago   ⬭ 3 or more years ago

18. How long has it been since your last Pap test?
⬭ I have never had one   ⬭ 1–2 years ago   ⬭ Don't know/Don't remember
⬭ Less than one year ago   ⬭ 3 or more years ago

19. When was the last time your breasts were examined by your doctor or nurse?
⬭ Never   ⬭ 1–2 years ago   ⬭ Don't know/Don't remember
⬭ Less than one year ago   ⬭ 3 or more years ago

20. How often do you examine your breasts for lumps?
⬭ Every month   ⬭ Every few months   ⬭ Rarely or never

21. Are you currently pregnant?
⬭ Yes   ⬭ No   ⬭ Not sure

22. Are you planning to become pregnant in the next year?
⬭ Yes   ⬭ No   ⬭ Not sure

23. Have you ever had a baby that weighed over nine pounds at birth?
⬭ Yes   ⬭ No

24. Have you gone (or are you going) through menopause?
⬭ Yes   ⬭ No   ⬭ Not sure

25. Have you had a hysterectomy?
⬭ Yes   ⬭ No   ⬭ Not sure

FIGURE 9.2. (*continued*)

Questions 26 and 27 Are for Men Only:

26. How long has it been since your last prostate exam?
    - ⬭ I have never had one   ⬭ 1–2 years ago   ⬭ Don't know/Don't
    - ⬭ Less than one year ago   ⬭ 3 or more years ago   remember

27. Was your PSA (prostate specific antigen) level measured at your last prostate exam?
    - ⬭ Yes   ⬭ No   ⬭ Don't know/Don't
    remember

28. When was the last time you had either a rectal exam or a test for blood in your bowel movement?
    - ⬭ I have never had one   ⬭ 1–2 years ago   ⬭ Don't know/Don't remember
    - ⬭ Less than one year ago ⬭ 3 or more years ago

29. Has any member of your birth family had a history of any of the following health problems? (Mark **all** that apply. Leave blank if you don't know.)

	Father/Mother	Sister/Brother	Grandparent
High Blood Pressure	⬭	⬭	⬭
High Cholesterol	⬭	⬭	⬭
Heart Attack (before age 55)	⬭	⬭	⬭
Diabetes	⬭	⬭	⬭
Cancer of the colon or rectum	⬭	⬭	⬭
Overweight/Obesity	⬭	⬭	⬭

30. Considering your age, how would you describe your overall physical health?
    - ⬭ Excellent   ⬭ Very Good   ⬭ Good   ⬭ Fair   ⬭ Poor

31. During the past 3 months, how often has your physical health or emotional problems interfered with what you do at work or at home?
    - ⬭ Not at all   ⬭ Slightly   ⬭ Moderately   ⬭ Quite a bit   ⬭ Extremely

32. During the past 3 months, how often has your physical health or emotional problems interfered with how you relate to your family or friends?
    - ⬭ Not at all   ⬭ Slightly   ⬭ Moderately   ⬭ Quite a bit   ⬭ Extremely

33. During the last year, how many times have you gone to either an emergency room or urgent care center for treatment?
    - ⬭ None   ⬭ 1 time   ⬭ 2 times   ⬭ 3 or more times

34. During the past year, how many days have you missed from work due to personal illness or injury?
    - ⬭ 0   ⬭ 1–2   ⬭ 3–5   ⬭ 6–10   ⬭ 11–15   ⬭ 16 or more

35. Have you received a shot for:

Flu (**last year** during the fall?)	⬭ Yes	⬭ No	⬭ Not sure
Pneumonia (age 65 or older?)	⬭ Yes	⬭ No	⬭ Not sure
Tetanus (in the last 10 years?)	⬭ Yes	⬭ No	⬭ Not sure
Hepatitis B (ever, as an adult?)	⬭ Yes	⬭ No	⬭ Not sure

(*continued*)

FIGURE 9.2. (*continued*)

Health Habits:

36. Do you currently use any of the following tobacco products? (Please answer yes or no for each item. For cigarettes, mark how many per day. Please don't skip any items.)

	Use?	**How many per day?**
Cigarettes:	◯ No ◯ Yes ➡	◯ 1–9 ◯ 10–20 ◯ 21–39 ◯ 40 or more
Cigars:	◯ No ◯ Yes	
Pipes:	◯ No ◯ Yes	
Snuff/Chewing Tobacco:	◯ No ◯ Yes	

37. Do you live or work with anyone who often smokes around you?   ◯ Yes   ◯ No

38. If you used to smoke cigarettes but quit, how long ago did you quit?
◯ I have never smoked   ◯ 6 months–3 years ago   ◯ 7–15 years ago
◯ Less than 6 months ago   ◯ 4–6 years ago   ◯ 16 or more years ago

39. What was the average number of cigarettes per day that you smoked in the 2 years before you quit? (Leave blank if you have never smoked.)
◯ 1–9   ◯ 10–20   ◯ 21–30   ◯ 31–39   ◯ 40 or more

40. Mark the oval which best matches your plans about smoking.
◯ I have never smoked or I do not currently smoke
◯ I have no plans to quit smoking in the next 6 months
◯ I am thinking about quitting smoking within the next 6 months
◯ I am making plans to quit smoking within the next month

41. How many alcoholic drinks do you usually have in a typical week?

◯ I do not drink	**One drink is:**
◯ Less than 1 drink	
◯ 1–7 drinks	1 glass of wine
◯ 8–14 drinks	1 can or bottle of beer
◯ 15 or more drinks	1 mixed drink or shot of liquor

42. Please answer each statement below as it applies to you.
I sometimes feel I should cut down on the amount I drink.   ◯ Yes   ◯ No
Sometimes people annoy me by criticizing me for drinking.   ◯ Yes   ◯ No
I sometimes feel guilty about the amount I drink.   ◯ Yes   ◯ No
Sometimes I have a drink in the morning to get myself going.   ◯ Yes   ◯ No

43. **On how many days** do you exercise *for at least 10 minutes* in a typical week? Exercise includes walking.
◯ 0 days per week ◯ 2 days per week ◯ 4 days per week ◯ 6 days per week
◯ 1 day per week   ◯ 3 days per week ◯ 5 days per week ◯ Every day

44. **How many minutes** do you usually exercise on a typical day? Be sure to count all types of exercise, including walking, even if you do it for short periods of time.
◯ 0 min   ◯ 10 min   ◯ 20 min   ◯ 30 min
◯ 40 min   ◯ 50 min   ◯ 60 min   ◯ Over 60 min

FIGURE 9.2. (*continued*)

45. How hard do you work when you exercise? MARK ONLY ONE OVAL
Very Easy ⊙ ○ ○ ○ ○ ○ ○ ○ ○ ○ ○ ○ ○ ○ ○ ○ ○ ⊙ **Very Hard**
      Stretching Walking Jogging/Cycling/Swimming Running/Stair Climbing

46. Do you lift weights or circuit train 3 or more times each week?
      ⊙ Yes   ⊙ No

47. Do you do stretching exercises 3 or more times each week?   ⊙ Yes   ⊙ No

48. Mark the oval that best matches your exercise plans.
      ⊙ I have no plans to increase my exercise in the next 6 months
      ⊙ I am thinking about increasing my exercise in the next 6 months
      ⊙ I am making plans to increase my exercise within the next month
      ⊙ I already do a total of 30 minutes or more of moderate exercise on 6–7 days each
          week, **or** I do an equal amount of more intense exercise on 3–5 days each week

49. How many servings of fruits and/or vegetables do you eat during a typical **day?**

> **One Serving:** 1 cup **fresh** vegetables; **or** 1/2 cup **cooked** vegetables, peas,
> beans; **or** 1 cup fruit; **or** 1 medium piece of fruit; **or**
> 3/4 cup fruit juice

      ⊙ 1 or fewer servings per day   ⊙ 3 servings per day   ⊙ 5 or more servings
      ⊙ 2 servings per day   ⊙ 4 servings per day   per day

50. How many meals **per week** do you usually eat in fast-food restaurants?
      ⊙ Less than 1   ⊙ 1–3   ⊙ 4–7   ⊙ 8–14   ⊙ 15 or more

51. Using the examples below, mark the oval that best matches how often you choose
      high- versus low-fat foods during a typical day (the typical American range is shown
      for a reference).

Low-Fat Examples:	**High-Fat Examples:**
Lean meats, skinless poultry, fish (not fried), skim milk, low-fat dairy products, fruit, vegetables, pasta, gelatin desserts	Hamburgers, hot dogs, luncheon meats, cheese, whole milk, eggs, butter, mayonnaise, salad dressings (not diet), cakes, pastries, ice cream, chocolate, deep fried foods, many fast foods

Mostly ○ ○ ○ ○ ○ ○ ○ ○ ○ ○ ○ ○ ○ ○ ○ ○ ○ ○ **Mostly**
Low Fat   **High Fat**
                    Average American

52. Mark the oval that best matches your plans about eating low-fat foods.
      ⊙ I already eat low-fat foods most of the time
      ⊙ I have no plans to eat **more** low-fat foods in the next 6 months
      ⊙ I am thinking about eating **more** low-fat foods in the next 6 months
      ⊙ I am making plans to eat **more** low-fat foods in the next month

(continued)

FIGURE 9.2. (*continued*)

53. Mark the oval that best matches your plans about the amount of fruit and vegetables you eat.

- ⬭ I already eat 5 or more servings of fruits and vegetables each day
- ⬭ I have no plans to eat **more** fruits and vegetables in the next 6 months
- ⬭ I am thinking about eating **more** fruit and vegetables in the next 6 months
- ⬭ I am making plans to eat **more** fruit and vegetables in the next month

54. What is your current height (to the nearest inch; without shoes) and weight (to the nearest pound; in light clothing, without shoes)? Fill in your percent body fat if you know it.

Height		Weight	% Fat
Ft.	Inches	Pounds	

55. Mark the oval that best matches your plans about weight loss.

- ⬭ I have no plans to start a weight loss program within the next 6 months
- ⬭ I am thinking about starting a weight loss program within the next 6 months
- ⬭ I am making plans to start a weight loss program within the next month
- ⬭ I am currently involved in a weight loss program

Stress and Life Satisfaction:

56. How satisfied are you with your personal and work life?
- ⬭ Completely satisfied
- ⬭ Mostly satisfied
- ⬭ Partly satisfied
- ⬭ Not satisfied

57. How often do you feel stress in your life?
- ⬭ Seldom stressed
- ⬭ Sometimes stressed
- ⬭ Often stressed
- ⬭ Very Often stressed

58. How well are you coping with stress in your life?
- ⬭ Coping very well
- ⬭ Having trouble coping at times
- ⬭ Coping fairly well
- ⬭ Often have trouble coping

FIGURE 9.2. (*continued*)

59. Mark the oval that best matches your plans for managing the stress in your life.
- ⬭ I have little stress in my life, so I have no plans to work on my stress level
- ⬭ I have no plans to work on my stress level within the next 6 months
- ⬭ I am thinking about working on my stress level within the next 6 months
- ⬭ I am making plans to work on my stress level within the next month
- ⬭ I am currently working on my stress level

60. Do you have family or friends who you can count on for help if you need it?
- ⬭ Yes   ⬭ No   ⬭ Not Sure

61. How often does being angry, irritated, or annoyed affect you in your work and/or your personal life?
- ⬭ Never/Rarely   ⬭ Sometimes   ⬭ Often   ⬭ Almost always/Always

62. During the past 6 months, have you had any periods lasting as long as 2 weeks during which you were so depressed that you had trouble functioning in your job or personal life?
- ⬭ Yes   ⬭ No

63. How satisfied are you with your job?
- ⬭ Very satisfied   ⬭ Somewhat satisfied
- ⬭ Somewhat unsatisfied   ⬭ Very unsatisfied

64. How many hours of sleep do you usually get most nights?
- ⬭ Less than 7 hours   ⬭ 7–8 hours   ⬭ 9–10 hours   ⬭ More than 10 hours

65. Do you often feel tired, even after a good night's sleep?
- ⬭ Yes   ⬭ No   ⬭ Not sure

Safety:

66. On a typical day, how do you usually get to places (for example, to stores or to work)? (Mark only one oval)
- ⬭ Mostly stay home   ⬭ Subcompact or compact car
- ⬭ Walk   ⬭ Midsize or full-size car
- ⬭ Bicycle   ⬭ Truck or van
- ⬭ Motorcycle   ⬭ Bus, subway or train

67. How many thousands of miles will you probably travel this year?
- ⬭ Less than 2000   ⬭ 11,000–15,999   ⬭ 31,000 to 50,000
- ⬭ 2000–5999   ⬭ 16,000–20,999   ⬭ Over 50,000
- ⬭ 6000–10,999   ⬭ 21,000–30,999

68. Do you usually wear a seat belt when you drive or ride in a car?
- ⬭ Almost always (80–100% of the time)
- ⬭ Sometimes (1–79% of the time)
- ⬭ Never

69. How many times in the last month did you drive or ride in a motor vehicle when the driver had perhaps too much alcohol to drink?

⓪ ① ② ③ ④ ⑤ ⑥ ⑦ ⑧ ⑨ ⑩ ⑪ ⑫ ⑬ ⑭ ⑮+

(continued)

FIGURE 9.2. (*continued*)

70. How close to the speed limit do you usually drive?
  ⬭ Within 5 mph of limit   ⬭ 11–15 mph over limit   ⬭ I do not drive
  ⬭ 6–10 mph over limit   ⬭ More than 15 mph over limit

71. How often do you wear a helmet when riding a motorcycle or bicycle?
  ⬭ Does not apply to me   ⬭ 26–74% of the time
  ⬭ 0–25% of the time   ⬭ 75–100% of the time

72. If you spend a lot of time in the sun, do you usually wear a protective sunscreen (SPF 15 or higher)?
  ⬭ Yes   ⬭ No   ⬭ Does not apply to me   ⬭ Not sure

Thanks for filling out this survey!

> This is the end of the survey. Take a minute now to check that you have answered each question. We need all the information to help you. Thank you for taking the time to fill out this health survey and to invest in YOUR health!

See Appendix G. for example of feedback formula.

Assessment of Health Status—The Duke Health Profile (DUKE)

Assessment of health status can be carried out using a variety of paper-and-pencil approaches. Nearly all instruments to assess health status use the same approach. Questions are asked about the various aspects of health, and the responses are processed to arrive at a score. A good example of this type of health status assessment is the Duke Health Profile (DUKE).

The DUKE is a seventeen-item questionnaire that can be completed by individuals themselves or with the assistance of an interviewer. It can be completed by telephone as well. It is designed to assess functional health status during a one-week time period. It is easy to complete, having only three response options for each item. The DUKE has 11 scales, including physical health, mental health, social health, general health, perceived health, self-esteem, anxiety, depression, anxiety-depression, pain, and disability (see figure 9.3).

Validity, reliability, and usability of the DUKE have been established and confirmed through numerous projects (Parkerson, 1996). Usability of the DUKE is quite good. Literate individuals usually require less than five minutes to answer the

FIGURE 9.3. Duke Health Profile (The DUKE) Copyright © 1989 and 1994 by the Department of Community and Family Medicine, Duke University Medical Center, Durham, N.C., U.S.A.

Date Today: _____ Date of Birth: _____ Female: ___ Male: ___ ID Number: _____

INSTRUCTIONS: Here are a number of questions about your health and feelings. Please read each question carefully and check (√) your best answer. You should answer the questions in your own way. There are no right or wrong answers. (Please ignore the small scoring numbers next to each blank.)

	Yes, describes me exactly	Somewhat describes me	No, doesn't describe me at all
1. I like who I am...	12	11	10
2. I am not an easy person to get along with.....	20	21	22
3. I am basically a healthy person.....................	32	31	30
4. I give up too easily...	40	41	42
5. I have difficulty concentrating.......................	50	51	52
6. I am happy with my family relationships......	62	61	60
7. I am comfortable being around people..........	72	71	70

TODAY would you have any physical trouble or difficulty:

	None	Some	A Lot
8. Walking up a flight of stairs..........................	82	81	80
9. Running the length of a football field........	92	91	90

DURING THE PAST WEEK: How much trouble have you had with:

	None	Some	A Lot
10. Sleeping...	102	101	100
11. Hurting or aching in any part of your body...	112	111	110
12. Getting tired easily..	122	121	120
13. Feeling depressed or sad...............................	132	131	130
14. Nervousness...	142	141	140

DURING THE PAST WEEK: How often did you:

	None	Some	A Lot
15. Socialize with other people (talk or visit with friends or relatives)..............................	150	151	152
16. Take part in social, religious, or recreation activities (meetings, church, movies, sports, parties)..	160	161	162

DURING THE PAST WEEK: How often did you:

	None	1–4 Days	5–7 Days
17. Stay in your home, a nursing home, or hospital because of sickness, injury, or other health			

(continued)

FIGURE 9.3. (*continued*)

SCORING THE DUKE HEALTH PROFILE*

Copyright © 1994 by the Department of Community and Family Medicine
Duke University Medical Center, Durham, N.C., U.S.A.
(Revised October 1994)

Item		Raw Score
8	=	____ PHYSICAL HEALTH SCORE
9	=	____
10	=	____
11	=	____
12	=	____
Sum	=	____ × 10 =

To calculate the scores in this column the raw scores must be revised as follows:
If 0, change to 2; if 2, change to 0; if 1, no change.

Item		Raw Score →	Revised	
2	=	____	→ ____	ANXIETY SCORE
5	=	____	→ ____	
7	=	____	→ ____	
10	=	____	→ ____	
12	=	____	→ ____	
14	=	____	→ ____	
Sum		=	____ × 8.333 =	

Item		Raw Score
1	=	____ MENTAL HEALTH SCORE
4	=	____
5	=	____
13	=	____
14	=	____
Sum	=	____ × 10 =

Item		Raw Score →	Revised	
4	=	____	→ ____	DEPRESSION
5	=	____	→ ____	SCORE
10	=	____	→ ____	
12	=	____	→ ____	
13	=	____	→ ____	
Sum		=	____ × 10 =	

Item		Raw Score
2	=	____ SOCIAL HEALTH SCORE
6	=	____
7	=	____
15	=	____
16	=	____
Sum	=	____ × 10 =

Item		Raw Score →	Revised	
4	=	____	→ ____	ANXIETY-
5	=	____	→ ____	DEPRESSION
7	=	____	→ ____	(DUKE-AD)
10	=	____	→ ____	SCORE
12	=	____	→ ____	
13	=	____	→ ____	
14	=	____	→ ____	
Sum		=	____ × 7.43 =	

GENERAL HEALTH SCORE

Physical Health score	=	____
Mental Health score	=	____
Social Health score	=	____
Sum	=	____ ÷ 3 =

PERCEIVED HEALTH SCORE

Item		Raw Score
3	=	____ × 50 =

PAIN SCORE

Item		Raw Score →	Revised
11	=	____	→ ____ × 50 =

SELF-ESTEEM SCORE

Item		Raw Score
1	=	____
2	=	____
4	=	____
6	=	____
7	=	____
Sum	=	____ × 10 =

DISABILITY SCORE

Item		Raw Score →	Revised
17	=	____	→ ____ × 50 =

*Raw Score = last digit of the numeral adjacent to the blank checked by the respondent for each item. For example, if the second blank is checked for item 10 (blank numeral = 101), then the raw score is "1", because 1 is the last digit of 101.

Final Score is calculated from the raw scores as shown and entered ino the box for each scale. For physical health, mental health, social health, general health, self-esteem, and perceived health, 100 indicates the best health status, and 0 indicates the worst health status. For anxiety, depression, anxiety-depression, pain, and disability, 100 indicates the worst health status and 0 indicates the best health status.

Missing Values: If one or more responses is missing within one of the eleven scales, a score cannot be calculated for that particular scale.

seventeen items. Of course, individuals who have difficulty reading are likely to require assistance, and it is recommended that an informed source be available to answer questions in all cases. Scoring of the DUKE can be done manually, or by computer, with guidance from the User's Guide (Parkerson, 1996). The final score on each scale ranges from 0 to 100. Interpretation of scores from the DUKE is helped if you have scores from a reference population. For example, if the DUKE was to be used in assessing results from a program in a particular worksite population, it would be helpful if scores from a sample of individuals employed at the worksite before the program were implemented. These scores would provide a reference point for change that may occur with the program. Comparison of the mean (average) score obtained from the groups would provide the basis for examining any changes that could occur.

Nutritional Assessment

Nutritional assessment is used widely in worksite health promotion programs (Glanz, Sorensen, and Farmer, 1996). Focusing on cardiovascular risk reduction (cholesterol) for the most part, nutrition-related worksite health promotion programs involve assessments that are often quite complex. Worksite programs focusing on nutrition have historically fit into two main categories; those that are designed to encourage behavior change in individuals and those that focus on making changes in the work environment that facilitate changes in diet (Glanz and Seewald-Klein, 1986).

Many instruments are used to assess individual nutritional practices, but the most widely used are based on individual reports of consumption of food and beverages. Figures 9.4 and 9.5 illustrate two of the most commonly used approaches to nutritional assessment; a twenty-four-hour recall and a three-day food record. Note that for each instrument, validity and reliability are highly dependent on the ability of the individual to accurately record the food and beverages that are consumed.

As you might imagine after reviewing the information in figures 9.4 and 9.5, collection of diet/nutrition information can be challenging in the worksite setting. The instruments ask for a considerable amount of detail and are time-consuming to complete. In addition, in many cases an interviewer is required to provide assistance and ensure that the information is recorded appropriately.

In addition to the nutritional assessment approaches shown previously, there has been considerable activity in developing brief instruments. These instruments are designed for use in settings where relatively little time is available for complex assessment—which is typical of many worksite settings. Two examples of these instruments are the Block Screening Questionnaire for Fat and Fruit/Vegetable/Fiber Intake, and the 5 A Day for Better Health instrument (Thompson and Byers, 1994).

The items used in the Block Screening Questionnaire for Fat and Fruit/Vegetable/Fiber Intake are a subset of items from a much longer instrument. The general form of the Block Screening Questionnaire is shown in figure 9.6.

Scoring of the Block questionnaire is designed to provide individuals with a characterization of the category that they fit into. Figure 9.7 shows the scoring and interpretation guide.

FIGURE 9.4. Twenty-four-hour Dietary Recall Instrument

Name:
Interviewer:

I am going to ask you about the foods that you have eaten in the past twenty-four hours. We will begin with the present time and work backwards. Please include any condiments (salt, sugar, ketchup, etc.) that was added to foods. Please give as much detail about how the food was prepared as you can.

Meal (Breakfast, Lunch, Supper, Snack):_____
Time of Day:_____
Foods Eaten   Amount

_____   _____

_____   _____

_____   _____

_____   _____

Meal (Breakfast, Lunch, Supper, Snack):_____
Time of Day:_____
Foods Eaten   Amount

_____   _____

_____   _____

_____   _____

_____   _____

Repeat for as many separate meals as needed for the twenty-four-hour period.

FIGURE 9.5. Three-Day Food Record

Name: _____
Interviewer: _____

Instructions

1. Please record all the foods and beverages that you eat and drink for three nonconsecutive twenty-four-hour periods. At least one of the three twenty-four-hour periods should be a weekend day (Saturday or Sunday).
2. Please write down at the top of the page the day and date of each day that you are recording. Try to use days that are typical for you in terms of food consumption (i.e., don't record consumption if you attend a special event such as a party).
3. Begin each recording day in the morning with your first meal and end it with the last food you eat before you go to bed (do not overlap days). Try to record each food immediately after eating so it will be accurate and complete.

(*continued*)

FIGURE 9.5 (*continued*)

4. Please record the following for each food:
   Time of day
   Meal (Breakfast, Lunch, Supper, Snack)
   Amount using standard household units (cup, slice, tablespoon, ounce)
   Condiments used (salt, pepper, etc.)
   Brand name of store-bought items
   Restaurant name if eaten outside the home
5. For mixed dishes such as casseroles and desserts, record the approximate amounts of the main ingredients. For sandwiches, list the ingredients separately.
6. Please be as descriptive as possible in recording each food and beverage. Include preparation method (baked or fried, for example).
7. Please be as descriptive as possible in recording your eating of the foods and beverages. Indicate how much you ate and drank of each item.

Day 1
Meal: _____   Time of day: _____
Food(s)   Amounts

_____   _____

_____   _____

_____   _____

Meal: _____   Time of day: _____
Food(s)   Amounts

_____   _____

_____   _____

_____   _____

Meal: _____   Time of day: _____
Food(s)   Amounts

_____   _____

_____   _____

_____   _____

Meal: _____   Time of day: _____
Food(s)   Amounts

_____   _____

_____   _____

_____   _____

Repeat for Days 2 and 3.

FIGURE 9.6. The Block Screening Questionnaire. To obtain more extensive dietary analysis, call 510-704-8514, or consult a dietitian. © Block Dietary Data Systems 97á

Your name: _____ **Age:** _____ **Sex:** M   F

Think about your eating habits over the past year or so. About how often do you eat each of the following foods? Remember breakfast, lunch, dinner, snacks and eating out. Mark an 'X' in one column for each food.

	(0)	(1)	(2)	(3)	(4)	
Meats and Snacks	1/MONTH or less	2–3 times a MONTH	1–2 times a WEEK	3–4 times a WEEK	5+ times a WEEK	**Score**
Hamburgers, ground beef, meat burritos, tacos	O	O	O	O	O	_____
Beef or pork, such as steaks, roasts, ribs, or in sandwiches	O	O	O	O	O	_____
Fried chicken	O	O	O	O	O	_____
Hot dogs, or Polish or Italian sausage	O	O	O	O	O	_____
Cold cuts, lunch meats, ham (not low-fat)	O	O	O	O	O	_____
Bacon or breakfast sausage	O	O	O	O	O	_____
Salad dressings (not low-fat)	O	O	O	O	O	_____
Margarine, butter or mayo on bread or potatoes	O	O	O	O	O	_____
Margarine, butter or oil in cooking	O	O	O	O	O	_____
Eggs (not Egg Beaters or just egg whites)	O	O	O	O	O	_____
Muffins or biscuits	O	O	O	O	O	_____
Cheese, cheese spread (not low-fat)	O	O	O	O	O	_____
Whole milk	O	O	O	O	O	_____
French fries, fried potatoes	O	O	O	O	O	_____
Corn chips, potato chips, popcorn, crackers	O	O	O	O	O	_____
Doughnuts, pastries, cake, cookies (not low-fat)	O	O	O	O	O	_____
Ice cream (not sherbet or non-fat)	O	O	O	O	O	_____
					Fat Score =	

(continued)

FIGURE 9.6 (*continued*)

Fruits and Vegetables	(0) Less than 1/WEEK	(1) Once a WEEK	(2) 2–3 times a WEEK	(3) 4–6 times a WEEK	(4) Once a DAY	(5) 2+a DAY	Score
Fruit juice, like orange, apple, grape—fresh, frozen or canned. (Not sodas or other drinks)	O	O	O	O	O	O	_____
How often do you eat any fruit, fresh or canned (not counting juice?)	O	O	O	O	O	O	_____
Vegetable juice, like tomato juice, V-8, carrot	O	O	O	O	O	O	_____
Green salad	O	O	O	O	O	O	_____
Potatoes, any kind, including baked, mashed or french fried	O	O	O	O	O	O	_____
Vegetable soup, or stew with vegetables	O	O	O	O	O	O	_____
Any other vegetables, including string beans, peas, corn, broccoli or any other kind	O	O	O	O	O	O	_____

Fruit/Vegetable Score = [   ]

Do you take vitamins, like One-a-Day or vitamin C?   O Never   O Once in a while
O A few times a week   O Almost every day

FIGURE 9.7. Scoring and Interpretation of Block Screening Questionnaire
©BDDS. Scoring for 1-page BBDS Screener dated 97á

How well are you doing?

How to score your answers:

▶   Check one column for each food.
▶   At the top of each column is a number. Write the number of the column you
      checked, on the right side of the page beside each food.
▶   Add up these numbers, separately for the Meat/Snacks Score and for the
      Fruit/Vegetable Score.

Scoring for the **Meat/Snacks section** of the screener*:

If your score is
0–7:   Your fat intake is very low, probably less than 25% of calories. Congratulations!
8–14:   Your fat intake is about like most Americans, probably between 30% and 35% of
         calories. Experts recommend that it be less than 30%. Try eating some of your
         high-scoring foods less often, and eat more fruits and vegetables.

FIGURE 9.7. (*continued*)

How well are you doing?

15–22: Your diet is quite high in fat, probably higher than the U.S. average of 35% of
calories. Look at the foods you scored highest on. You don't have to give up
your favorites, just eat them less often or in smaller portions. Try lower-fat milk,
low-fat salad dressing. And fill up on grains, fruits and vegetables!

23+:   Your diet is very high in fat, probably 40–50% of calories! Look at the foods you
scored highest on, and eat them less often. Switch to 2% milk, and low-fat lunch
meats and salad dressing. Most of the food you eat should come from bread,
rice, cereals, fruits and vegetables.

Scoring for the **Fruit/Vegetables section** of the screener*:

If your score is

0–10:   You are not eating enough fruits and vegetables! You are probably eating fewer
than 3 servings a day, but experts recommend 5 or more. You may be low in
important vitamins, and fiber. Pick a few fruits or vegetables you like, and eat
more of them. Green salad counts, too, and fruit juice or vegetable juice.

11–12: Your diet is like most Americans—low in fruits and vegetables! You're eating
fewer than 4 servings, but experts recommend 5 or more. Pick some you like,
and eat them more often. Green salad counts, and fruit juice or vegetable juice.

13–15: You are doing better than most people, but you are still not eating 5 servings of
fruits and vegetables every day. Try adding fruit or vegetable juice, or salad—or
just any fruit or vegetable you like.

16+:   You're doing very well in fruits/vegetables, probably around 5 servings a day!
Congratulations! The best score on this screener is 19 or more. Go for it!

Eat a low-fat diet, that has five servings a day of fruits and vegetables.
For a detailed dietary analysis, see your health care provider or dietitian,
or call BDDS at 510-704-8514.

Back Injury Prevention

Back injuries are a consistent source of concern for worksite health promotion professionals. Such injuries often include extensive need for medical assistance, physical therapy, and lost time from the worksite. Some may even result in long-term
disability. Assessment related to back injury prevention often begins with collection
of information that describes the injuries themselves and their effects on workers.
The instruments that are used for this application are focused on specific activities
of daily living that are affected by the injury. Typical components of such instruments include sections focusing on the injury itself, and how it affects different activities. Figure 9.8 illustrates the types of items that are typically included in instruments designed for this type of assessment.

FIGURE 9.8. Back Injury Assessment Instrument

Pain Intensity
__I do not require pain medication
__Pain medication gives moderate relief
__Pain medication gives very little relief
__Pain medication does not provide relief
Personal Care
__The pain does not prevent me from taking care of myself
__Taking care of myself increases the pain
__Pain prevents me from taking care of myself
__I require help from others to take care of myself
__Because of the pain, I do not get out of bed
Lifting
__I can lift heavy weights without pain
__Lifting heavy weights increases my pain
__Pain prevents me from lifting heavy weights
__Because of the pain, I can only lift light weights
__The pain prevents me from lifting

Adapted from (Fairbank, Couper, Davies, and O'Brien, 1980).

Other sections of the instrument include items focusing on walking, sitting, standing, sleeping, sex life, social life, and traveling. Scoring of such instruments is carried out by summing the number of statements that are checked and calculating the proportion compared with the total number of items.

SELECTING AN ASSESSMENT INSTRUMENT

As you can see from reviewing the information provided in this chapter, many different assessment instruments are available. Given the wide array available, one of the issues to be faced is how to select an instrument, or instruments, for a particular situation. Although there are no hard-and-fast rules to guide you in making such decisions, general principles can be applied that will help in this task. The general principles are as follow:

- *What is the nature of the program and the characteristics of participants?* A key factor in deciding on assessment instruments is the nature of the program. Programs that have very specific objectives require assessment instruments that focus on measuring the extent to which the objectives were achieved. For example, a program that is designed to increase fruit and vegetable consumption would require an instrument to measure diet. The characteristics of the participants go hand in hand with the objectives of the program. Are the participants highly literate, or do some have limited reading ability? Do the participants speak, read, and write in English? Are they members of different cultures? Considerations of literacy and cultural issues are critical to selecting an appropriate instrument. For low-literate groups, it may be necessary to administer the assessment verbally, which will require additional resources. For groups who don't use English as their primary language for communication, an interpreter will be needed. In such circumstances, it will be necessary to carefully review the assessment instruments with the interpreter and include the ability to translate the items as one of the criteria for selecting an instrument.

- *What is wanted from evaluation, who wants it, and what do they want the evaluation to show?* The sponsors supporting the program and its evaluation often have specific questions that they would like to have answered by evaluation. For a program in which a mobile van was used to provide low-cost mammography for women at a worksite, it was critical to learn the relative influence of health status and cost on decisions to participate by women. In this case, an instrument that assessed health status in a general sense would be needed.

- *What will be done with the results of assessment?* In some cases, the results of assessment are only used by program sponsors for internal accountability. That is, the results are shared with worksite management and others as an internal document. In other cases, however, the results of assessment will be used directly in making decisions about the program. It is important to learn what the results will be used for in selecting an assessment instrument, and to match the level of detail and sophistication of the instrument with the needs of the sponsors. In some cases, merely counting participants will suffice; in others much more detail is needed.

- *What is the setting in which assessment will occur?* Logistical considerations are always a primary concern in selection of assessment instruments. Instruments that require extensive time to complete will require that participants have

Profiles in Health Promotion

HRAs have many uses. For individuals, they may be used to identify behaviors that increase the risk of disease. For employers, they may be used to identify individuals with special needs. Should an employer have access to the results of HRAs? Consider the following scenario.

Female employees were asked to voluntarily complete an HRA. The appraisal covered many different areas, including family history of disease. One group of items focused on family history of cardiovascular disease. It is well known that a family history increases risk of heart disease. What is less clear, however, is what should be done in cases where women

have increased risk. Recommendations range from cholesterol screening, screening for other risk factors, and changes in diet and exercise. When the women who completed the HRA received their results, it became clear that they were surprised to learn of their increased risk of cardiovascular disease.

Imagine yourself in this situation in the role as a worksite health promotion professional. What would you recommend for the women whose HRAs indicated an increased risk for cardiovascular disease? What about those without any indication that they were at increased risk? How much "faith" should the women place in the results of the HRA?

Check It Out

Use an existing assessment instrument or create one of your own for a sample worksite situation. It should be easier to use an existing assessment instrument than make up your own. That's right, but the established instrument has to be appropriate for the people and the setting if assessment is going to be worthwhile. Unfortunately, there aren't any easy ways to decide whether an instrument is appropriate or not. You have to make an "educated guess." To illustrate how you might go making such a guess about whether it is better to use or adapt an existing instrument or make up your own, let's go through the process step by step.

The first step is to identify instruments that could be used or adapted for use in our situation. We can begin by consulting broad-based sources of literature on worksite health promotion. The Internet would be a good place to start. It may take awhile to cover your subject area(s) on the Web, but it is usually well worth the time spent. After tracking down and reviewing promising articles, you will find yourself more familiar with the assessment instrument commonly used in situations like yours.

Once you have found articles that refer to assessment instruments that look promising, the next step is to find out more about the instrument itself. (Only rarely are instruments included in articles.) The article should identify the author(s) for you to contact. Phone calls and E-mail messages are usually the easiest ways to make such contacts. When you contact the author(s), find out about the population that they worked with and decide whether your population is similar to theirs. If it is similar, then their experience with the instrument will probably be a good guide for you. If your population is different, their experience may not provide much guidance at all. Based on this information, you should find yourself in a position to make an educated guess about using the instrument "as is," adapting it to some extent for your population, or deciding not to use it at all.

It is important to know that you need the permission of the author(s) if you decide to use their instrument. Some well-established instruments can be purchased, some are published in entirety and are in articles (they are then in the "public domain"), and some are sensitive and you can't even buy them. Finally, you should realize that it will be necessary to pilot test any instrument that you decide to use or to change for your population.

such time available. At many worksites, time away from one's job means a loss of productivity. Consequently, it is important that the sponsors of evaluation understand what is required for evaluation and that an appropriate level of resources—time away from the workstation—be available. In the best situations, the assessment instruments are selected to match the time available for completion as closely as possible.

Summary

- This chapter has presented an overview of assessment instruments that can be used in evaluation of health promotion programs.
- Validity, the extent to which the instrument assesses as intended, is perhaps the most important quality in an instrument. Without a high degree of validity, the instrument will not produce useful results.

- Reliability, the extent to which the instrument performs consistently, is also important for evaluation. Factors that contribute to high reliability are simplicity in design and clear language, both of which minimize the need to interpret instructions and items.
- Usability, the extent to which the instrument will be applicable to the environment where assessment will occur, is also very important.
- The selection of instruments is a key factor in making evaluation successful, and the main point to remember is to match the instrument with the nature of the program, the expectations from evaluation, the characteristics of the program participants, and the setting.

Bibliography

AMLER, R., EVANS, R., JACOBS, T., SCEIGAJ, M., and SLIGH, D (Eds.). 1991. *Healthier People version 4.0.* Atlanta: The Carter Center of Emory University.

ANDERSON, D. R., and STAUFACKER, M. J. 1996. The impact of worksite-based health risk appraisal on health-related outcomes: A review of the literature. *American Journal Health Promotion* 10(6): 499–508.

Centers for Disease Control. 1981. Health risk appraisal. *Morbidity and Mortality Weekly Report* 30(11): 133–135.

CRONBACH, L. J. 1951. Coefficient alpha and the internal structure of tests. *Psychometrika* 16: 297–334.

CRONBACH, L. J. 1970. *Essentials of psychological testing* (3rd ed.). New York: Harper and Row.

FAIRBANKS, J. C. T., COUPER, J., DAVIES, J. B., and O'BRIEN, J. P. 1980. The Oswestry low back pain disability questionnaire. *Physiotherapy* 66: 272.

GLANZ, K., and SEEWALD-KLEIN, T. 1986. Nutrition at the worksite: an overview. *Journal of Nutrition Education* 18(Suppl 1): S1–S12.

GLANZ, K., SORENSEN, G., and FARMER, A. 1996. The Health Impact of Worksite Nutrition and Cholesterol Intervention Programs. *American Journal Health Promotion* 10(6): 453–470.

PARKERSON, G. R. 1996. *User's guide for the Duke Health Profile (DUKE).* Durham, NC: Department of Community and Family Medicine, Duke University Medical Center.

PETERSON, J. A. (Ed.). 1997. *ACSM's health/fitness facility standards & guidelines* (2nd ed.). Champaign, IL: Human Kinetics Press.

THOMPSON, F. E., and BYERS, T. 1994. Dietary assessment resource manual. 1994. *Journal of Nutrition* 124(115): 2296S–2305S.

USPHS. 1991. *Healthy People 2000: National health promotion and disease prevention objectives.* Publication (PHS) 91-50212. Washington, DC: U.S. Department of Health and Human Services.

VOGT, W. P. 1993. *Dictionary of statistics and methodology: A nontechnical guide for the social sciences.* Newbury Park, CA: Sage.

Appendix A:
Web Sites for Health Promotion

HEALTH PROMOTION–RELATED WEB SITES

American Cancer Society
http://www.cancer.org/frames.html

American Diabetic Association
http://www.diabetes.org/default.htm

The American Medical Association
http://www.ama-assn.org

American Psychological Association
http://www.apa.org/

Association for Worksite Health Promotion
http://www.awhp.com

Center for Disease Control
http://www.cdc.gov/

C. Everett Koop's Shapeup America
http://www.shapeup.org/sua

Change Assessment Research Project
http://firenza.uh.edu/Departments.htmid/psychology.htmid/change/change

Dietary Guidelines for Americans
http://www.odphp.dhhs.gov/pubs/dietguid/defai;t.htm

Duke University's Healthy Devil On-Line
http://h-devil-www.mc.duke.edu/h-devil

Emory University Resources
http://www.cc.emory.edu/WHSCL/medweb.html

Federal Government—Statistical Data
Fedstatshttp://www.fedstats.gov

Fitness Link
http://www.fitnesslink.com

Gatorade Sport Science Institute
http://www.gssiweb.com

Harvard Medical Web
http://www.med.harvard.edu/

Healing Passages
http://www.healingpassages.com

Health Finder
http://www.healthfinder.gov/

Health Finder Libraries
http://www.healthfinder.gov/libraries.htm

Health and Medical Libraries
http://www.arcade.uiowa.edu/hardin-www/hslibs.html

Human Anatomy On-Line
http://www.innerbody.com

Infoseek Health Channel
http://www.infoseek.com/Topic?tid=1207

Mayo Clinic Health Oasis
http://www.mayohealth.org/

Medscape
http://www.medscape.com

MedScope
http://davidgel.ab.umd.edu/medscope/

OSHA
http://www.osha.gov

National Health Observances
http://www.nhic~.health.org/nho97a.htm

The New England Journal of Medicine
http://www.nejm.org/

Pharmaceutical Information Network
http://www.pharminfo.com/

Reducing Occupational Stress
http://www.workhealth.org/prevent/prred.htm

Surgeon General's Report on Physical Activity
http://www.cdc.gov/nccdphp/sgr/sgr.htm

UC Irvine Health Promotion Center
http://www.socecol.uci.edu~socecol/depart/research/hpc/hpc.html

Welcome to Internet FDA
http://www.fda.gov/

WellTech
http://com/workplacehealth

World Health Organization
http://www.who.com

Your Business Your Health
http://www.siu.edu/departments/bushea/

Your Health Daily
http://yourhealthdaily.com

SEARCH ENGINE WEB SITES

WebCrawler
http://webcrawler.cs.washington.edu/WebCrawler

WWWW—The World Wide Web Worm
http://www.cs.colorado.edu/home/mcbryan/WWWW.html

The Whole Internet Catalog
http://nearnet.gnn.com/wic/newrescat.toc.html

The Well-Connected Mac
http://rever.nmsu.edu/~elharo/faq/macintosh.html

What's Cool
http://home.mcom.com/home/whats-cool.html

EINet Galaxy
http://www.einet.net/

Yahoo
http://www.yahoo.com

Appendix B:
Guidelines for Worksite Health
Promotion Directors

Developed by the AWHP Professional Standards Task Force

The proliferation of worksite health promotion programs over the past two decades has resulted in the maturation of this field into a discipline of its own. As in most emerging disciplines, the development of professional and program guidelines are a prerequisite for defining the profession and ensuring its integrity.

In 1990, the AWHP board of directors recognized the need for development of professional and program guidelines. In 1992, the board appointed a Professional Standards Task Force, consisting of worksite professionals and academics, to begin the process. Due to resource limitations, the task force chose to limit the scope of its initial work to role delineation, guideline development and validation of guidelines for worksite health promotion directors who supervise at least one full-time professional. Information concerning the task force's role delineation and validation work was previously published.

The following guidelines should be viewed as a reference from which worksite health promotion professionals and their programs can be assessed, and quality and professional growth can evolve. The intention behind the development of the guidelines is to provide professionals with a clearer understanding of the competencies that are required to effectively manage a company health promotion program.

At this time, the guidelines are not being used in any context other than providing direction for professionals and their programs. However, the task force believes that these guidelines will provide a basis for future credentialing of individual worksite health promotion professionals. Currently, AWHP is cooperating with other nationally recognized health organizations in an industrywide effort to develop worksite health promotion program standards that may eventually lead to a program accreditation process.

The main functions of the worksite health promotion director are delineated into three broad areas: business management, program management, and human resource management. This delineation provides professionals and employers with a framework for enhancing the overall quality of worksite health promotion programs and the professionals who oversee them.

BUSINESS MANAGEMENT

The health promotion director must be able to implement good business practices, policies, and procedures to operate a successful health promotion program. To accomplish this task, the health promotion director must be able to effectively use technology, understand up-to-date facility design and maintenance plans and procedures, utilize accepted financial management practices, establish internal operating policies and procedures, develop strong communications, assure quality in all areas, use an effective marketing strategy, and provide consistent business planning.

Technological Applications

Technological applications involve selection and utilization of appropriate computer hardware and software programs and other technologies to make the health promotion program more efficient and effective in its operation. To be technologically competent, the health promotion director should be able to:

1. Identify organization and management data needs common to a worksite health promotion program;
2. Select appropriate computer software and other technologies for a worksite health promotion program; and
3. Integrate technological applications into the program design and worksite environment.

Facility and Equipment

Management of facility (structures including meeting rooms, resource areas, labs, and exercise areas) and equipment (including educational materials and exercise equipment) involves the ability to establish up-to-date facility design and equipment layout plans and procedures that offer and maintain an environment conducive to stimulating good health. To be competent in facility and equipment management, the health promotion director should be able to:

4. Develop an effective system for inventory control in a health promotion program;
5. Develop an equipment and facility maintenance schedule for a health promotion program;
6. Identify environmental, structural, and legal design issues that facilitate optimum delivery of health promotion services; and
7. Identify appropriate equipment and space needs.

Financial Management

Financial management involves the ability to apply accepted financial management practices to the health promotion program to maintain a consistent program operation. To be competent in this area, the health promotion director should be able to:

8. Use a budgeting process to develop operating and capital budgets for a health promotion program;
9. Present and defend a budget;
10. Interpret financial statements; and
11. Manage a budget.

Organizational Policies and Procedures

Organizational policies and procedures involve the ability to establish standardized policies and procedures that provide for safe, effective, and consistent administration and operation of a health promotion program. To be competent in this area, the health promotion director should be able to:

12. Determine administrative and program policies and procedures in the worksite environment;
13. Integrate a health promotion program's policies and procedures with those of the company;
14. Update policies and procedures based on current standards; and
15. Describe how to adhere to organizational and professional standards concerning confidentiality of information.

Communications

Communications involve establishing a process that provides for the sharing of information, ideas, comments, and complaints among staff, employees and management. To be competent in this area, the health promotion director should be able to:

16. Describe the program in a written form suitable for publication in a newsletter, trade journal, or peer-reviewed publication;
17. Write appropriate management communications (memos and reports) with accepted business-writing form;
18. Describe and demonstrate the oral presentation skills necessary to deliver an effective presentation;
19. Describe different communication styles that can be used with various audiences (such as management, professionals, employees, or dependents);
20. Develop written and/or oral proposals for a budget, program, policy statement, business plan, and marketing plan;
21. Write appropriate marketing communication pieces for a health promotion program (press releases, brochures, newsletters, flyers, and bulletin board announcements);
22. Use a variety of methods to facilitate effective meetings (rules of order, facilitating skills, small-group dynamics, agendas, and minutes);
23. Develop, review and analyze an overall communication strategy; and
24. Demonstrate effective interpersonal communication skills.

Quality Management and Assurance

Quality management and assurance involves a process that establishes a commitment to excellence through efficient and effective task accomplishment. To be competent in this area, the health promotion director should be able to:

25. Develop a strategy that will define for the health promotion program a quality management and assurance process that is consistent with the worksite environment;
26. Define the health promotion employee's role in a quality assurance process;
27. Identify recognized and accepted standards of programming quality;
28. Identify potential liability areas and develop a system for legal and risk management; and
29. Identify and influence the organization's stance on health and safety issues.

Marketing

Marketing involves directing the flow of health promotion goods and services to consumers. The goals of marketing are satisfying customers and meeting the goals and objectives of the organization. To be competent in this area, the health promotion director should be able to:

30. Use marketing analysis to implement appropriate health promotion program offerings;
31. Describe an appropriate marketing strategy for the target population; and
32. Describe how to position the health promotion program in its competitive environment.

Business Planning

Business planning involves using an accepted business-planning process to develop a focused mission statement—with supportive goals and objectives—that results in the ability to effectively manage the short- and long-range operation of the health promotion program. To be competent in this area, the health promotion director should be able to:

33. Define the mission, goals, and objectives of a health promotion program;
34. Develop a work plan, including action steps and policies to carry out the goals and objectives;
35. Develop health promotion program strategies that are acceptable to the corporate population;
36. Establish interdepartmental collaboration;
37. Influence the design of a benefit package to support health promotion;
38. Develop a strategic planning process and direct the development of a departmental strategic plan;
39. Develop a strategic-planning process and influence positioning of a company through health promotion strategic planning;
40. Establish himself/herself as the corporate health promotion expert and advocate;
41. Propose new concepts, directions, and opportunities for health promotion; and
42. Describe how business planning is used for evaluating and refining the health promotion program.

PROGRAM MANAGEMENT

The director of a health promotion program must be able to effectively manage all the activities and services of the program. To accomplish this task, the director must be able to systematically identify, plan, implement, and evaluate the services and activities offered to achieve maximum impact and positive outcomes.

Needs Analysis

A needs analysis involves collecting and interpreting data to determine appropriate program activities and services. To be competent in assessing the needs of his/her constituents, the health promotion director should be able to:

43. Conduct an audit of the organization's priorities and external and internal resources;
44. Formulate a needs-assessment process;
45. Define a target population;
46. Formulate or identify a cost-effective and appropriate needs-assessment methodology;
47. Collect and analyze organizational data related to the development of the health promotion program;
48. Analyze and synthesize the results of the needs assessment; and
49. Summarize and document the results of the assessment.

Program Design

Program design involves developing a plan to meet the goals of the health promotion program and complement the mission of the organization. To be competent in this area, the health promotion director should be able to:

50. Define the program's mission, goals, and objectives utilizing needs-assessment data;
51. Define and prioritize the appropriate mix of services and activities to meet the program's goals and objectives based on the population needs;
52. Identify and interpret the results of important studies and apply those results to program design;
53. Identify relevant model programs and apply the knowledge obtained to program design;
54. Plan a program that complements the organizational culture, structure, and environment;
55. Develop a plan that effectively accounts for action steps, resource allocation, assignment of personnel, and time frames for accomplishing program objectives;
56. Develop a marketing strategy;
57. Design incentive and motivational reinforcements for the program; and
58. Select the appropriate evaluation design that is consistent with the program's goals, objectives and resources.

Program Implementation

Program implementation involves providing program activities and services in a cost-effective and efficient manner. To be competent in this area, the health promotion director should be able to:

59. Implement and follow operational and administrative policies and procedures;
60. Market program services and activities;
61. Deliver program services and activities to assure accessibility and maximum utilization; and
62. Apply process-evaluation procedures and modify the program appropriately.

Program Evaluation

Program evaluation involves evaluating the measurable outcomes and impacts of the activities and services provided by the health promotion program. To be competent in this area, the health promotion director should be able to:

63. Apply the appropriate designs for impact and outcome evaluation;
64. Utilize the appropriate methods of data collection and analysis;
65. Interpret the data, draw conclusions, and make recommendations; and
66. Disseminate the results of an evaluation to the appropriate individuals within the organization.

HUMAN RESOURCE MANAGEMENT

The director of a health promotion program must be able to effectively manage the health promotion professionals who work for him/her. To accomplish this task, the director must understand and possess superior leadership skills. In addition, sound management practices are required to maximize the potential of all personnel. The personnel management skills necessary for the health promotion director include the ability to define to management the needs for personnel, hire the best individuals possible, train and develop the personnel, and provide effective day-to-day management. In addition, the health promotion director must be able to effectively manage his/her own organization and professional and personal responsibilities.

Staffing the Health Promotion Program

Staffing the health promotion program involves determining staff needs related to services and activities provided by the health promotion program and identifying the skills necessary to accomplish these tasks. To be competent in this area, the health promotion director should be able to:

67. Determine staffing needs based on a health promotion program plan;
68. Conduct a job analysis;
69. Write a job description;
70. Develop performance standards;
71. Evaluate candidates for a job;
72. Review applications and resumes;
73. Conduct a job interview;
74. Evaluate references;
75. Obtain the approval to hire;
76. Orient new health promotion employees to the job, program, and worksite culture; and
77. Manage staffing changes using proper legal procedures and policies of the organization.

Train and Develop Personnel

Training and developing personnel for the health promotion program involves providing the appropriate education and experience to assure a high level of competency for the health promotion staff. To be competent in this area, the health promotion director should be able to:

78. Determine and evaluate staff training and development needs;
79. Provide or support training and development opportunities for staff;
80. Promote personal and career development; and
81. Delegate appropriate responsibilities and authority to the staff.

Manage Human Resources

Effective human resource management involves the ability to effectively direct and lead employees' activities. To be competent in this area, a health promotion director should be able to:

82. Establish goals, objectives and a work plan with each employee on at least an annual basis;
83. Provide ongoing feedback to employees and conduct regular performance appraisals;
84. Prepare staff schedules and assign responsibilities;
85. Anticipate and resolve conflicts;
86. Motivate personnel to enhance productivity;
87. Maintain open communication channels between and among management and employees;
88. Utilize appropriate leadership styles for specific situations;
89. Determine the criteria for selection of consultants and vendors;

90. Identify need for consultant and vendor services;
91. Negotiate consultant and vendor services contracts;
92. Identify and comply with company policies and legal procedures relating to consultants and vendors; and
93. Evaluate the performance of consultants and vendors.

Personal Management

Personal management involves the ability of the health promotion director to maintain high standards of performance for all aspects of his/her career. To be competent in this area, the health promotion director should be able to:

94. Develop a personal career plan to promote self development;
95. Model healthy behaviors; and
96. Demonstrate service to the profession and the community.

HOW DO YOU MEASURE UP?

In addition to the guidelines presented above, the health promotion director is expected to possess a bachelor's, master's, or doctorate degree in a field related to health promotion from an accredited institution of higher education. Although the competencies described in this document are management-oriented and, therefore, may require course work or training in business, the activities and services provided by a worksite health promotion program fall in the areas of health promotion and physical fitness. As such, the worksite health promotion director must possess appropriate knowledge in the content areas within health promotion and physical fitness.

The publication of these guidelines represents an important step forward for the worksite health promotion professional. For the first time, a set of guidelines is available that describes the behaviors which characterize individual excellence within this field. We encourage all worksite health promotion directors, and aspiring directors, to use them as a benchmark to evaluate their individual performances.

The AWHP Professional Standards Task Force received financial support from Union Pacific Railroad Co. and American Corporate Health Programs Inc. In-kind support was received from Tenneco, University of Nebraska, MetLife, DINE Systems Inc., Pennsylvania State University, University of Cincinnati and MediFit Corporate Services.

Appendix C:
PAR-Q and Health Histories

Physical Activity Readiness Questionnaire (PAR-Q)

Name of participant_____Signature_____Date_____

PAR-Q and You

PAR-Q is designed to help you help yourself. Many health benefits are associated with regular exercise, and the completion of PAR-Q is a sensible first step to take if you are planning to increase the amount of physical activity in your life.

For most people physical activity should not pose any problem or hazard. PAR-Q has been designed to identify the small number of adults for whom physical activity might be inappropriate or those who should have medical advice concerning the type of activity most suitable for them.

Common sense is your best guide in answering these few questions. Please read them carefully and check the correct answer opposite the question if it applies to you.

Yes No

❑ ❑ 1. Has your doctor ever said you have heart trouble?

❑ ❑ 2. Do you frequently have pains in your heart and chest?

❑ ❑ 3. Do you often feel faint or have spells of severe dizziness?

❑ ❑ 4. Has a doctor ever said your blood pressure was too high?

❑ ❑ 5. Has your doctor ever told you that you have a bone or joint problem such as arthritis that has been aggravated by exercise or might be made worse with exercise?

❑ ❑ 6. Is there a good physical reason not mentioned here why you should not follow an activity program even if you wanted to?

❑ ❑ 7. Are you over age 65 and not accustomed to vigorous exercise?

If you answered **Yes to one or more questions**

If you have not recently done so, consult with your personal physician by telephone or in person before increasing your physical activity and/or taking a fitness appraisal. Tell your physician what questions you answered "yes" to on PAR-Q or present your PAR-Q copy.

Programs

After medical evaluation, seek advice from your physician as to your suitability for

• unrestricted physical activity starting off easily and progressing gradually, and

• restricted or supervised activity to meet your specific needs, at least on an initial basis. Check in your community for special programs or services.

No to all questions

If you answered PAR-Q accurately, you have reasonable assurance of your present suitability for

• a graduated exercise program—a gradual increase in proper exercise promotes good fitness development while minimizing or eliminating discomfort—and

• a fitness appraisal—the Canadian Standardized Test of Fitness (CSTF)

Postpone

If you have a temporary minor illness, such as a common cold.

The Fitness and Wellness Center

Center for Fitness & Wellness

HEALTH HISTORY

Name_____Date_____

Address_____City_____Zip_____

Business Phone (   )_____Home Phone (   )_____

Occupation_____Sex_____Age_____Birth date_____

Employer_____

A. GENERAL

1. Have you had a physical exam in the past year? Yes_____No_____
   If yes, when?_____Physician_____
2. Have you had an x-ray in the past year? Yes_____No_____
   If yes, what was x-rayed?_____Date_____
3. Have you had a serious illness, health problem, or injury in the last TWO years?
   Yes_____No_____
   If yes, please describe:_____
   _____
   _____
4. Please list all medications that you take regularly:_____
   _____
5. Allergies:_____

B. HISTORY

Please check yes or no for each question on your own health history:

Yes	No			Yes	No		
____	____	1.	High blood pressure	____	____	23.	Back pain or injury
____	____	2.	Heart disease	____	____	24.	Hernia
____	____	3.	Chest pain (angina)	____	____	25.	Knee injury
____	____	4.	Rheumatic fever	____	____	26.	Muscle weakness
____	____	5.	Shortness of breath	____	____	27.	Varicose veins
____	____	6.	Emphysema	____	____	28.	Swollen ankles
____	____	7.	Asthma	____	____	29.	Head injury
____	____	8.	Hay Fever	____	____	30.	Severe headaches
____	____	9.	Abnormal chest x-ray	____	____	31.	Mental or nervous disorders
____	____	10.	Lung disease	____	____	32.	Anemia
____	____	11.	Stroke	____	____	33.	Hemophilia
____	____	12.	Dizziness or Fainting	____	____	34.	Sickle Cell anemia
____	____	13.	Epilepsy	____	____	35.	Kidney disease
____	____	14.	Stomach ulcers	____	____	36.	Venereal disease
____	____	15.	Diabetes	____	____	37.	Cancer
____	____	16.	Hypoglycemia	____	____	38.	Muscular Dystrophy
____	____	17.	High cholesterol	____	____	39.	Cerebral Palsy
____	____	18.	Thyroid problems	____	____	40.	Multiple Sclerosis
____	____	19.	Eye problems	____	____	41.	Parkinson's disease
____	____	20.	Ear or hearing problems	____	____	42.	Surgery
____	____	21.	Skin conditions	____	____	43.	Other
____	____	22.	Arthritis				

Please explain all "YES" answers (identify by number):_____

_____

_____

C. WOMEN'S HEALTH

1. Number of pregnancies_____
2. Number of live births_____
3. Complications of past pregnancies?_____
   Complications of current pregnancy?_____
4. Date of last menstrual cycle_____
5. Currently breast feeding?_____
6. Menstrual problems?_____
7. Date of last breast exam_____Date of last pap smear_____

D. HISTORY OF CHILDHOOD OR INFECTIOUS DISEASES:

Yes	No	Immunized	
___	___	___	1. Mumps
___	___	___	2. Measles
___	___	___	3. Rubella (German Measles)
___	___	N/A	4. Chicken Pox
___	___	___	5. Whooping Cough (Pertussis)
___	___	N/A	6. Tuberculosis Skin test result _____
___	___	___	7. Hepatitis type A_____ type B _____
___	___	N/A	8. Herpes
___	___	___	9. Polio
___	___	___	10. Tetanus Date of last booster _____

E. FAMILY HISTORY

	Age, if living	Age at death	Casue death
1. Mother	_____	_____	_____
2. Father	_____	_____	_____
3. Maternal grandmother	_____	_____	_____
4. Maternal grandfather	_____	_____	_____
5. Paternal grandmother	_____	_____	_____
6. Paternal grandfather	_____	_____	_____
7. Sibling	_____	_____	_____
8. Sibling	_____	_____	

9. Is there a history of the following in your family?

_____Heart disease   _____High blood pressure   _____Stroke

_____Diabetes   _____Cancer   _____Arthritis

_____Kidney disease   _____Tuberculosis   _____Other:_____

F. HEALTH HABITS

1. SMOKING (including cigarettes, cigars, pipe)

_____never smoked   _____used to smoke   _____currently smoke

Years since you quit smoking_____

Years you smoked prior to quitting_____

How many packs of cigarettes per day do you smoke?_____

How many cigars per day do you smoke?_____

Do you chew tobacco?_____ Do you dip snuff?_____

2. ALCOHOL

Do you drink socially? Yes_____ No_____

If one beer = 6 oz. wine = 11/2 oz. liquor, how many drinks do you have daily_____

weekly_____ monthly_____?

3. CAFFEINE

Average servings per day? Tea_____Coffee_____Cola_____

4. DIETARY HABITS

Do you regularly eat any of the following? (3 times a week or more)

_____cheese _____eggs _____whole milk _____skim milk _____margarine _____butter _____fried foods _____processed/canned foods _____sweet snacks _____salty snacks _____red meat: How many times weekly_____ _____meals at fast-food places: How often per week_____

5. EXERCISE:

	Average times per week	Average minutes per session
___Jogging/running	_____	_____
___Walking	_____	_____
___Swimming	_____	_____
___Cycling	_____	_____
___Aerobic dance	_____	_____
___Weight training	_____	_____
___No regular exercise	_____	_____
___Team sport played regularly Specify:	_____	

6. STRESS

	Never	Sometimes	Often	Always
a. Do you feel a great deal of impatience with delays (lines, traffic)?	_____	_____	_____	_____
b. Do you often try to do two things at once, such as eat and read business papers?	_____	_____	_____	_____
c. Does it bother you to watch someone perform a task that you could do faster?	_____	_____	_____	_____
d. Do you feel vaguely guilty when you do nothing for hours or days?	_____	_____	_____	_____

e. Have you suffered a personal loss or misfortune in the past year (such as job loss, divorce or separation, death in family)?

_____yes, one serious loss   _____yes, two or more such losses   _____no

G. Have you ever collected workman's compensation?_____ Are you currently receiving disability payments?_____ If ever in the military, type of discharge:_____

H. Is there any additional health information you would like to add?_____

_____

_____

THE INFORMATION GIVEN ON THIS ENTIRE FORM IS TRUE TO THE BEST OF MY KNOWLEDGE:

_____
(signature)

_____
(date)

Physician Referral_____Yes

_____No

HEALTH HISTORY PRESCREENING EVALUATION
Fitness & Wellness Center—University of Memphis

NAME:_____   MEMBER#:_____

AGE:_____ SEX: MALE ( )   FEMALE ( )   DATE:_____

To find out whether you should consult a physician prior to beginning your exercise program, the following checklist is provided.

PLEASE CHECK(√) YOUR RESPONSES TO THE FOLLOWING QUESTIONS: IF YES, PLEASE EXPLAIN:

Yes   No

( )   ( )   1. Has your doctor ever said you have heart trouble?

( )   ( )   2. Do you have frequent pains or pressure in your chest, neck, shoulder(s) or arm(s) during or immediately after exercise?

( )   ( )   3. Do you have a history of fainting or having spells of severe dizziness?

( )   ( )   4. Has a doctor ever said your blood pressure was high and/or not under control? Or don't you know whether your blood pressure is normal?_____

( )   ( )   5. Has anyone in your immediate family had a heart attack before the age of 50?_____

( )   ( )   6. Has a doctor ever told you that you have a bone or joint problem such as arthritis that has been aggravated by exercise, or might be made worse with exercise?

( )   ( )   7. Do you have a physical or medical condition (i.e., insulin-dependent diabetes) not mentioned previously, which might need special attention in an active exercise program?

_____

_____

( )   ( )   8. Are you over the age of 60 and not regularly engaged in an active exercise program at present?_____

( )   ( )   9. Are you currently taking medications? If yes, please list._____

If you answered *NO* to all questions above it gives a general indication that you may participate in both the fitness testing and an aerobic exercise program tailored to your needs. The fact that you answered *NO* to the above questions does not guarantee that you will have no abnormal response to exercise.

If you answered *YES* to any question above, then you will need a physician's approval before participating in the Living Well Program.

HEALTH HISTORY

Check those boxes that apply to you or your family history. When appropriate, describe.

Personal   Family
History   History

Check the symptoms that currently apply to you.

SYMPTOMS

( ) ( ) Allergy
( ) ( ) Anemia
( ) ( ) Arthritis
( ) ( ) Asthma
( ) ( ) Bladder
        Infection
( ) ( ) Bronchitis or
        Emphysema
( ) ( ) Cancer
( ) ( ) Cirrhosis
( ) ( ) Diabetes
( ) ( ) Ulcers
( ) ( ) Disability
( ) ( ) Gout
( ) ( ) Heart Disease
( ) ( ) High Blood
        Pressure
( ) ( ) Insomnia
( ) ( ) Overweight
( ) ( ) Surgery
( ) ( ) Stroke
( ) ( ) Kidney Disease
( ) ( ) Lung Disease
( ) ( ) Pneumonia
( ) ( ) Rheumatism
( ) ( ) Seizures
( ) ( ) Skin Rashes
( ) ( ) Thyroid, Low
( ) ( ) Thyroid, High
( ) ( ) Other Serious
        Problems_____
_____
_____
_____

(   ) Pain or discomfort in chest after
       exercising, eating, or exposure to cold.
(   ) Frequent heart palpitations or
       fluttering.
(   ) Pain in legs when walking or climbing
       stairs.
(   ) Unusual shortness of breath
       from brisk walking or climbing stairs.
(   ) Poor exercise tolerance
(   ) Dizziness
(   ) Chronic cough
(   ) Cough up blood
(   ) Frequent colds or flu (more than 1/year)
(   ) Frequent headaches
(   ) Frequent aches or pains in joints
(   ) Frequent backache
(   ) Frequent digestive upsets

LIFESTYLE FACTORS

Smoking Status

(   ) Have never smoked
(   ) Have quit smoking
(   ) Smoke pipe or cigar only
(   ) Smoke_____pack(s)/day

Drinking Status (alcoholic beverages)

(   ) Never drink
(   ) Seldom ever drink
(   ) 1–2 time(s)/week
(   ) 3–6 time(s)/week
(   ) Daily

INDICATE MEDICINES YOU CURRENTLY USE.

Birth Control Pills_____
Hormones _____
Sleeping Pills/Sedatives _____
Tranquilizers_____
Thyroid _____
Laxatives_____
Cortisone_____

Blood Pressure_____
Heart Medicine _____
Vitamins _____
Aspirin_____
Other Drugs_____
_____
_____

Appendix D:
Sample Consent Forms

INFORMED CONSENT AND RELEASE

I wish to voluntarily engage in the University of Memphis's Program for Health Promotion and Fitness. I understand that I am free to participate in any of the educational programs, and any questions I may have about my program will be answered by the Health Promotion staff.

I hereby expressly release the University of Memphis's Program for Health Promotion & Fitness and its employees from any and all responsibility or liability to me for injuries that might be sustained while doing any of the exercises or utilizing any of the facilities and equipment of the Program. I also expressly acknowledge that any and all fitness testing undergone was done merely for informational purpose to develop my fitness program and, said testing and the results thereof in no way declare my fitness or lack of fitness for participation in the Health Promotion Program.

In addition, I understand that participation in the exercise programs are contingent upon my truthful responses to the health history prescreening questionnaire. _____(initial)

Participant's Signature	Date

Witness	Date

Witness	Date

INDIVIDUALS REQUIRING A PHYSICIAN'S PERMISSION TO PARTICIPATE

I hereby verify that I have received approval from my physician to participate in the Health Promotion & Fitness Program and a letter of verification is on file with the program office in the Department of Health & Movement Science.

Participant's Signature	Date

****************OFFICE USE ONLY BELOW THIS LINE****************

FORM ON FILE

Verified _____
      Staff Signature   Date

Express Assumption of Risk Form
Fitness and Wellness Center
University of Memphis

I, the undersigned, hereby expressly and affirmatively state that I wish to participate in_____. I realize that my participation in this activity involves risks of injury, including but not limited to _____ (list)_____ and even the possibility of death. I also recognize that there are many other risks of injury, including serious disabling injuries, that may arise due to my participation in this activity and that it is not possible to specifically list each and every individual injury risk. However, knowing the material risks and appreciating, knowing, and reasonably anticipating that other injuries and even death are a possibility, I hereby expressly assume all of the delineated risks of injury, all other possible risk of injury, and even risk of death, which could occur by reason of my participation.

I have had an opportunity to ask questions. Any questions I have asked have been answered to my complete satisfaction. I subjectively understand the risks of my participation in this activity, and knowing and appreciating these risks I voluntarily choose to participate, assuming all risks of injury or even death due to my participation.

_____   _____
Witness   Participant

                                    Dated_____

Notes of questions and answers

_____
_____
_____

This is, as stated, a true and accurate record of what was asked and answered.

                                    _____
                                    Participant

                    To be checked by program staff

                                                        Checked   Initials

  I. Risks were orally discussed.   _____   _____

 II. Questions were asked, and the participant indicated
     complete understanding of the risks.   _____   _____

III. Questions were not asked, but an opportunity to ask
     questions was provided and the participant indicated
     complete understanding of the risks.   _____   _____

_____
Staff member   Dated

Note. The law varies from state to state. No form should be adopted or used by any program without individualized legal advice.

Appendix E:
Addresses of Professional Associations, Organizations, and Health Promotion Vendors

ADDRESSES OF PROFESSIONAL ASSOCIATIONS AND ORGANIZATIONS

Amateur Athletic Union AAU House
3400 W. 86th Street
Indianapolis, IN 46268

American College of Sports Medicine
P.O. Box 1440
Indianapolis, IN 46206

Association for Worksite Health
Promotion (AWHP)
60 Revere Drive, Suite 500
Northbrook, IL 60062

Canadian Association for Health,
Physical Education, and Recreation
333 River Road
Ottawa, Ontario, CN KIL 8H9

Wellness Councils of America (WELCOA)
Historic Library Plaza
1823 Harney Street, Suite 201
Omaha, NE 68102

Washington Business Group on Health
777 N. Capitol St., NE
Suite 800
Washington, DC 20002

Fitness Management*
3923 West Sixth Street
Los Angeles, CA 90020

American Alliance of Health, Physical
Education, Recreation & Dance
1900 Association Drive
Reston, VA 22091

Athletic Institute
200 N. Castlewood Drive
North Palm Beach, FL 33408

Aerobics and Fitness Association (AFAA)
15250 Ventura Blvd
Suite 200
Sherman Oaks, CA 91403

National Strength & Conditioning Assoc.
P.O. Box 81410
Lincoln, NE 68501

National Wellness Institute
South Hall, 1319 Fremont Street
Stevens Point, WI 54481

Club Industry**
1415 Beacon Street, C9122
Boston, MA 02146

*Provides an excellent source book for products
and services
**Provides an annual buyer's guide that is free to
magazine subscribers

241

VENDORS FOR HEALTH PROMOTION MATERIALS

The following groups offer for sale a variety of health promotion–related materials.

Adventure North, Inc.
P.O. Box 128
Pillager, MN 56473

Advocate Fitness
205 Touhy, Suite 122
Park Ridge, IL 60068

American Corporate Health Programs
30445 Northwestern Hwy., #350
Farmington Hills, MI 48334

American Institute for Preventive Medicine
30445 Northwestern Highway
Suite 350
Farmington Hills, MI 48334

Health Awareness, Inc.
53526 Hunters Crossing
Utica, MI 48315

Healthy Achievers
22 Hayes Road
Madbury, NH 03820

Hope Publications
350 E. Michigan Avenue, Suite 301
Kalamazoo, MI 49007

Krames Communications
1100 Grundy Lane
San Bruno, CA 94066-3030

Biedna and Company
499 Flora Place
Fremont, CA 94536-4408

Cardio Theater
12 Piedmont Center, Suite 105
Atlanta, GA 30305

Corporate Fitness Works
18558 Office Park Drive
PGaithersburg, MD 20879

Corporate Health Designs
P.O. Box 55056
Seattle, WA 98115

Denice Ferko-Adams & Associates
Wellness Resources
Cooperburg, PA 18036-1514

Futrex, Inc.
6 Montgomery Village Ave., Suite 620
Gaithersburg, MD 20879

Great Performances
14964 NW Greenbrier Parkway
Beaverton, OR 97006

Healing Resources
P.O. Box 670174
Dallas, TX 75367

TerraCom Medical Communications
266 Harristown Road, Suite 106
Glen Rock, NJ 07452

Welltech International
P.O. Box 411183-251
St. Louis, MO 63141

Whole Person Associates
201 W. Michigan
Duluth, MN 55802

LifeCare Resources, Inc.
540 N. Golden Circle Five, #300
Santa Ana, CA 92705

Mayo Health Information
200 First Street, SW
Rochester, MN 55905

Office Workouts, Inc.
29399 Agoura Road, Suite 113
Agoura Hills, CA 91301

Parlay International
Box 8817
Emeryville, CA 94662-0817

Personal Growth Technologies
404 E. Ten Mile Road
Pleasant Ridge, MI 48069

Pro Source Fitness
3500 W. 80th Street, Suite 130
Bloomington, MN 55431

Rodale Press, Inc.
33 E. Minor Street
Emmaus, PA 18098

Tanita Corporation of America
2625 S. Clearbrook Drive
Arlington Height, IL 60005

Appendix F:
Health Risk Appraisal Results

To illustrate the type of results that are obtained from paper-and-pencil administration of a Health Risk Appraisal, we simulated responses that might be seen from a 26 year old male. He reports his height as 5'10" tall and weight as 180 pounds. He exercises rarely, eats a fairly high fat diet, smokes at least one half pack of cigarettes a day, and uses seat belts most of the time. He has a history of asthma, but no other chronic diseases. No blood specimen was collected on this individual. ASAP! processed a health risk appraisal for this hypothetical individual. **Excerpts** of their report on him are shown below and on the pages that follow:

Action Steps Assessment Programs

Individual Health Report
ID: 000001615   Date: 08/19/98   Age/Sex: 26/Male

Health Strengths and Opportunities to Improve Your Health

You have 7 medical and/or lifestyle areas that increase your risk for future health problems. These are opportunities for you to improve or maintain your health. They are shown in the table below in boldface. Taking action steps to reduce or get rid of even one of these risks can have important effects on your future health and quality of life! Use the section called "How Do I Start?" to make an action plan.

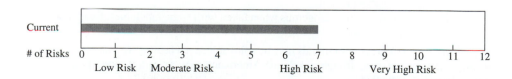

Health Opportunities*	Current	Recommended
Medical:		
• TC: HDL Ratio	NA	< 5.0
• Triglycerides	NA	< 150 mg/dl
• Blood Sugar	NA	< 160 mg/dl
• Systolic Blood Pressure	NA	< 140 mmHg
• Diastolic Blood Pressure	NA	< 85 mmHg
• Weight	**180 lbs**	125–164 lbs
Lifestyle:		
• Exercise	**120 min (light)**	420 min (light)**
• Dietary Fat	**Moderate Fat**	Low Fat
• Fruits/Vegetables	**3 servings/day**	5 servings/day
• Smoking	**Smoker**	No Smoking
• Stress	**High Stress**	Low Stress
Coping	Coping well	Coping well
Sleep	7–8 hours	7 hours or more
• Alcohol Use	8–14 drinks/week	0–14 drinks/week
• Auto Safety	**Sometimes use seat belt**	Always use seat belt

Risks with dot (•) contribute to total score. (Systolic/Diastolic = 1)
**Time depends on intensity: Light = 420 min; Moderate = 210 min; Heavy = 140 min; Very Heavy = 120 min

Special
Considerations

*You reported that you have or have had asthma. Since you have a health problem, much of the information in this report is especially important for you. HOWEVER, due to your condition, it is equally important that you talk with your physician as you take action steps to improve health. He or she may have special instructions for you.

Action Steps to Better Health

Here are important action steps that you already do. Keep up the good work!

Alcohol Use

Congratulations! You report having fewer than 15 drinks per week. This places you in a generally safe range. (0–14 drinks per week for men; 0–7 is safest for women) There is some evidence that people who have 1 or 2 drinks per day may have a lower risk of heart disease. However, alcohol is not necessary for good health, and there are times for caution:

- During pregnancy, or if you have an illness, consult with your doctor.
- If family or friends are worried about your drinking, or if you cannot stop at 1 or 2.
- If you binge drink ("I don't remember what I did last night").
- If you drink and drive. 40%–50% of all automobile fatalities may involve alcohol.
- Alcohol is dangerous when taken with some medicines. Read labels; ask questions.

A drink with friends may be enjoyable, even healthy. But alcohol is not free of risk. Roughly 1 in 10 Americans may have a serious problem with alcohol.

The following action steps require extra effort, but they're important. Think about the benefits you might get by giving them a try.

Smoking

You say you are smoking between 10 and 20 cigarettes per day, but you are thinking about quitting. This is a great idea! There are literally hundreds of benefits that can be achieved by not smoking. These benefits include being at lower risk for heart disease, stroke, many cancers, and lung disease. By not smoking, you will also help to protect the health of your family and friends by:

- Not exposing them to the harmful effects of tobacco smoke.
- Setting a good example of how to live a healthy life.

The most important step for you to take right now is to make a list of your personal reasons for quitting. This list can help you stay focused on the pros of quitting if you find yourself tempted to start smoking again. Also, consider using nicotine replacement (gum or patch). These products can really make the job of quitting a lot easier. Discuss your plans with your doctor. He/she may have other helpful ideas. Good luck!

Seat Belts

You already buckle your seat belt some of the time. We ask you to think about buckling up all the time. Here are the facts!

- Auto accidents are a leading cause of injury and death in the USA.
- Most of these accidents take place within 20 miles of home and at low speeds.
- If you drive for 38 years, you have a 50/50 chance of being in a bad accident.
- Seat belts prevent about 60% of serious injuries and deaths.

Choosing to always buckle up is a 5 second Action Step that could save your life. And getting into the habit is easy. To get started, make a promise to buckle up every time you drive for just 3 days. If you forget, pull over and take 5 seconds to buckle up. After 3 days, ask yourself if you could do it for the rest of the week. After a week, try it for a month. By then you have will probably have made seat belt buckling a life-long habit.

Exercise

You are currently doing little or no exercise. But, you are thinking about doing more. That's great! Exercise is a powerful action step for good health! Regular exercise helps to:

- Protect your heart's health   • Control weight   • Manage stress
- Improve sleep   • Set a good example for family and friends

Fitting exercise time into your day may take some effort at first, but most people find the rewards are worth it. What benefits could you get from doing more exercise? Write down your ideas, then post them as a reminder. When you are ready to make a change start small—add 5–10 minutes of extra exercise somewhere in your week. Then gradually add more. Remember, all exercise counts—no matter how little. Good luck!

If you are pregnant, have a serious health problem or have had previous injuries, ask your doctor for safe exercise guidelines.

Fruit &
Vegetables

Eating five or more servings of fruits and vegetables every day is a great Action Step to best health. You eat 3–4 servings per day, so you are almost at that level. Getting enough fruit and vegetables helps to:

• Keep your heart healthy • Reduce your risk for developing certain cancers • Control cholesterol • Control weight • Control blood pressure • Set a healthy example for your family

Eating more fruits and vegetables may be easier than you think, and it doesn't have to take extra time from your day. Here are some ideas that might help you reach a goal of 5 or more servings every day:

• Fix extra for later   • Take them to work   • Keep a can opener handy
• Add vegetarian meals   • Buy extra canned and frozen vegetables
• Make your plan for eating extra servings, then post it as a reminder

How Do I Start?

• Talk with your doctor. He or she may have other Action Steps to recommend to you, based on your personal medical history.
• Pick one or two changes that you are willing to start on today. An example is shown to assist your plan making.

Getting Started

WHAT WILL I DO?	WHY?	HOW WILL I DO IT?
Stop Smoking	No more smoker's cough; good example for my kids; lower risk of cancer	Talk to my doctor; get the nicotine patch to help me

Write your Action Steps and post them where you can see them.
Life can be very busy. Written notes can help you stay focused.

Remember These Important Points

• Remember, this report does not replace your doctor's advice or make guarantees about your future health.
• Everyone can benefit from healthy Action Steps. Even if you feel great or have the best genes in the world, your body and mind can benefit from healthy lifestyle habits.
• It's never too late. You're never too old and rarely too sick to improve your health!
• Never give up! Making lasting changes can be hard. But keep trying until your Action Steps become a natural part of your life.
• Celebrate your success. Reward yourself when you make changes.
• Start today! Good health can be just an Action Step away.

Index